THE

ECONOMICS
OF THE
GHETTO

THE
ECONOMICS
OF THE
GHETTO

CAROLYN SHAW BELL

PEGASUS · NEW YORK

ACKNOWLEDGMENTS

THIS BOOK stems out of a research seminar developed at Wellesley College: I owe much to my students and to my colleagues Marshall Goldman, Rodney Morrison, and Donald Polk. I wish also to acknowledge the rich sources of the college library, especially its documents collection, and the able assistance there of Marion Kanaly and Jeanne Doherty. Miss Doherty's untimely death has robbed us all of a helpful and cheerful presence. For insight and encouragement I would like to thank Mary Jane Latsis and my husband.

CONTENTS

LIST OF DIAGRAMS

LIST OF TABLES

THE

ECONOMICS

OF THE

GHETTO

CHAPTER ONE

ECONOMICS
AND THE GHETTO

WITH ALL that has been written about the ghetto, why read a book called *The Economics of the Ghetto?* What can it add to the testimony offered to the Kerner Commission, the witnesses of *Dark Ghetto* or *Down These Mean Streets* or *The Other America,* the newspaper reports of violence in city streets, and the demonstrations in city welfare offices? What does the economist have to contribute?

THE ROLE OF ECONOMISTS

The term "economics" lends itself handily to a variety of topics: the economics of pollution, of national defense, of transportation, urban economics, international economics, consumer economics—and all these uses refer to economics as a method of analyzing any given subject, a system of thought. Some have criticized economists for thinking rather than feeling; this comment is typical:

> Economists . . . have a built-in bias to see social problems in wholly rational, nonemotional, and static terms because they are preoccupied and almost solely focused on the concepts of macroeconomics, the Gross National Production, the economics of the country as a whole rather than

any of its . . . social subdivisions. . . . What about values; what about the justice of distributing national resources solely in terms of the status quo; what, in short, about priorities? The economists in their macroeconomic cloisters presume these will be taken care of in the long run.[1]

Such a challenge deserves some answer if the economist is to comment on the ghetto, one of the gravest social problems of our day.

Over the past forty years, as the quotation suggests, economists have concentrated on macroeconomic problems; but over this time period the central concern of our society has been with such problems. A generation ago, one out of three people were unemployed, and factories and farms were idle: the pressing need was not to distribute the few goods and services available but to get the economy out of depression into full production. A decade later, World War II, the cold war, and the Korean War posed new problems for the country as a whole: how to expand and strengthen a defense economy. The question about priorities was peremptorily answered during the forties by diverting resources from consumer goods companies to war plants, and it dramatizes the extent of the unemployment that still existed to realize that demands for war production never threatened civilian *needs*. The simple expansion of Gross National Product not only provided the weapons for war but also vastly improved living conditions for families whose poverty had stemmed from unemployment. In these concerns, economists shared the value judgments of the general public; during these years one deeply felt emotion was paramount, and *everyone* worried about macroeconomics, although the term was rarely used. Depression and war have been the critical issues of two-thirds of a lifetime, and they are macroeconomic in scope.

It is true, of course, that ghetto problems do not fall easily into the framework of macroeconomics or aggregate analysis: the country as a whole grew at an unprecedented rate during the sixties, yet these were the years when we became increasingly aware that economic growth was not enough. It is not true that economists are almost solely focused on these concepts: microeconomic analysis—the economics of particular subdivisions of the country—supplements macroeconomics, the economy as a whole. And this book should, therefore, explain more about the system of thought that is economics, while it applies economic analysis to the ghetto.

To begin with, much of what has been written about the ghetto depends on the work of economists. Take, for example, the following sentence from *Black Power:* "Even after completing college and spending at least one year in graduate school, a nonwhite man can expect to do about as well as a white person who only completed high school."[2] Carmichael and Hamilton, the authors, cite as their source *The American Negro Reference Book,*[3] edited by J. P. Davis, which in turn quotes an article by Andrew F. Brimmer entitled "The Negro in the National Economy." Although Mr. Brimmer is an economist, the statement is not original with him, either. This comparison between white high school graduates and nonwhite college graduates required innumerable calculations, and while Mr. Brimmer's competence to do such research is unquestioned, as a member of the Federal Reserve Board of Governors he has other things to do. His footnote refers to Herman Miller of the Bureau of the Census, who presented figures illustrating the statement to a subcommittee of the Senate Committee on Labor and Public Welfare on July 31, 1963.[4] Mr. Miller himself credits the Census Bureau and the Social Science Research Council for sponsoring the necessary research; his findings were first published in a Census monograph[5] and then, in other versions, in two books, *Rich Man Poor Man*[6] and *Income Distribution in the United States,*[7] all under Miller's authorship. In the last volume mentioned, in Table 2 of Appendix E, can be found the specific data documenting the differences in earnings by education and race. And even here the story of economic research does not end, for obviously the data were compiled by others. So Mr. Miller cites his obligation to Selma Goldsmith, another distinguished economist, and to the Census Bureau staff. And the Census Bureau itself relies on methods evolved by still other economists and statisticians.

The statement on earnings comes in many versions (not all as impeccably documented as Carmichael, Hamilton, Brimmer, and Miller have done) and illustrates the quantitative nature of economic analysis: it is a precise* statement supported by empirical data that is collected and analyzed by rigorous methods. To some extent this preoccupation with figures is the real heart of the complaint about the seeming unconcern of economists with human values. It is even discussed, from time to time, by members of the profession. Boulding, for example, points out that "The major impact of economics on ethics, it can be argued, has come because it has developed broad, aggregative concepts of general welfare which are subject to quantification."[9] Certainly using lifetime earnings to compare nonwhites and whites, or college graduates and high school graduates, illustrates just such a concept—we argue that the men with higher earnings are "better off" than those with less. But this does not mean, as Boulding goes on to point out, either that economists think that money (or earnings) is everything in life or that dollar measurement implies "an insensitivity to the large issues of malevolence, benevolence, the sense of community and so on."[10]

To illustrate, let us analyze the statement about earnings: the fact that a nonwhite college graduate earns less than a

---

*Precision frequently involves terminology. Although the words "nonwhite," "Negro," "Black," and "Afro-American" are no longer neutral, objective terms, a book like this, which attempts to help people study economic problems, cannot discuss connotation and usage; economic analysis has nothing to contribute to the subject. In most cases, this book deals with published data and follows the terminology of the primary source. The Bureau of the Census, for example, has this to say:

> The three major race categories distinguished in this report are white, Negro, and other races. . . . In addition to persons of Negro and of mixed Negro and white descent, the category "Negro" includes persons of Negro and of mixed Negro and white descent unless the Indian ancestry very definitely predominates or unless the person is regarded as an Indian in the community.[8]

For statements drawn from this source, therefore, it is simply not correct to substitute the word "Afro-American" or "Black" for the word "nonwhite." That is why Messrs. Carmichael and Hamilton used the term "nonwhite," although they titled their book *Black Power*. Nor is it correct to change the word "Negro" to "Black" or to "Afro-American," for these alternatives were not offered at the time people were classified as "white, Negro, or other nonwhite." There is no way of knowing that people would choose, in every case, to identify "Negro" as "Black," and if any did not so choose, the content of the statements themselves would be altered. For the chapters to follow, it should be clear from the context when the term "Negro" or "nonwhite" or "Black" occurs whether or not it depends on similar usage by another source.

white high school graduate. First, what are the exact quantities involved? Data from the 1960 Census show an association between income and education such that white males with four years of high school could be expected to earn $253,000 during their lifetime, while nonwhite males with five years or more of college could anticipate lifetime earnings of $246,000, or $7,000 *less*. Second, the "payoff" from a college education can be estimated. The white man with some college courses can expect to earn $301,000 during his working years; but if he gets a college diploma, the figure goes up to $395,000. A crude estimate of the return on his investment, therefore, suggests that the white high school graduate will gain almost $50,000 by going to college, and that by finishing the four years of college he will receive almost $100,000 more over a lifetime. But for nonwhites the "payoff" amounts to much less. The nonwhite male with a high school diploma can expect to earn $152,000 during his working years, and if he has one to three years of college, he can anticipate some $162,000 of lifetime earnings. If he graduates from college, the figure goes up—but only to $185,000. The black high school graduate who continues his education, therefore, finds his efforts rewarded by less than a third of what accrues to the white high school graduate who goes on to college.

Before continuing, it is essential to understand what these data do and do not show. First, they tell nothing about any *individual*, or his expected lifetime earnings; as averages, the figures apply to large groups of people. Furthermore, years of education do not absolutely dictate the dollars of income, even for large groups: earnings depend partly on age, occupation, and location. And people's motivation, their intelligence, and their educational opportunities affect both their learning and earning. Finally, since the estimates are based on 1960 data, they need not be appropriate for 1970; indeed, economists frequently hope that by making estimates and predictions they can change policy so that future conditions will differ, and the estimates will not hold true.

The data allow, however, many other comparisons. Lifetime earnings differ for people in different occupations and regions of the country, and the payoff from college or graduate school

Table I-1

Estimated Lifetime Earnings

Education, Color, Occupation, and Region (thousands of dollars, earnings from 18 to 64 years)

Occupation		Years of School Completed				Region	
		High School 4 years	1–3 years	College 4 years	5+ years	North and West	South
Experienced civilian labor force,	white	253	301	395	466	251	213
	nonwhite	151	162	185	246	154	91
Professional, technical, and kindred,	white	292	305	357	481	367	348
	nonwhite	188	179	192	264	236	167
Civil Engineers, total		285	310	377	387	347	308
Chemists, total		277	300	328	371	326	329
Physicians & surgeons, total		–	–	730	727	847	727
Teachers,	white	–	220	230	279	268	219
	nonwhite	–	–	164	213	216	170
Farmers & farm managers,	white	169	215	276	252	157	129
	nonwhite	147	–	–	–	166	41
Managers, officials & proprietors,	white	350	420	556	561	384	328
	nonwhite	210	211	243	–	206	129
Clerical and kindred workers,	white	222	229	264	276	221	208
	nonwhite	172	176	182	–	170	144

Occupation		Years of School Completed				Region	
		High School 4 years	1-3 years	College 4 years	5+ years	North and West	South
Craftsmen, foremen and kindred,	white	247	258	320	353	240	197
	nonwhite	166	167	–	–	171	106
Carpenters,	white	212	211	232	–	211	146
	nonwhite	147	–	–	–	164	81
Cement and concrete finishers,	white	237	–	–	–	236	168
	nonwhite	–	–	–	–	161	110
Automobile mechanics and repairmen,	white	207	201	–	–	204	161
	nonwhite	168	–	–	–	164	96
Painters, construction and maintenance,	white	194	190	–	–	189	141
	nonwhite	–	–	–	–	132	83
Bus drivers,	white	198	179	–	–	191	145
	nonwhite	–	–	–	–	187	83
Truck and tractor drivers,	white	219	217	–	–	215	155
	nonwhite	139	–	–	–	154	94
Service workers,	white	192	194	216	–	176	249
	nonwhite	123	127	–	–	126	90
Farm laborers and foremen,	white	134	155	–	–	102	71
	nonwhite	86	–	–	–	84	42

Source: U.S. Bureau of the Census, *Income Distribution in the United States*, by Herman P. Miller (A 1960 Census Monograph). U.S. Government Printing Office, Washington, D.C., 1966. pp. 270–296.

varies considerably, depending on the field of study. Table I-1 provides some figures for the reader to analyze for himself; he will conclude that the financial return from education for non-whites falls considerably below that for whites.

The data also show that the costs of education for nonwhites and whites are dissimilar. Anyone getting educated must consider the alternative uses for his time: if he doesn't spend four, six, or eight years in school and college, he can get a job and earn four, six, or eight years' pay. A prospective student should add this income given up to the tuition charges and expenses of his education to figure its total cost. The earnings lost by not being employed make up the *opportunity cost* of education. And this loss, the opportunity cost, is not the same for whites and nonwhites, although they may face the same tuition charges and expenses. The high school graduate who is white gives up (on the average) four years of earning $4,000 per year, while his black classmate loses only $2,800 a year. It is cheaper, in terms of opportunity costs, to educate the black man than the white. The economist might conclude, therefore, that resources should be shifted from educating white students to educating nonwhites until the costs (in terms of income foregone) become more nearly equalized between the two groups.

This minor bit of analysis (oversimplified but nonetheless suggestive) follows from what some might call a "wholly rational, nonemotional" approach. But why condemn this approach? It argues for improving the educational facilities for nonwhites on stronger grounds than any appeal for "revising our priorities to make up for a hundred years of neglect." The economist, unlike the politician or polemicist, rarely uses the word "priority," which is becoming extraordinarily fashionable these days. The stateman promises "first priority" to the plight of cities; the college president declares "faculty salaries must take priority"; and neither statement means much. Such remarks offer no guidance whatever about how to use our limited resources: to say that rebuilding the slums should take priority over sending a man to Mars provides not a clue about how many construction workers should be trained, whether or not to expand steel or lumber production, where to let building contracts—in short, how to divide up the available supplies of men and materials and machinery. These are quantitative problems and require quantitative answers. But it is not a valid criticism to equate precision with heartlessness, for it was not random intellectual curiosity that set economists to measuring poverty, or to correlating measures of housing with health, or to comparing education and income between ethnic and racial groups.

THE MEANING OF A CITY

So we may return to the ghetto, and pose an economist's questions about it. The Kerner Commission's definition will serve to start: "The term 'ghetto' as used in this Report refers to an area within a city characterized by poverty and acute social disorganization and inhabited by members of a racial or ethnic group under conditions of involuntary segregation."[11] How do we measure "poverty"? and "acute social disorganization"? What data about these conditions exist? What methods can be used to collect more? Do the "members of a racial or ethnic group" share common economic characteristics? or problems? What effect does segregation have on the economy? What are the economic dimensions of a ghetto? For that matter, what are the economic dimensions of a city, if that is where ghettos are found?

It is important first to acquire some technical expertise with terms like "city," "urbanization," "metropolitan area," and even "suburb"—a word in such common use that few people ever stop to think of its precise meaning, or of the knotty distinctions between "towns" and "townships" in different regions.

One major division of the places where people live separates *urban* residence from *rural* residence. The Census Bureau defines the former, however, to include places with 2,500 or more inhabitants; and in many areas a "place" with two to four thousand residents strikes most people as "countryfied" rather than "citified." To say that seven out of ten Americans now live in urban areas, or that by 1980 85 per cent of the population will be urbanites does not mean, therefore, that big *cities* are growing at any significant rate. In fact, between 1950 and 1960 while the total population increased by almost one-fifth, the major cities grew by half that much. During the decade when the population increased by 29 million, some nine million persons were added to places with less than 25,000 inhabitants. Nor can these figures be dismissed with a simple reference to suburbia, for that phenomenon itself is complex.

The Census Bureau recognizes that a "metropolitan area" need not (and in these politically defined United States probably will not) coincide with any municipality or other state or county subdivision; analysts therefore work with a *Standard Metropolitan Statistical Area* (commonly known as SMSA). Each such geographical entity contains a *central city* (or two "twin cities") of at least 50,000 inhabitants and a surrounding area that forms an integrated social and economic system with the city. Specific criteria define the term *metropolitan:* the majority of the labor force must be employed outside agriculture, and the majority of the population must live in areas with a population density of at least 150 persons per square mile. Equally precise is the notion of *integrated,* defined primarily in terms of where people live and work, although counts of telephone service, newspaper circulation, retail charge accounts, and other types of activities can also demonstrate the intermingling of the population. Obviously, not all the people in such a metropolitan area live in a city—either in the central city that identifies the SMSA or in any outlying city that may appear in the area. Between 1950 and 1960 the metropolitan population grew by 25 per cent (compared to a total population increase of 18.5 per cent), but the number living *outside* the central cities grew much more, by some 36 per cent. Nearly one-fourth of the metropolitan population, outside the central cities, lives in rural areas.

To define suburbia, we need still another concept, that of the *urbanized area,* (sometimes abbreviated to UA), a Census term for the SMSA central city (or twin cities), plus its *urban fringe* of heavily settled areas. The *SMSA ring,* then, becomes the urban fringe plus what is left in rural nonfarm and farm areas, and makes up the entire metropolitan district. Either the urban fringe *or* the SMSA ring can be used to identify suburban areas near a central city; rates of growth and all the associated problems will obviously show great variation, depending on the definition that is chosen.

The United States economy therefore encompasses many different types of localities, and the several regions of the country reveal many different combinations of central cities, urban fringe, SMSA ring, rural nonfarm, and farming areas, as well as different growth rates for each component. Almost everyone knows that the population has grown most rapidly in the Pacific and Mountain states during recent years, but it may not be such common knowledge that most of the urban population gain there has occurred in cities numbering from 100,000 to a quarter of a million people. Almost everyone knows that during the past fifteen years population growth in the South has been less than the national average (and in some states an absolute decrease), but not as many are aware that the same years saw a major shift of Southerners from rural to urban areas, with the large cities and metropolitan areas of the South growing rapidly.

In Census terminology it is the *inner city* which is most frequently associated with the ghetto. But such usage may be too narrow: there may be pockets of "poverty and acute social disorganization" and "conditions of involuntary segregation" in rural nonfarm or suburban areas, to say nothing of the isolated communities of Indian reservations and migrant labor camps. And little is gained by facile generalization or model-building: "the ghetto" comes in many sizes and shapes. Before trying to apply the lessons learned in one area to the problems of another, it is essential to delineate the specific locality involved.

AN INTRODUCTION TO SOME DATA

All too frequently the current interest in urban affairs or social problems prompts an immediate rush of scholars to the streets ("studies in the field") to investigations and interviews that, no matter how well-meaning the research worker, may generate opposition and resentment from people who see such studies as at best misdirected and at worst an invasion of privacy. It is one object of this book to help people avoid asking unnecessary questions, by learning from published data, and to help people design more efficient field studies when the need for these is proved.

Any research project should begin with what is already known: the economist working with the microeconomic units of localities uses data from the U.S. Census tracted areas. A *Census tract* is a small area of a city or its environs; one tract generally contains about 4,000 people but obviously can vary widely in geographical size. In some suburbs a tract may contain four or five square miles; in central cities it may consist of only a few blocks. Both local experts and Census authorities help to set the boundaries of a tract so that it will comprise a reasonably homogeneous population, in terms of economic status and living conditions. The concept of census tracts originated early in the twentieth century, and the Census Bureau has published 1960 population and housing statistics for 180 tracted areas.

Except for two areas in New Jersey, every Census tract lies within a standard metropolitan statistical area. In most of the country, SMSA's consist of a county, counties, or parts of counties; in New England the SMSA contains towns and cities rather than counties. For example, the Portland, Oregon SMSA contains parts of four counties: Clackamas County, Oregon; Multnomah County, Oregon; Washington County, Oregon; and Clark County, Washington. The city itself takes up part of the first two counties; Census tracts have been drawn for the entire city and part of each of the four counties. In Connecticut, the Hartford SMSA contains one city and twenty-one towns that spread over parts of three counties. Table I–2 reproduces, from Census tract data, the general characteristics of the population for tracts in the Portland, Oregon, SMSA; and Table I–3 reproduces data on housing for Census tracts in the Hartford, Connecticut, SMSA, two of which happen to be entire towns. Other details provided for each Census tract include characteristics of the labor force—employment, occupation, and so on, in addition to age, color, and marital status by sex, and information on population movements. For some Census tracts, the data are tabulated for all inhabitants and separately for the nonwhite population. The reports contain, therefore, a mine of material useful for studying any small or large area and for isolating the economic characteristics of a ghetto.

On the other hand, using Census data to pinpoint one small

area raises problems that do not exist in analyzing totals for a state or country. The Census tracts are small enough so that usually one enumerator records all the data for the people and houses within any individual tract. Consequently any misunderstanding of instructions would lead to a wider margin of error for an individual tract than for an entire city or region. In some areas, however, the householders themselves supplied Census information by filling out forms which were either collected by the enumerator or mailed to the local Census office; errors on these forms would, of course, be more random than those made by one enumerator. A more serious fault, not only with the tract data but with certain nationwide totals, lies in underreporting certain groups of people. Nonwhites are more apt to be overlooked than whites, males than females, and people at either end of the age distribution rather than the middle-aged. Two kinds of faulty counting occur: missing the household itself and failing to list everyone living in a household. Most of the white people omitted by the Census fall into the first category; less than 5 per cent of white males are overlooked, and less than 3 per cent of white females, except for women in their early fifties and sixties. But among nonwhites the Census fails to count all the individuals rather than omitting households. Over ten per cent of all nonwhite males between the ages of 15 and 54 were left out, with the largest omission among those aged from 20 to 34 and 50 to 54. These differences in counting mean, among other things, that calculated rates of unemployment or even births and deaths can be faulty.[12]

A number of reasons seem responsible. Census enumerators who find no member of a household at home may obtain information from landlords or neighbors, although only after repeated efforts to reach the family. But despite careful training and supervision, some enumerators neglect call-backs, especially in the evening, and in districts where overcrowding or racial tension seem threatening. Information from other people of course must be less reliable than what would be provided by the family itself. Poor communication between enumerator and resident means that not everyone is counted in places where two or more families share living quarters. And

Census Tracts

Table I-2—GENERAL CHARACTERISTICS OF THE POPULATION, BY CENSUS TRACTS: 1960

[Asterisk (*) denotes statistics based on 25-percent sample. Population per household not shown where less than 50 persons in households. Median not shown where base is less than 200]

SUBJECT	BALANCE OF CLACKAMAS COUNTY--CON.							PORTLAND (PART IN MULTNOMAH COUNTY)					
	TRACT C-0037	TRACT C-0038	TRACT C-0039	TRACT C-0040	TRACT C-0041	TRACT C-0042	TRACT C-0043	TRACT 0001	TRACT 0002	TRACT 0003-A	TRACT 0003-B	TRACT 0004-A	TRACT 0004-B
RACE AND COUNTRY OF ORIGIN													
TOTAL POPULATION	1 986	3 347	2 755	923	1 808	2 467	2 942	6 008	5 164	2 868	7 850	4 008	3 368
WHITE	1 974	3 331	2 754	915	1 807	2 457	2 936	5 965	5 149	2 823	7 785	3 956	3 291
NEGRO	5	4	...	...	...	5	...	18	5	13	11	15	39
OTHER RACES	7	12	1	8	1	5	6	25	10	32	54	37	38
BORN IN PUERTO RICO*	...	...	...	...	...	...	...	...	...	...	...	...	...
PUERTO RICAN PARENTAGE*	...	...	...	...	...	...	...	...	...	...	...	...	...
TOTAL FOREIGN STOCK*	346	590	407	135	362	276	426	1 530	1 415	885	2 077	1 025	883
FOREIGN BORN*	62	90	94	24	80	31	95	152	397	218	485	244	679
NATIVE, FOR. OR MIXED PARENTAGE	284	500	313	111	282	245	331	1 098	1 018	667	1 592	781	664
UNITED KINGDOM	12	24	50	26	11	41	64	174	174	94	218	54	54
IRELAND (EIRE)	7	12	19	4	4	12	...	45	36	29	42	42	16
NORWAY	4	113	18	21	35	21	34	100	89	63	92	37	58
SWEDEN	24	16	28	5	90	24	16	124	136	48	120	46	39
GERMANY	119	140	82	44	49	67	104	283	197	100	302	161	130
POLAND	4	7	7	...	7	3	...	49	39	56	37	24	...
CZECHOSLOVAKIA	11	...	...	...	11	...	4	18	15	8	12	8	8
AUSTRIA	9	15	4	4	4	12	12	63	28	21	93	34	50
HUNGARY	...	39	20	8	...	...	8	18	27	15	31	30	24
U.S.S.R.	31	...	11	4	9	11	7	63	74	52	31	86	82
ITALY	...	12	78	3	8	12	30	71	136	108	215	108	104
CANADA	12	...	...	...	58	45	10	102	224	132	260	161	151
MEXICO	74	97	...	...	...	...	66	223	...	...	325	...	3
ALL OTHER AND NOT REPORTED	51	112	86	16	55	45	71	265	240	159	326	199	164
HOUSEHOLD RELATIONSHIP													
POPULATION IN HOUSEHOLDS	1 986	3 338	2 719	923	1 780	2 457	2 890	5 932	5 138	2 320	7 843	4 008	3 346
HEAD OF HOUSEHOLD*	549	993	893	276	543	764	900	2 098	1 854	767	2 342	1 322	1 107
HEAD OF PRIMARY FAMILY	488	878	735	239	462	623	751	1 611	1 505	651	2 114	1 129	934
WIFE OF HEAD	61	115	158	37	81	141	149	487	349	116	228	193	173
PRIMARY INDIVIDUAL	464	814	682	226	415	580	693	1 377	1 329	590	1 975	1 031	807
CHILD UNDER 18 OF HEAD	784	1 161	963	334	654	893	1 050	1 761	1 373	753	2 902	1 287	1 074
OTHER RELATIVE OF HEAD	164	311	165	70	147	180	207	542	492	168	544	321	305
NONRELATIVE OF HEAD	25	59	126	17	21	10	40	154	90	42	80	47	53
POPULATION IN GROUP QUARTERS	...	9	36	...	28	10	52	76	26	58	67	...	22
INMATE OF INSTITUTION*	...	...	29	...	25	...	...	20	...	5	...	...	...
OTHER*	...	...	7	...	3	10	52	5	5	58	7	...	22
POPULATION PER HOUSEHOLD	3.62	3.36	3.04	3.34	3.28	3.22	3.21	2.83	2.77	3.02	3.35	3.03	3.02

MARRIED COUPLES*	470	827	225	440	597	700	1 345	1 343	599	2 027	999	783
WITH OWN HOUSEHOLD	139	200	148	134	235	215	305	255	162	538	263	233
WITH OWN CHILDREN UNDER 6	300	422	148	260	400	407	661	618	339	229	557	446
WITH OWN CHILDREN UNDER 18	202	289	76	195	249	307	501	468	259	916	440	371
WITH HUSBAND UNDER 45	83	157	61	167	238	278	406	389	223	836	364	319
WITH OWN CHILDREN UNDER 18			39	107	153	227	596	368	610	259	194	287
UNRELATED INDIVIDUALS*												
PERSONS UNDER 18 YEARS OLD**	842	1 223	375	675	949	1 059	1 880	1 448	817	2 971	1 376	148
LIVING WITH BOTH PARENTS**	806	1 155	341	644	877	992	1 578	1 306	743	2 854	1 262	938
*SCHOOL ENROLLMENT												
TOTAL ENROLLED, 5 TO 34 YEARS OLD	570	864	255	477	615	730	1 333	1 114	1 060	2 332	967	809
KINDERGARTEN	...	...	...	...	25	15	115	38	45	164	61	74
PUBLIC	...	...	...	...	25	15	115	35	45	150	61	71
ELEMENTARY (1 TO 8 YEARS)	418	607	165	327	426	540	897	737	343	494	586	517
PUBLIC	407	596	165	327	416	540	714	624	276	130	430	451
HIGH SCHOOL (1 TO 4 YEARS)	148	229	60	144	158	158	272	267	172	531	260	182
PUBLIC	148	209	90	138	148	158	246	214	131	447	223	154
COLLEGE	4	28	...	6	6	17	49	72	500	143	60	36
*YEARS OF SCHOOL COMPLETED												
PERSONS 25 YEARS OLD AND OVER	1 050	898	527	1 021	1 341	1 652	3 765	3 409	1 500	4 579	2 436	2 023
NO SCHOOL YEARS COMPLETED	19	19	8	23	5	23	29	24	...	34	28	45
ELEMENTARY: 1 TO 4 YEARS	40	53	25	22	32	52	132	82	94	70	59	82
5 TO 7 YEARS	115	213	86	144	157	185	454	201	92	429	189	186
8 YEARS	290	611	152	248	272	432	912	702	256	532	486	360
HIGH SCHOOL: 1 TO 3 YEARS	238	294	104	217	327	466	768	732	332	412	509	514
4 YEARS	283	508	116	265	366	468	1 052	1 054	387	958	753	636
COLLEGE: 1 TO 3 YEARS	31	138	32	81	88	103	242	373	211	1 015	270	121
4 YEARS OR MORE	31	62	34	41	94	67	176	181	198	87	142	79
MEDIAN SCHOOL YEARS COMPLETED	10.0	9.5	9.0	10.3	10.9	10.3	10.4	11.6	12.1	12.8	11.7	11.0
*RESIDENCE IN 1955												
PERSONS 5 YEARS OLD AND OVER, 1960	1 769	2 044	831	1 622	2 159	2 660	5 502	4 769	2 659	7 108	3 615	3 030
SAME HOUSE IN U.S.	803	959	531	963	1 047	1 136	3 096	2 807	344	073	209	715
DIFFERENT HOUSE IN U.S.	957	1 081	297	651	1 018	369	2 265	911	944	944	369	272
CENTRAL CITY OF THIS SMSA	131	52	36	52	80	199	176	133	485	204	217	805
OTHER PART OF THIS SMSA	564	573	65	285	538	641	455	399	617	221	248	191
OUTSIDE THIS SMSA	262	456	196	314	400	529	634	360	617	979	206	276
NORTH AND WEST	262	441	188	314	400	516	593	19	40	40	42	261
SOUTH	...	15	8	...	...	13	19	32	36	87	28	15
ABROAD	3	...	3	...	5	13	83	19	24	4	9	30
MOVED, RESIDENCE IN 1955 NOT REPORTED	6	4	...	3	94	150	58					13
*FAMILY INCOME IN 1959												
ALL FAMILIES	490	880	241	476	638	760	1 646	1 572	647	2 138	1 136	913
UNDER $1,000	41	61	12	37	44	39	80	80	12	29	59	76
$1,000 TO $1,999	41	113	42	55	44	60	125	83	16	38	50	28
$2,000 TO $2,999	39	117	56	48	60	79	140	98	11	54	82	58
$3,000 TO $3,999	47	116	22	49	65	92	155	112	36	73	59	93
$4,000 TO $4,999	69	92	37	46	110	115	181	118	52	93	105	150
$5,000 TO $5,999	85	115	19	80	93	134	302	264	68	181	199	127
$6,000 TO $6,999	73	107	26	53	98	74	169	185	84	251	109	136
$7,000 TO $7,999	46	48	8	33	71	45	121	91	68	173	135	80
$8,000 TO $9,999	42	36	8	25	34	19	122	87	44	208	98	46
$10,000 TO $14,999	12	24	...	21	24	39	95	223	117	479	28	70
$15,000 TO $24,999	8	32	8	13	21	17	138	44	17	212	...	...
$25,000 AND OVER	4	12	...	10	30	7	50	...	12	126	...	15
MEDIAN INCOME: FAMILIES	$5 294	$4 359	$3 477	$5 038	$5 430	$4 957	$5 470	$6 314	$7 405	$8 746	$6 284	$6 138
FAM. & UNREL. INDIV.	$4 870	$3 671	$2 911	$4 175	$4 961	$4 280	$4 543	$5 649	$4 335	$8 149	$5 895	$5 420

Census Tracts

Table I-3—OCCUPANCY AND STRUCTURAL CHARACTERISTICS OF HOUSING UNITS, BY CENSUS TRACTS: 1960

SUBJECT	BALANCE OF SMSA IN HARTFORD COUNTY													
	TRACT AV-0168	TRACT BL-0115	TRACT BL-0116	TRACT BL-0117	TRACT BL-0118	TRACT CA-0189	TRACT EW-0175	TRACT EW-0176	TRACT FA-0165	TRACT FA-0166	TRACT FA-0167	TRACT GL-0147	TRACT GL-0148	TRACT GL-0149
ALL HOUSING UNITS	1 576	1 008	812	867	998	1 551	1 392	792	632	1 259	1 260	819	1 585	1 151
TENURE, COLOR, AND VACANCY STATUS														
OWNER OCCUPIED	1 186	930	704	763	836	1 002	1 006	526	587	958	933	646	926	1 018
WHITE	1 184	867	597	762	827	1 001	984	525	586	954	933	646	924	1 015
NONWHITE	2	63	107	1	9	1	22	1	1	4	...	...	2	3
RENTER OCCUPIED	293	66	92	64	112	435	325	224	26	232	213	126	600	96
WHITE	292	54	80	64	111	434	312	216	26	231	262	125	595	94
NONWHITE	1	12	12	...	1	1	13	8	...	1	1	1	5	2
AVAILABLE VACANT	50	11	9	25	20	48	39	29	10	39	40	24	38	21
FOR SALE ONLY	34	9	2	22	16	26	12	14	9	26	25	19	18	14
FOR RENT	16	2	7	3	4	22	27	15	1	13	15	5	20	7
OTHER VACANT	47	1	7	15	30	66	22	13	9	30	24	23	21	16
CONDITION AND PLUMBING														
SOUND	1 455	970	755	829	936	1 488	1 178	719	628	1 165	1 209	731	1 489	1 131
WITH ALL PLUMBING FACILITIES	1 433	967	750	824	930	1 402	1 141	696	627	1 144	1 182	703	1 447	1 122
LACKING ONLY HOT WATER	1	1	1	...	2	2	8	17	...	6	7	7	10	1
LACKING OTHER PLUMBING FACILITIES	21	2	4	5	4	64	29	6	...	15	20	21	32	6
DETERIORATING	85	37	41	30	41	51	182	60	1	78	45	77	89	12
WITH ALL PLUMBING FACILITIES	64	36	34	27	28	39	120	41	1	73	32	48	69	9
LACKING ONLY HOT WATER	6	...	4	3	2	2	9	10	...	1	3	5	10	2
LACKING OTHER PLUMBING FACILITIES	15	1	3	...	11	10	53	9	...	4	10	24	10	1
DILAPIDATED	36	1	16	8	21	12	32	13	3	16	6	11	7	8
BATHROOMS														
1	962	873	629	264	358	1 145	1 184	658	298	788	1 004	489	1 292	513
MORE THAN 1	582	135	159	578	601	321	95	94	334	440	207	272	213	629
SHARED OR NONE	32	...	24	20	39	85	113	40	...	31	49	58	80	9
ROOMS														
1 ROOM	11	...	4	...	2	17	29	2	2	5	5	11	16	2
2 ROOMS	13	3	4	2	6	16	34	13	1	21	13	12	23	3
3 ROOMS	55	10	14	10	21	74	168	36	5	58	56	29	145	27
4 ROOMS	284	194	100	40	70	309	328	164	42	135	201	100	353	87
5 ROOMS	388	494	367	102	173	340	377	185	182	294	398	248	411	284
6 ROOMS	441	311	214	244	351	358	229	193	244	347	342	246	378	404
7 ROOMS	244	60	302	302	204	206	117	90	96	155	162	89	141	200
8 ROOMS OR MORE	190	16	35	167	171	231	110	109	60	244	123	84	118	144
MEDIAN	5.7	5.9	5.7											

	Col 1	Col 2	Col 3	Col 4	Col 5	Col 6	Col 7	Col 8	Col 9	Col 10	Col 11	Col 12	Col 13	Col 14
2	39	141	40	82	22	4	26	138	254	9	24	40	43	79
3 AND 4	5	64	.	67	5	.	21	21	87	9	10	10	.	25
5 TO 9	.	25	16	10	6	.	.	43	40	.	.	.	.	.
10 OR MORE	.	10	.	.	.	.	.	9	.	.	.	.	.	.
YEAR STRUCTURE BUILT														
1950 TO MARCH 1960	706	337	458	532	434	442	275	629	508	507	554	429	711	652
1940 TO 1949	157	381	61	188	200	99	46	145	214	128	120	135	88	264
1939 OR EARLIER	288	867	300	540	625	91	471	618	829	363	193	248	209	660
BASEMENT														
BASEMENT	1 022	1 434	765	1 148	1 129	618	754	991	1 340	916	822	723	777	1 468
CONCRETE SLAB	105	96	18	52	85	14	23	126	173	47	25	45	86	39
OTHER	26	55	36	62	45	.	15	275	138	35	15	44	145	69
HEATING EQUIPMENT														
STEAM OR HOT WATER	797	987	490	858	791	521	470	646	839	683	645	621	679	1 040
WARM AIR FURNACE	281	417	202	259	383	91	100	454	403	251	170	157	296	387
BUILT-IN ROOM UNITS	53	45	30	32	30	11	44	49	43	8	16	11	8	21
OTHER MEANS WITH FLUE	12	119	89	90	51	9	155	215	243	48	36	19	21	98
OTHER MEANS WITHOUT FLUE	8	17	4	4	.	.	20	21	9	8	.	.	4	23
NONE	.	.	4	17	4	.	3	7	14	.	.	4	.	7
ALL OCCUPIED UNITS	1 114	1 526	772	1 196	1 190	613	750	1 331	1 437	948	827	796	996	1 479
PERSONS														
1 PERSON	50	131	45	92	109	21	62	146	137	40	38	39	23	113
2 PERSONS	296	400	177	275	327	169	184	338	405	229	172	208	197	379
3 PERSONS	214	306	153	239	221	138	163	265	297	176	146	152	206	281
4 PERSONS	264	324	181	249	232	141	157	254	277	228	231	206	318	314
5 PERSONS	184	217	118	185	135	91	86	145	178	154	145	108	141	220
6 PERSONS OR MORE	106	148	98	156	166	53	98	183	143	121	95	83	111	172
MEDIAN														
ALL OCCUPIED	3.5	3.3	3.6	3.5	3.2	3.3	3.3	3.2	3.1	3.6	3.7	3.5	3.7	3.4
OWNER	3.6	3.1	3.8	2.7	3.4	3.3	3.5	3.1	3.2	3.7	3.9	3.4	3.8	3.4
RENTER	.	3.1		2.7	2.4		3.3	3.0	2.8					3.3
PERSONS PER ROOM														
0.50 OR LESS	506	582	290	462	595	279	335	486	690	433	366	301	282	637
0.51 TO 0.75	349	394	204	314	300	185	185	309	353	276	309	201	289	430
0.76 TO 1.00	225	430	227	333	224	136	165	384	305	200	131	243	350	334
1.01 OR MORE	34	120	51	87	71	13	65	152	89	39	21	51	75	78

the young male population, especially the nonwhite youth, frequently has no clearly defined place of residence. He is sometimes visiting his family or his friends, but sometimes sleeping in hallways or in all-night restaurants or theaters. By hiring enumerators more familiar with slum conditions and more responsive to the language and living conditions of the inner city, the 1970 Census will, it is hoped, provide a more accurate count.

Despite such cautionary qualifications to the Census tract data, we are extremely fortunate to have such extensive and, on the whole, reliable, information about people and places in the metropolitan areas of this country. Knowing what conditions exist is an essential prerequisite to understanding these conditions, how they came about, and what they imply for the future. Making use of available, published data is surely the most efficient way to begin learning about conditions as they exist.

PREVIEW AND PLAN

This book is designed to provide an introduction to primary data on ghetto economics. We study important characteristics —income, employment, living conditions—not in theoretical models, but with empirical facts and figures. It is, of course, impossible to investigate each of the hundreds of communities where urban ghettos might exist; so the chapters to follow include, as examples, material dealing with three cities in the United States, and specifically, with three neighborhoods within each metropolitan area. These data prove little but illustrate much; they can be duplicated for other communities in the country by any reader. Collecting such information is only the first step, and each chapter concerning a particular problem also presents methods of analysis: how to interpret data and draw conclusions from the material available.

The three cities remain anonymous in our discussion for two reasons. First, revealing their identities would probably distract the reader from learning about the economics of the ghetto to speculating on the problems of the particular city, which may or may not be typical of other areas. Second, the districts within each city are of course familiar to some readers, who might therefore add their own knowledge—or misconceptions—to the material presented, which is drawn from published sources and does not rely on special surveys. Indeed, anyone interested in making such a survey, or field study, can discover from the chapters to follow what "searching the literature" means, and what a wealth of data already exist. This is the plan of the first six chapters.

In Part Two, the book changes its viewpoint. If Part One says, "these conditions exist and this is what they mean," Part Two states the logical follow-up, "what are we going to do about it?" Here, economics means not the analysis of empirical data or theoretical reasoning but the appraisal of suggested programs or policies. Again, we make no pretense at dealing with all the ideas for solving ghetto problems, but choose some to illustrate the economist's approach.

CHAPTER TWO

INCOME AND POVERTY

WE TAKE income as a measure of well-being—affluence, poverty, or general economic status—in appraising a country, a firm, or an individual family. Thus it is common knowledge that "the United States is the richest country in the world"—meaning that the level of income, both aggregate and per capita, exceeds that elsewhere. *High income* may even be confused with *wealth,* although the first refers to a flow of resources (we measure income over time), while the second means a stock of capital, or valuable assets, at any one point in time. But we speak of a "wealthy" company and describe its substantial profits, (its net income), or a "wealthy" family and quote the sizable figures of its income. Although we rarely agree on exactly how many dollars constitute a "sizeable" income, there has recently been fairly widespread use of a dollar measure for the other end of the scale, poverty. Early in the 1960's the Council of Economic Advisers declared that an income of less than $3,000 represented poverty for a family of four, while a single individual with less than $1,500 annually was poor. Since then "poverty" has been redefined in dollar terms; in late 1969 the poverty level income for a family of four was $3,700. But any of these precise statements spawn all sorts of arguments about the number of poor people, whether they are

"really" poor, whether $3,500 isn't a good wage for a high
school dropout or for a housewife working part-time, and so
on. What sources exist to let us make statements about income?
How, having counted people and incomes, can we interpret
the statements?

COLLECTING THE FACTS

The Census of Population, discussed in the previous chapter,
provides both enumerated and sample data. The Constitution
requires that the population itself be enumerated, i.e., every
single human being in the country counted, as far as possible.
Such characteristics as age and sex and relationship to other
people living in the same household also refer to the enumerated
population. But the Census publishes income data which come
from a sample (as do some other details on housing and automobiles).

The basic unit for the Census enumerator is not a person
but a housing unit—a house, an apartment, a group of rooms,
or a single room—which consists of separate living quarters
for the occupants. In 1960 each housing unit and all the persons living there were listed by the Census taker, and every
fifth unit became part of the sample for more detailed information. (Aside from housing units, the Census also recognized
"group quarters": dormitories, hospitals, jails, military barracks,
fraternity houses, and the like—and here the sample included
every *fourth person*.) The theory of statistical sampling tells us
that taking roughly 25 per cent of the population in this fashion
provides an extraordinarily large sample but not one which
provides extraordinarily more accurate information than other,
smaller, samples. The Census enumerator asked about income
from all sources for every member of the household over fourteen years of age; the precise definitions enabled everyone to
calculate income in the same way, excluding, for example, gains
from a real-estate sale or an inheritance, but including wages
and salaries before taxes, rather than take-home pay. The
Census taker provided cards for those people who wished to
mail in income information in order to preserve complete
anonymity.

For a number of reasons, however, income data could not

be obtained from all the people who were asked to supply it: while this does not affect income figures for the entire country, it does for small areas, especially individual Census tracts, and more particularly for tracts in ghetto areas. The income data published for some localities cannot be used because the number of people who provided information was far too small to represent the whole locality. The previous chapter mentioned some of the difficulties in taking a Census in urban areas, especially in slum districts, with the regrettable result that large numbers of people went uncounted. But even where the Census gives a reasonably complete count of *people,* it does not always produce accurate *income* information. Economic research suffers because income data are difficult to come by and when they do exist we suspect their reliability.

Two major sources of error distort the evidence. The first is ignorance and this includes many kinds of ignorance. The interviewer or data-collector normally calls at the home during the day, and most often talks to a woman. We know that a significant number of wives are deliberately kept in ignorance by their husbands of the full amount of family income. (We may wonder whether men tend to conceal the total amount of income because they are also concealing expenditures.) The system of leaving cards to be filled out anonymously was designed partly to meet this problem. But mailed responses involve another problem—that of the person who speaks English adequately to answer questions, but who reads and writes the language poorly, if at all. To such a family member the card is an embarrassment best disposed of in the wastebasket.

Another sort of ignorance has to do (despite the best efforts of the Census Bureau's public relations staff) with the nature of a Census and the information gathered. Some people regard the Census as unwarranted snooping. Since some of the most strenuous objectors to so-called snooping are congressmen and senators, it does not seem appropriate to launch a government program to educate the untutored masses in the methods and uses of the Census, which is, after all, basic to the form of government prescribed in the Constitution. In recent months the press has quoted flaming statements by one or another congressman about preparations for the 1970 Census, who objects to this or that question as an "invasion of privacy." Among the questions that congressmen find objectionable are those about the condition of housing and the type of employment—both vital to any valid estimate of the extent of poverty.

Some reluctance to answer questions stems from confusing the Bureau of the Census with the Bureau of Internal Revenue —people refuse to give income information because they fear it will have repercussions on their tax liability. Whether this indicates a guilty conscience or not, it does demonstrate another kind of ignorance: it is a fact that no Census data about any individual, or family may be reported to any other agency, governmental or private.

Aside from ignorance, another source of difficulty in getting income data may include problems that are not for economists to dwell on. Some human behavior has nothing to do with rational calculation but rather with emotions—unformulated fears, feelings of self-esteem or deprecation, the wish to be admired or liked or respected; people may lie about their income or, more commonly, refuse to talk about their income. No matter what technique is used—anonymous cards, appeals to better judgment, avowals of utter secrecy—they all tend to fail before the overriding propensity to conceal the facts of personal income. This propensity, unlike those forms of ignorance discussed earlier, varies directly with the level of income; rich people have been less cooperative than poor people. It is even easier (judging from the response rate to the investigators for the first Kinsey report, and the experience of the staff at the Institute for Sex Research) to get people to talk about their sexual activities than it is to get them to describe their financial activities.

With these facts in mind, the income data for small areas, like a Census tract or a group of Census tracts defining a ghetto, demand respectful attention. Only the decennial Census provides such separate figures for every locality in the country. In other years the Census releases information about income for the entire population: these data come from a small sample that is carefully selected to represent everyone in the country, and the data cannot, therefore, be used for particular states, cities, or districts. On occasion, the Census also prepares

a special report for a particular area: thus in 1965 a survey of
Cleveland, Ohio, provided comparative data to those gathered
in 1960. After the Watts riot, the Bureau made a survey of the
East Spanish and South Negro areas in Los Angeles to find
out how conditions had changed since 1960. Perhaps the gravest defect of research based on Census data is due to the fact
that during the 1960's, conditions in cities *did* change, rapidly
and drastically, so that reliable information quickly became
obsolete, while more recent information lacked precision and
reliability. Thus the President's Advisory Commission on Civil
Disorder, reporting in 1968 on troubles that took place in 1967,
relied heavily on 1960 Census data in its discussion of the
cities and the areas within them where disorders occurred. The
1970 Census will not begin to provide tract data until 1971;
complete publication will take longer.

ANALYZING THE FIGURES

The economist looks at the income of any population with
the aid of a frequency distribution: a grouping of all the people into different income classes ranging from high to low.
Table II-1 shows an income distribution for the entire United
States, and nine other frequency distributions for three SMSA's,
each with three different districts containing roughly the same
number of people. The data show what percentage of all the
families in the area fall in each of several income classes; unrelated individuals have been excluded. Dividing all the families into just two classes gives an income figure called "the
median," which can be used to represent the entire distribution. The median income is higher than what fifty per cent of
the families receive, and lower than what the other fifty per
cent receive. Note that in areas with high median incomes
(III*A*, for example) there is a larger number of people in high
income classes and a smaller number in the lower income
classes than in areas with a lower median income (I*C*, for
example.) Calculating the median gives a more representative
figure than would the arithmetic mean (the sum of all incomes
divided by the number of families) because the distribution
itself is skewed, that is, there are many more small incomes
than large ones.

Table II-1
Distribution of Families, by Income,
United States and Selected Areas, 1960
1959 Income, before Taxes

Percentage of Families

Income Class	United States	SMSA I District			SMSA II District			SMSA III District			
		A	B	C	A	B	C	A	B	C	CN
Less than 1,000	5	3.3	3.4	9.8	1.9	2.4	9.3	1.1	3.5	4.6	4.2
1,000–2,999	16.7	5.4	2.1	44.8	5.8	18.8	30.1	2.9	17.0	20.5	16.2
3,000–4,999	20.3	10.6	22.1	25.9	8.0	28.4	29.9	6.1	32.1	26.4	21.3
5,000–6,999	23.6	17.3	27.6	11.3	21.3	27.7	16.1	13.0	26.8	27.5	15.8
7,000–9,999	20.6	27.6	23.5	6.2	26.8	16.8	9.7	21.8	15.2	14.9	7.3
10,000–14,999	11.3	22.2	9.9	1.4	19.4	5.6	3.5	23.2	4.7	5.3	3.8
15,000–24,999	3.5	10.3	1.3	.6	11.3	.7	.5	18.0	.6	.7	–
25,000 and over		3.1	–	–	5.4	.2	.9	14.0	.1	.2	–
Median	$5,625		$5,752		$8,300		$3,703		$4,851		$4,176
			$8,295		$2,785		$5,869		$13,890		$4,888

Source: U.S. Censuses of Population and Housing: 1960, Final Report PHC (1).

These figures and their skewedness reflect, of course, the well-known fact that incomes are not equal, and therefore some people are better off than others. But it is worthwhile to compare the inequality of income distribution *within* one area to that within another. Does the population contain very rich and very poor? Or is everybody about as well-off (or as destitute) as the next person? To answer these questions, we use the figures from column 1 of Table II-1 to calculate the share of total income received by the families in each income class. If income were equally distributed, each group of families would receive a share of income equal to its share of the population: for example, the 11.3 per cent of the families in the country with incomes between $10,000 and $14,999 would receive 11.3 per cent of the total income in the country. These calculations can be expressed mathematically with a number known as the Gini ratio, or pictorially with a diagram known as the Lorenz curve. Diagram II-1 shows the Lorenz curve for the income distribution in column 1 of Table II-1, that is, for the United States in 1960. Since the percentages of population measured along the horizontal axis equal 100, as do the percentages of income measured along the vertical axis, the data would fall along the 45-degree line shown, if income were exactly equally distributed. The degree of inequality in income, therefore, determines how far away the data will actually fall: the more unequal, the more bowed-out the Lorenz Curve. This relation between any income distribution and the 45-degree line is expressed numerically by the Gini ratio, defined as the proportion of the total area under the diagonal that lies between the diagonal and the Lorenz curve. Thus, the smaller the ratio, the closer the Lorenz curve is to the 45-degree line; of two Gini ratios, .5 and .2, the former represents a more unequal distribution of income. The ratio computed for all families in the United States was .369 in 1960, very close to what it has been since World War II.

Diagram II-1
**Distribution of Income, United States, 1960
and Two Hypothetical Economies,**
Lorenz Curves

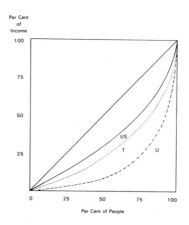

Diagram II-1 also shows two other lines that represent hypothetical data. A fascinating economic proposition exists about income distribution and development that stems from observations first made by Simon Kuznets.[1] He noted that income is more equally divided in mature than in developing economies: the distribution of income in the United States is more equal than that, say, in Mexico, which has reached the "take-off" stage in industrial development; and in Mexico, incomes are more equally distributed than in Haiti or some other under-developed economy. Line T on Diagram II-1 represents the distribution of income in a hypothetical developing country; line U, that in a poor stagnant economy. While data have been collected to illustrate this proposition, nobody really under-stands its relation to the process of development: that is, why do these differences in equality of distribution exist? More im-portant, do they mean that as a country progresses from rela-tive backwardness to maturity its people will share its income more evenly and if so, how? What happens to make the income distribution change over time in the process of development?

This proposition, and the literature that treats it, has two implications for the economics of the ghetto. First, some have argued that a ghetto resembles an underdeveloped country and requires technical assistance and capital investment for economic development in the same way that an underdeveloped country does. This hypothesis and its implications for policy will be discussed in Chapter Ten. It may be that one can use the Kuznets observation as a test of the "underdevelopedness" of a locality, specifically a ghetto area. Second, quite aside from questions of economic development, income inequalities tell us something about the relative *affluence* of different popula-tions. Within broad limits, richer groups of people have their total income more equally distributed than do poorer groups of people. In Kuznets' words, "The secular income structure is somewhat more unequal in underdeveloped countries than in the more advanced . . . the wider inequality in the secular income structure of underdeveloped countries is associated with a much lower level of average income per capita."[2] Dia-gram II-1 can depict not only three countries in different stages of economic development—the United States as a mature economy, Mexico as a developing economy, and Haiti as an undeveloped economy—but also three countries ranging from very poor to very rich. And in the richest country (the United

States) where average per capita income is eight times that of Mexico, incomes are much more equally distributed. The disparity between rich and poor is greatest in the *poor* countries; the poor people of the rich countries are not as widely separated from the rich people as are poor people in the poor countries. Consequently, economists have asked whether, *within* a given economy, areas with a high average income show a more even distribution of income than areas with a low average income. In this country, for example, the South, generally speaking, is a poor region compared to the Northwest. How does the distribution of income in the South compare to that in the Northwest? It is far more unequally distributed. The diagram could, equally well, stand for three regions in this, or any country, where the general economic level of well-being differs among the inhabitants.

Income inequality also appears among groups in the economy classified by occupation, age, employment, or other characteristic. For example, family income varies by age: where the head of the household was over 65, median income in 1960 was $2,862 compared to $6,385 in families headed by a man between 45 and 54. Income was distributed far more equally among the second group of families (Gini ratio of .357) than among the first (Gini ratio of .468). If we divide families according to whether or not they contain working wives, we find that in 1960 the median income of families where married women hold jobs outside the home was $6,808, while the median for families with nonworking wives was $5,448. The Gini ratios show marked inequality of income distribution for the families where wives did not work and a more equal distribution among the others: .378 and .294. Finally, we know that income figures for white families are about twice those for nonwhites, and we find that total income is more equally shared among white families than among nonwhites. In 1960 the median income for the latter group was $3,390; white families showed a median income of $6,190. The Gini ratios for the two groups were .410 and .357. The disparity between rich and poor was much greater for nonwhite families than for white families.

Such observations reinforce the correlation between low income and a high degree of income inequality, but they do little to explain it. We may ask, however, whether income inequality is also related to low incomes in neighborhood areas. The Census tract information suggests that such is the case, and that in an area where median income is high the distribution of income appears more equal than in an area where median income is low. The nine districts for which data is presented in Table II–1 show striking disparities of income distribution. As a general illustration, the Lorenz curves of Diagram II–1 represent fairly well (in exaggerated form) the three districts of each SMSA, using the curve of greatest equality (lying next to the diagonal) for district *A* where incomes are highest, and the other two curves, expressing more unequally shared income, standing for the poorer districts.

Diagram II–2 illustrates these differing income distributions in another way. This graph shows percentages of families on the vertical scale and relative incomes on the horizontal scale, where equal distances do not measure equal dollar *amounts* but equal proportions.* The curves delineating families of various incomes within the three *A* districts are much alike; they approximate a "normal" distribution with most of the families clustered within a fairly small range in the middle. In SMSA II and III, these A distributions contrast with those for district *B* where many more families appear at the low end of the distribution. But the curves for the *C* districts show the greatest dissimilarity with the other two. Most of the families in these areas receive a small percentage of income, and a small percentage of families receive incomes many times higher than those in the lower brackets.

These different ways of analyzing income suggest something of the complex nature of poverty, and of income as its measure. In most people's minds (according to the precise definition introduced in the previous chapter), the urban ghetto spells poverty. Certainly poverty adds to the problems of the ghetto. But most measures of poverty are necessarily relative: Table II–1 enables us to say, for instance, that the inhabitants of district A in each SMSA are better off than the other families

*Such a geometric or semi-logarithmic scale is best understood by comparing specific figures. Note that the distance between $2,000 and $4,000 equals the distance between $4,000 and $8,000 or between $5,000 and $10,000, because each of these pairs equals the same ratio, 1:2.

Diagram II-2
Distribution of Families by Income, Selected Areas, 1960

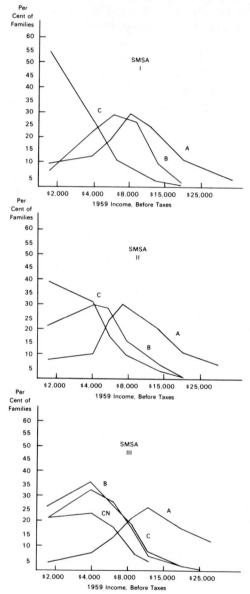

tabulated. It does not allow us to say that *any* of the groups shown is "poor" in any absolute sense. Diagram II–2 lets us say that income is more unequally distributed in low-income than in high-income areas: it does not measure poverty absolutely any more than dollar figures do. Unless, however, we take absolute income equality as our goal, poverty and wealth in a *relative* sense cannot be abolished: there will always be some families in the lower half of the income distribution; and we all know someone better off than we are.

This type of ranking does not pose a major problem for most people, and certainly not for society: it is rather the degradation and privation of the way poor families live that arouses our concern. We need, therefore, to turn from the dollar figures of income distributions to another way of looking at income and poverty.

DOLLAR INCOME AND REAL INCOME

What did it actually mean if your family had an income of, say, $5,625 in 1960? How do people with median incomes live? To use more recent figures, in 1968 the median family income was $8,632, well above that of 1960. Even after allowing for price rises, family income has increased over the past decade: the median level, in real terms or in constant dollars, is thirty per cent above that of 1960. Most families could buy almost one-third more, in 1968, than they could in 1960.

But the question remains, *what* can you buy with an average income, or a median amount? If half the families in the country received more than $8,632 in 1968 (or $5,625 in 1960), how much more food and clothing and cars and cosmetics did they buy than the bottom half of the families below the median income? How far does $8,600 go, these days? How far did the median income of families in district IC (about $3000) go in 1960?

Answers to these questions depend on what a family buys as well as the prices it pays, and the list of purchases depends on who the family is—that is, how many adults and children, of what ages, live together or are provided for by the family income. But it seems plausible that one could design a list of items—the "necessities of life," perhaps—that should be available to any particular kind of family. Such a list, for example, might stress milk for a family with young children and gasoline for one with teen-agers. This approach would measure poverty realistically, in terms of how the family lives, by the food and clothing and furniture they can buy, rather than by dollar sums. It would also, seemingly, provide an absolute rather than a relative standard with which to identify poor families. It would represent a generally agreed-upon minimum level that families or individuals would not be allowed to fall below.

Most people feel, from a wishful point of view, that such a level exists, but the American way of assisting those who lack a minimum income has taken many and varied forms over the years. In *From the Depths*,[3] historian Robert Bremner traces the American awareness of and the Americans' attitudes toward poverty, both of which shape the ways in which we have dealt with poverty. Bremner makes it clear that defining the minimum level of living has always been a controversial issue in any program to alleviate poverty or erase its causes.*

Some of the terms that have been used to describe such a minimum include "a standard of health and decency," "the bare necessities," "enough to live on," "the minimum requirements of health, decency, and self-respect, according to conditions actually prevailing," a "standard below which an average family could not fall without the sacrifice of something absolutely essential," and so on. These descriptions are qualitative, not quantitative, and therefore there can be disagreement over them. And there is even a sense of hysteria in these quotations: they move from the fairly calm statement about health and decency to a frenzied cry about sacrificing something *absolutely essential,* as if introducing adverbs like "absolutely" improved the definition.

The economist tries to avoid such terms because they are value judgments; he should search for quantitative data which he is competent to handle. This does not mean that we should not *make* value judgments, but only that it is simply more efficient to measure something than to argue interminably about whether it is large or small. But *having* measured it, we can then judge its size as desirable, or beautiful, or repulsive, or prohibitive, or anything else. We do not avoid this judgment

*Cf. Chapter Seven, pp. 169–172.

by insisting on measurement first, we simply make it clearer. What data exist, then, to express a minimum level of consumption or living?

BUDGETS AND STANDARDS

Around the turn of the century, when social workers and other people investigated conditions in the slums and poverty areas of American cities, the customary way of defining a minimum level was to prepare a budget: a list of articles selected by an expert in household management. Newly arrived immigrant families learned, in settlement houses, to prepare nutritious meals from the suggested foods and to shop for the durable furniture and sturdy clothing itemized. The budget-makers leaned heavily on the actual experiences of actual families, however, and from surveys of family expenditures, they discovered what items and quantities were customarily bought.

The history of consumer surveys probably begins with Ernst Engel in the middle of the nineteenth century; certainly Engel's laws, as they are called, play a vital role in our current definitions of poverty. Engel discovered from analyzing data on European family income and spending that food purchases amounted to a smaller proportion of large incomes than of small incomes. Since this relationship appears in all sorts of different populations and time periods, we celebrate it by calling the ratio between food expenditure and income an "Engel coefficient." For example, among urban families in the United States in 1960, this coefficient amounted to .24, compared to .30 in 1950 when the average family income was smaller.*

*These particular figures, and most Engel coefficients, calculate expenditures as a percentage of *total consumption expenditure*, rather than of *total income*. In other words, the average family in 1950 spent $3.00 on food out of every $10.00 spent in current consumption; in 1960 food purchases took only $2.40 out of every $10.00 spent. Since total spending is obviously higher at higher income levels, the relationship is the same whether we use total income or total consumption expenditure. But it is wise to use the latter figure in comparing expenditures among families at different income levels. For one thing, families at very low income levels frequently spend more than their total income, while families with large incomes save a substantial amount. So the fraction of *income* spent on food would understate its importance to poor families, and overstate it for rich families. Based on total consumption expenditures, the Engel coefficient for urban families in 1960 ranged from .30 for families with incomes of less than $2,000 to .24 for those with incomes between $7,500 and $10,000 and to .19 for families with incomes above $15,000.

These figures come from surveys of incomes and expenditures conducted by the Bureau of Labor Statistics in the Department of Labor; such studies provide a wealth of detail on types and amounts of income, spending, and saving for many different kinds of families, classified by size, location, age, and occupation. Special surveys of food purchases and consumption habits add more data; in 1955 and in 1965 the Agricultural Research Service of the Department of Agriculture conducted Household Food Consumption Surveys. They show, for example, that in 1965 the average family spent $33.06 weekly for food, but the families with incomes from $2,000 to $3,000 spent less than this, $21.15, while families with incomes between $8,000 and $9,000 spent almost double that sum, or $42.02. This latter represents, of course, a smaller *proportion* of total income or spending. The surveys furnish many details: for example, in 1965 American families averaged weekly purchases of almost a pound of fresh tomatoes, less than half a pound of canned tomatoes, about the same quantity of tomato juice, and half a cup of condensed tomato soup.[4]

Over the years since 1875 when Carroll Wright made the first reliable large-scale survey of incomes and expenditures in Massachusetts, the nutritionists as well as the statisticians have been working to improve our knowledge about food consumption. Our notions of a proper diet have altered with the discovery of vitamins and trace elements in foods, with analyses of types of proteins, fats, and starches, and with improved methods of food processing and of quality control. Between 1900 and 1965 the American diet changed markedly, as suggested in Diagram II–3. The new knowledge of nutrition has also made it possible to draw up minimum standards for food consumption in terms of the nutrients required to maintain health and growth. The National Research Council has worked out recommended daily allowances of calories and of the fats, carbohydrates, and proteins which provide them: these criteria come very close to an objective measurement of a minimum level of consumption, with none of the overtones of quality implicit in earlier descriptions of "absolutely essential" and the like.

Diagram II-3
Trends in our Eating Habits*

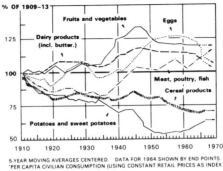

5-YEAR MOVING AVERAGES CENTERED.   DATA FOR 1964 SHOWN BY END POINTS.
*PER CAPITA CIVILIAN CONSUMPTION (USING CONSTANT RETAIL PRICES AS INDEX WEIGHTS).

U.S. DEPARTMENT OF AGRICULTURE   NEG. ERS 93X-64 (11) ECONOMIC RESEARCH SERVICE

But to say that a minimum level of income should provide at least 3000 calories a day for an adult male in a sedentary job and 2200 calories for a mildly active adult female does not entirely satisfy our search for an absolute measure of *food* consumption, below which people are poor. We cannot yet buy packaged calories and other nutritional needs in the supermarket. A recent analysis[5] dramatizes this problem of defining a minimum level:

> A good diet can be bought for very little money. Many inexpensive foods are good sources of nutrients. For example, the following foods eaten daily would provide a man with a good diet . . . : two cups of milk made from nonfat dry milk, two cups of cooked dry beans, five medium-size potatoes, 10 slices of enriched white bread and six ounces of margarine fortified with vitamin A. These foods cost about 40 cents in a Washington supermarket. Meals for a week would cost less than $3.00.

But the thought of eating three meals a day, 365 days a year, from these unvaried ingredients is insupportable.

So nutritional standards have to provide palatable food that people will eat, including some variety—if not from day to day then at least occasionally. To do this, experts at the Bureau of Human Nutrition and Home Economics in the Department of Agriculture have prepared low-cost menus, using food-stuffs

that are commonly in local markets, to provide the homemaker
with suggestions for how to feed a family economically but
nutritiously.

However, at this point, alas, we have left the realm of ob-
jectivity and technical standards, for once we move to choosing
actual foodstuffs, we confront human differences and likes and
dislikes. One family may like to eat oatmeal for breakfast
seven days a week and may even revel in it sugarless and with
skim milk—and this is an extremely nutritious and inexpensive
meal. But another family may rebel and demand poached eggs
and buttered toast, with a glass of whole milk or hot milk in
coffee. And while this is the same nutritionally, it costs more.
Now if we agree that the "good diet" described above is impossible, is oatmeal for breakfast equally untenable? How do
you decide which foods are acceptable for a minimum-cost diet
and which are too distasteful? Economics has no magic answer
to such questions.

The food plans can, however, be used with Engel coefficients
to calculate poverty-level incomes without specifying whether
these are "minimal," "absolutely essential," or whatever. The
Department of Agriculture prepares five food plans listing various foods in appropriate weekly amounts for different family
members: excerpts from the *least* expensive of these appear in
Table II–2. It suggests, for example, five eggs and one and
one-half pounds of citrus fruits, weekly, for each child between
six and eight, with fewer eggs and more fruit for each woman
over fifty-five years old. With such precise quantities, the expenditures required for a given food plan can be computed
from current market prices: in September 1969, the cost of
food at home under the Economy Plan amounted to $20.60
weekly for a family of four (man and woman between twenty
and thirty-five years old, two children under six). Turning now
to the survey data on *actual* expenditures for food, the Engel
coefficient (percentage of total expenditures taken by food purchases) can be calculated for such a four-person family. The
1955 Household Food Consumption Survey showed that similar families used approximately 35 per cent of their total
expenditures for food. If, therefore, the $20.60 required by the
Economy Food Plan is figured at 35 per cent, a total repre-

senting the "poverty level" can be calculated—in this case about $3060 annually. This is the procedure, first evolved and described by Mollie Orshansky in a classic article,[6] which makes it possible to vary the "poverty level" income depending on the number and age of family members, as well as their residence on farms or in urban areas.

Table II-2
Economy Food Plan, Amounts of Food for a Week

Food Plan Groups	Quantities for Family Members				
	Man, 35-54	Woman, 35-54	Girl, 9-11	Boy, 15-19	Child, 1-2
Milk, cheese, ice cream, quarts	3	3	5	6	4
Meat, poultry, fish, pounds	1¾	1¾	1¾	2½	1¼
Eggs, number	5	6	5	5	4
Dry beans, peas, nuts, pounds	½	⅝	⅝	⅝	¼
Flour, cereals, bakery products, pounds	4¼	2½	2¾	5	2¼
Citrus fruit, tomatoes, pounds	1½	1½	1¾	1¾	1¼
Dark-green, deep-yellow vegetables, pounds	¾	1½	¾	¾	¼
Potatoes, pounds	3½	2½	2½	4¾	1½
Other vegetables, fruits, pounds	3¼	2¾	3¼	3½	2½
Fats, oils, pounds	¾	⅜	½	1	⅜
Sugars, sweets, pounds	⅞	½	⅝	⅞	⅜

Source: U.S. Department of Agriculture, Washington, D.C.

Any such definition depends for its dollar values, of course, on the prices currently prevailing, so poverty level incomes have been revised periodically. For 1968, the average poverty income was calculated at $1,742 for a single person, $2,242 for two people, $3,531 for a four-member family, and $5,722 for a family with seven or more. These figures prompted the proposal in 1969 to remove such poor families from the federal income tax rolls. The definitions also influenced the administration's plan, voiced late in 1969, to allow income supplements for families of the so-called "working poor," such as the father of seven who can not earn more than $5,000.

The poverty index is not the only budget that has been evolved from expenditure data and Engel coefficients. In early 1969, the Bureau of Labor Statistics published lists of specifications for three living standards—moderate, higher, and lower, together with the dollar income required to maintain each of these standards in various cities throughout the country. Like the index of poverty income, these lists include food plans prepared by the Department of Agriculture to carry out the National Research Council's recommendations for good nutrition, but the moderate and higher budgets allow more expensive foods. Similar "objective" standards determined the specifications for shelter, medical care, and so on. For many items the budgets merely specify quantities or dollar amounts that result from consumer choice itself—the amounts bought by families with sufficient income to search for better quality rather than quantity. For example, survey data show that clothing expenditures are higher at successively higher income levels; at some point, however, the *rate* of increase falls off as clothing needs become less pressing in the estimation of the buyers. Purchases at this level represent the clothing budget for the moderate living standard; adjustments up and down provide clothing allowances for the other two budgets.

Table II-3 gives some examples of budget quantities for a four-person family: the difference in the three food plans shows up clearly in the pounds of meats and vegetables; the figures for personal care and furniture suggest that even the "higher living standard" is not exactly luxurious. For durables like furniture, the suggested quantities are best thought of in terms of replacements: thus the .04 living-room sofa, annually, means a sofa that lasts for twenty-five years; and the .10 vacuum cleaner suggests that the appliance has a ten-year life. These standards suggest one answer to our earlier question, what can the "average" family buy? The *moderate* standard shown costs more, in most cities, than the median family income. Half the families in the country, therefore, lack the means to buy these items.

Table II-3
Three Standards of Living, Selected Items, For an Urban Family of Four Persons

Item[1]	Unit	Budgeted Quantity		
		Lower Standard	Moderate Standard	Higher Standard
Milk and milk products[2]	quarts	18.00	19.00	20.50
Meat, poultry, and fish	pounds	11.25	17.50	20.75
Eggs	dozen	2.08	2.25	2.42
Dry beans, peas, and nuts	pounds	1.38	.88	.88
Grain products[3]	pounds	13.00	12.25	11.00
Citrus fruits and tomatoes	pounds	7.50	9.00	11.75
Potatoes	pounds	10.00	8.50	7.75
Other vegetables and fruits	pounds	22.50	25.00	27.75
Fats and oils	pounds	2.12	2.75	2.75
Sugar and sweets	pounds	2.75	3.38	4.25
Haircut, husband		18.9	23.2	24.9
Wife:				
Haircut		1.6	3.0	3.8
Permanent wave		–	.9	1.1
Shampoo and set		.7	4.6	16.3
Boy, Haircut		10.4	12.8	13.3
Girl, Haircut		.7	1.3	2.2
Toilet soap	medium bar	105.1	116.2	142.1
Toothpaste	ounce	64.4	64.4	64.4
Shaving cream	ounce	21.1	21.1	21.1
Cleansing tissue	box 200 double	25.3	27.3	32.3
Shampoo	ounce	47.5	47.5	47.5
Home permanent kit	refill	1.5	.6	.6
Sanitary supplies	box of twelve	20.7	20.7	20.7
Furniture:				
Living room suite		.01	.04	.04
Chair, fully upholstered		.09	.09	.11
Table		–	.08	.08
Sofa		.02	.04	.04
Bedroom suite		.03	.03	.05

[1]For food items, quantities shown are *weekly* purchases; for all other items, *yearly* quantities. Weekly quantities provide for 84 meals at home or 4,368 meals annually.
[2]Includes fluid whole milk and milk products.
[3]Weight in terms of flour and cereal.
Source: U.S. Department of Labor, Bureau of Labor Statistics, Bulletin No. 1570-5, "Three Standards of Living" (Washington, D.C.: U.S. Government Printing Office, 1969), pp. 53, 55, 64.

Table II-3 continued

Item[1]	Unit	Budgeted Quantity		
		Lower Standard	Moderate Standard	Higher Standard
Bed		.01	.02	.04
Mattress and bedspring		.26	.36	.36
Dresser and chest		.01	.01	.04
Dining room suite		–	.01	.01
Dining room table		.03	.04	.04
Dining room chairs		–	.05	.06
Dinette set		.02	.03	.04
Porch and Garden		.25	.30	.91
Vacuum cleaner		.05	.07	.10
Washing machine		.09	.15	.15
Clothes dryer		–	–	.05
Dishwasher		–	–	.02
Waste disposal		–	–	.02
Toaster		.03	.03	.06
Fryer, food mixer, etc.		.04	.10	.19
Iron		.09	.09	.13
Sewing machine		.04	.04	.05
Fan		.06	.06	.08

Although the low-cost budget shown on Table II–3 (or various adaptations of it) has been used by state and local welfare agencies to spell out goods and services available to families receiving various forms of welfare assistance, it was not designed primarily for this purpose. The poverty-level income figures have been used to make aggregate estimates of poverty, counting the number of poor people and the total amount of income deficiency in any one year. Neither the budget nor the calculated poverty income figures can be relied upon to identify poverty in ghetto areas, because of two problems. Dollar figures cannot adequately portray affluence or poverty, no matter how they are calculated or analyzed; these terms describe ways of living, or at least of consuming goods and services.

The low-cost food plan, for example, assumes that the homemaker is not only a good manager, with ample knowledge of nutrition and food planning, but that she has time to shop and the skill to keep waste to a minimum. The menus require considerable home cooking, which assumes not only adequate kitchen facilities, utensils, and good working conditions, but also the time and skill to prepare nutritious and appealing meals. All these attributes are not easily come by: the 1965 Household Food Consumption Survey found, for example, that among those families who spent the amounts recommended by the low-cost food plan, only three out of ten had a nutritionally adequate diet.

The specifications in the entire low-cost budget assume similar domestic skill on the part of shopper and homemaker as well as an adequate marketing system giving the low-income consumer access to good quality merchandise at budget prices. In a later chapter we can look more closely at the consumption and marketing patterns of ghetto residents, but here we may merely remark that income dollars have to be *spent* in order to achieve any standard of living. The measures of income discussed in this chapter give us a better understanding of how to compare rich and poor, although we may wish to agree with Mollie Orshansky[7] that

> Counting the poor is an exercise in the art of the possible. For deciding who is poor, prayers are more relevant than calculations because poverty, like beauty, lies in the eye of the beholder. Poverty is a value judgment; it is not something one can verify and demonstrate, except by inference and suggestion, even with a measure of error. To say who is poor is to use all sorts of value judgments. The concept has to be defined by the purpose which is to be served by the definition. There is no particular reason to count the poor unless you are going to do something about them. Whatever the possibilities for socioeconomic research in general, when it comes to defining poverty, you can only be more subjective or less so. You cannot be unsubjective.

Following this adjuration, our purpose is not to define poverty per se, but to analyze ghetto conditions.

CHAPTER THREE

HOUSING

To ANALYZE the economics of ghetto housing requires three types of data. There are, first, facts on the condition of housing; second, summary information about housing tenure; and third, some knowledge of the residents—how many families with how many people living together, and how many single individuals. For any group of people, housing characteristics show certain correlations with income, with the distribution of ethnic groups, and with the type of families according to their composition, the age and education of family members, and so on.

How Much Does Housing Cost?

We begin with a crude relationship between housing and income. In the previous chapter, the meaning of "real" income —the quantities of goods and services that can be bought with a given sum of dollars—was defined by some very specific budget lists that help dramatize the differences in how people at different income levels live. Such budgets always include detailed specifications about housing, because next to food, housing cost bulks the largest in determining the level of real income obtainable with a given money income. And like expenditures on food, the portion of income devoted to housing has been closely studied with surveys of consumer behavior. But unlike Engel's law for food, there is no clear relation between total housing expenditures and total income, so we cannot speak of Engel coefficients with respect to housing.*

Engel and his immediate followers in the late nineteenth century did, however, collect data on housing that settled a number of questions; and they built up a structure of analysis which is still used. These investigators of the poverty and urban ghettos of their time studied city planning and the economic impact of discrimination. They included Charles Booth and Seebohm Rowntree, who surveyed London, York, and other industrial British cities, and Charles B. Spahr and Robert Chapin in the United States.[1] Their early findings agree that housing *expenditures* depended more than anything else upon housing *tenure*—that is, whether the family rented or owned its dwelling.

In the second half of the twentieth century, housing tenure has much to do with the meaning of a ghetto. First, the original term "ghetto" referred to a place where people *lived* (the location of their housing) and to where people *had* to live (in other locations their housing tenure was restricted). The contemporary term "ghetto" implies a similar restriction on housing tenure. The definition of the Commission on Civil Disorders, quoted in the first chapter, refers to "conditions of involuntary segregation." Second, if the ghetto is an urban phenomenon, so are certain problems of housing, because housing tenure differs significantly in the city from that in suburbs, villages, or farms. Finally, insofar as housing expenditures express real income, they clarify the notion of poverty in the ghetto.

Housing has a dual impact on real income. Since housing expenditures take a significant fraction of total income, the amount left over for other things depends on the rent or other

---

*To confuse matters, one or more statements of a *so-called* Engel's law of housing do exist. One version says that housing expenditures, like food, take a smaller share of larger incomes than of smaller incomes. Another version says that the percentage of income spent on housing is constant over small and large incomes. Any such broad statement is wrong on two counts: first, Engel never drew any conclusions about housing expenditures, and second, survey data do not reveal any consistent relationship between housing and income.

current payment for housing. This argument may sound circular, in that *any* type of spending determines how much is "left over," but in the entire consumption pattern—the way a family disposes of total income—housing expenditures change least often. It is possible to vary the amount spent on, say, entertainment with that spent for transportation, and to do this in the course of a week. One can economize on a fall wardrobe or put off buying a new car in order to pay an unexpected dentist's bill. But housing expenditures reflect decisions that are made infrequently and usually commit the consumer for over a year or even longer; one cannot "cut down" this month and splurge next month. Consequently, the amount spent for housing does in a very real sense, or over the short term, determine how much is "left over."

Housing expenditures also determine real income by shaping the family's entire way of life. Housing regulates how far the wage earner travels to his job and the shopper to food and clothing stores, how long it takes to get to church or school, what kinds of places one walks by on the way home and whether, once there, the view is of trees or concrete. The technical terms "housing expenditures," "conditions of health and cleanliness," cover intensely personal living conditions, like whether the child has a room of his own and the wife sufficient counter space in the kitchen, whether the baby can play safely on the floor, and how much time and effort must be spent on house cleaning. Housing tenure also affects real income by influencing other types of expenditures. Home owners differ from renters in their purchases of many different types of consumer goods and their use of services. It seems obvious that renters would spend less on kitchen appliances and garden tools, but perhaps it would be unexpected that they spend more on alcoholic beverages, even within the same income class and location.

What data exist on housing expenditures, tenure, and income? The nation-wide survey of 1960–61, mentioned in the previous chapter, disclosed that the average family spent 29 per cent of its total expenditures for housing. This term "housing" must be subdivided: one set of categories distinguishes *shelter, household operations,* and *house furnishings and equipment.* In turn, shelter includes: (1) either rent or home ownership costs like mortgage payments and taxes, and (2) the utilities used to provide heat, light, water, and sanitation. Household operations consist of cleaning and laundry supplies plus such services as repairs for furniture and equipment, telephone, and dry-cleaning. Some examples of expenditures for house furnishings and equipment occur on Table II–3 in the previous chapter; the term also includes household textiles, kitchen utensils, china and glass, and so on.

The figures for shelter exclusive of utilities—that is, how much the family pays for the housing unit in which it lives—show that this cost to *renters* takes about 15 per cent of total consumption expenditures while the amounts spent by *owners* come to 11 per cent. (Neither of these figures resembles the familiar rule-of-thumb that housing costs should equal one-fifth of income because we are quoting percentages of total expenditures, not income, and because many items of household operation and utilities are included in the "rule-of-thumb" ratio.) The difference between owners and renters exists partly because owners tend to have higher incomes (and therefore higher total expenditures) than renters, and partly because some home owners, with no mortgage, make no payments for principal and interest, whereas rent payments occur with monotonous regularity.

The housing *tenure* which determines these expenditures can be broadly described by some figures for the country as a whole. First, we are a nation of home owners: in 1969, 64 per cent of all families owned their homes. Second, there is wide variation by area. Part of this country consists of *farms,* where three-fourths of the families own their home, and part of it consists of *nonfarm rural areas,* where 72 per cent of the people are home owners. These two kinds of areas, however, contain only about twenty per cent of the entire population, for the Standard Metropolitan Statistical Areas include 63 per cent of the population and the rest live in urban places outside them. Within each SMSA, the proportion of renters is highest in the urban core, where only 48 per cent of all families owned their homes in 1969. Note that all these statements refer to *families,* including single individuals, or one-person families; such figures come from surveys where the consumer or family is the basic unit counted.

Census tract data refer to *housing units,** the separate dwelling-places of families or individuals, and consequently provide other types of information, including the number of units in the structure, their value and gross rent, which allows some analysis of shelter costs for families with different incomes. In 1960, 62 per cent of all housing units were occupied by owners, with much the same variation by regions or areas as that described for families. In any area where the Census data show a high percentage of single-unit structures, the percentage of owner occupancy will also be high. In this country, "ownership" nearly always means single-unit houses, and rentals mean multiple-unit dwellings; and this has an important bearing on the type and condition of housing in different areas.

WHAT DOES THE HOUSING DOLLAR BUY?

Census data also include statistics on housing *quality,* which must be appraised according to some type of standard. As always, economists hope that technical experts will furnish some objective definitions (like the nutrients in food), but they do not yet exist. In the meantime precise knowledge of the Census definitions is essential. Three basic categories describe the condition of housing: *sound, deteriorating,* and *dilapidated.* Four categories for *plumbing facilities* distinguish various toilet, bathing, and water-heating arrangements. The details of these definitions follow:[2]

> Sound housing is defined as that which has no defects, or only slight defects which are normally corrected during the course of regular maintenance. Examples of slight defects include: lack of paint; slight damage to porch or steps; small cracks in walls, plaster, or chimney; broken gutters or downspouts; slight wear on floors or doorsills.
>
> Deteriorating housing needs more repair than would be provided in the course of regular maintenance. It has one or more defects of an intermediate nature that must be corrected if the unit is to continue to provide safe and adequate shelter. Examples of intermediate defects in-

*Cf. Chapter One, pp. 24–26

clude: shaky or unsafe porch or steps; holes, open cracks or missing materials over a small area of the floors or doorsills; broken or loose stair treads or missing balusters. Such defects are signs of neglect which lead to serious structural deterioration or damage if not corrected.

Dilapidated housing does not provide safe and adequate shelter. It has one or more critical defects; or has a combination of intermediate defects in sufficient number to require extensive repair or rebuilding; or is of inadequate original construction. Critical defects result from continued neglect or indicate serious damage to the structure. Examples of critical defects include: holes, open cracks, or missing materials over a large area of the floors, walls, roof, or other parts of the structure; sagging floors, walls, or roof; damage by storm or fire. Inadequate original construction includes structures built of makeshift materials and inadequately converted cellars, sheds, or garages not originally intended as living quarters.

Plumbing. The category "With all plumbing facilities" consists of units which have hot and cold piped water inside the structure, and flush toilet and bathtub (or shower) inside the structure for the exclusive use of the occupants of the unit. Equipment is for exclusive use when it is used only by the persons in one housing unit, including any lodgers living in the unit.

The category "Lacking some or all facilities" consists of units which do not have all the plumbing facilities specified above. Units without hot water, toilet, or bathtub (or shower) are included in this category. Also included are units whose occupants share toilet or bathing facilities with the occupants of another housing unit.

The category "Lacking some or all facilities—with flush toilet" consists of units which do not have all plumbing facilities but do have a flush toilet inside the structure. The toilet may be for the exclusive use of the occupants of the unit or shared with the occupants of another housing unit.

The category "Lacking some or all facilities—without flush toilet" consists of units for which there is no flush toilet available in the structure. These units may lack other plumbing facilities also.

The next question is to determine minimum standards: which conditions are unacceptable in American living? Two attempts at defining minimum standards follow:

"Social welfare demands for every family a safe and sanitary home; healthful surroundings; ample and pure running water inside the house; modern and sanitary toilet conveniences; adequate sunlight and ventilation; reasonable fire protection; privacy."[3]

"The primary objective of housing is health . . . that term includes not only sanitation and safety from physical hazards but also those qualities of comfort and convenience and aesthetic satisfaction essential for emotional and social well-being."[4]

The two seem quite similar, yet the first introduces a set of detailed specifications written in 1912 and the second prefaces a study in 1951. They suggest that the Census definitions are not unreasonable, despite their use of words like "considerable," "normal," "slight," "serious," and "sufficient" which occur without quantitative reference. If these definitions seem ambiguous, the Census warns that subjective interpretation is impossible to overcome completely, despite the detailed instructions and illustrative examples used in training enumerators.

The first standard of quality, therefore, assesses the condition of the structure—sound, deteriorating, or dilapidated—and the basic plumbing facilities available. "Substandard housing" has a very precise meaning: *either* it is dilapidated by the Census definition *or* it lacks hot running water, or a private flush toilet, or a bathtub or shower for private use. "Standard housing" must therefore include all plumbing facilities but it may require some repair. This definition represents, in a way, the current translation of the statements quoted about sanitation and safety for every family. The percentage of homes that fail to meet this standard has been declining over the past two decades: preliminary figures suggest that in 1966 about 10 per cent of all housing units would be classified as substandard, down from 16 per cent in 1960.

Another quality standard evaluates the space and privacy available for each family member or individual; these are also mentioned in general terms in the two standards quoted, and in terms of square and cubic feet per person in the detailed specification. "Privacy," however, implies something about individuals and the rooms available to them, not just the space inside a structure. The number of persons per room is a criterion of privacy or of crowding; in 1960 12 per cent of the units housed more than one person per room. (Group quarters have different specifications from those for housing units, so none of these standards apply to institutions.)

The most recent review of housing standards, by the National Commission on Urban Problems, suggests that these quality measures, of structures and occupancy rates, are insufficient:

> Decent housing has a far more subjective definition. . . . For middle-class Americans at the end of the 1960's, decent housing implies a high level of amenity, both in the house and within its immediate environment, a level of amenity none of the rest of the world, outside the rich, enjoys in its housing.
>
> To meet middle-class aspirations, decent housing may mean, for instance, enough bathrooms so there are no morning lineups as the family gets ready for work and school; uncrowded bedrooms; and a kitchen with a sink, range, oven, refrigerator, counter space, and outlets for portable appliances. Many even would include as minimum requirements dishwashers, clothes washers and dryers, garbage disposals, and, in areas of hot climate, air conditioning.
>
> Even such housing does not meet many people's idea of what is decent unless, in the neighborhood, there is recreation for children, shopping, and public transportation. Cultural or entertainment facilities within easy reach, trees, grass, flowers, and other features that make a neighborhood pleasant and liveable are expected. In short, the house that is adequate in itself ceases to be adequate for the middle-class family when dropped in the middle of a slum or otherwise unsuitable surroundings.[5]

The Commission here raises some of the same problems mentioned in the previous chapter in dealing with so-called "objective" standards or "minimum" levels. But despite the dissatisfaction with the existing definition of *substandard* housing, it is still used, as are other dimensions of quality, to appraise the housing of a given area. Table III–1 suggests that, like income figures, housing data provide considerable insight into the economic status of a neighborhood or small district. The table refers to the same SMSA's as the income distributions in the previous chapters: In SMSA I each district, *A, B,* and *C,* contains about 19,000 people; in SMSA II each district contains about 12,000 people; and in SMSA III from 10,000 to 14,000.

Table III-1
Housing Quality, Selected Areas, 1960

	I			II			III		
	A	B	C	A	B	C	A	B	C
Population, thousands	19.5	19.1	19.6	12.0	13.0	12.1	10.6	14.1	14.0
Families, thousands	5.7	4.9	3.9	3.4	3.6	2.8	2.8	3.7	3.4
Housing units, thousands	8.3	7.1	7.1	3.7	5.2	4.4	3.1	5.6	4.5
Percentage of units:	100°	100	100	100	100	100	100	100	100
Owner occupied	11.9	20.6	5.7	91.0	37.1	42.6	94.3	4.5	36.9
Renter occupied	82.9	73.0	83.0	7.5	55.4	48.4	2.8	87.3	57.6
Available vacant	4.3	4.6	7.8	–	6.0	6.5	1.4	6.8	3.7
Sound	97.6	76.0	56.0	96.9	69.0	61.6	99.3	91.0	63.2
Deteriorating	2.3	17.8	29.6	2.8	27.9	30.8	.6	8.7	28.9
Dilapidated	–	6.1	14.3	–	3.0	7.6	–	–	7.9
Other substandard	1.2	33.1	36.5	–	11.8	21.9	–	20.0	7.4
One bath only	89.5	62.2	48.7	56.5	75.8	72.6	31.0	79.7	82.8
Shared or no bath	1.1	35.7	48.9	–	19.1	22.9	–	19.0	8.4
Built before 1939	86.5	98.8	86.3	26.5	94.5	93.9	50.0	95.0	9.9
Percentage of units,									
persons per room	100	100	100	100	100	100	100	100	100
.50 or less	50.2	38.9	16.2	51.6	44.1	46.3	59.2	45.4	49.5
.51 to 1.00	46.4	42.5	50.3	42.9	38.6	29.3	39.7	45.9	37.5
1.01 or more	3.5	12.2	33.5	3.7	9.9	14.4	1.1	8.7	7.7
Percentage of units,									
occupants moved in	100	100	100	100	100	100	100	100	100
1958 to March, 1960	37.5	30.2	36.8	22.9	37.2	33.0	24.8	33.1	28.1
1954 to 1957	29.8	22.7	42.5	28.7	19.7	23.1	25.5	25.0	21.7
1940 to 1953	24.2	26.7	16.7	41.5	24.3	33.1	34.4	20.4	27.4
1939 or earlier	8.5	14.1	3.8	7.5	8.9	10.8	15.3	21.5	17.5

Table III-1 Continued
Housing Quality, Selected Areas, 1960

	I			II			III		
	A	**B**	**C**	**A**	**B**	**C**	**A**	**B**	**C**
Median value, owned units		$13,450			$7,800			$8,425	
	$22,139		$12,351	$16,635		$7,130	$22,120		$8,300
Median rent, rented units		$54.80			$63.40			$58.40	
	121.10		$65.31	–		$63.40	–		$73.40
Ratio, median rent to median family income		11.3%			13.0%			14.4%	
	16.9%		28.1%	–		21.0%	–		17.6%

Source: Census of Population and Housing, 1960.

Housing in each district *A* clearly represents a high level of real income: practically no homes are substandard, only a tiny fraction are deteriorating, and very few units house more than one person to a room. In SMSA I and III, where most of the *houses* have two or more baths, the median value of owned units turns out (coincidentally) to be about the same—almost twice the median value of all owned homes in the country. In the *A* districts of SMSA II and III, single-family dwellings predominate; in SMSA I these are in the minority, but the median rent of $121 represents for the apartment dweller the same type of superiority as the median value of the home. Evidently the district in SMSA I lies well within the inner city; whereas in II and III, district *A* represents suburbs where over half the families had lived for eight years or longer, although III *A* contains more new homes than II *A*. Fewer families and more single individuals live in I *A*, with a substantial turnover in the population, although the bulk of the *housing* is pre-World War II.

The contrast with the *B* and *C* districts is significant, although each SMSA warrants separate analysis. In district I*B*, one-fifth of the housing units are occupied by their owners, but most of them were built before 1939 and lack proper maintenance. Only a small amount of housing was judged dilapidated, so most of the substandard housing is due to inadequate plumbing facilities. The percentage of sound housing is higher than that in district I*C* where the families are clearly much worse off, with a higher percentage of both crowded and dilapidated quarters. Unlike *B,* the district's residents are fairly new to the area; eight of ten moved in during the preceding five years. The situation in SMSA II presents a somewhat different picture, with more home ownership in the poorest district *C* than in *B,* although both show a paucity of homes built since 1939. The amount of housing classified as either sound or deteriorating is not too dissimilar between the two districts—both fall well below the higher-income suburb in this respect—but district *C* has twice as many dilapidated housing units, and the lack of interior plumbing facilities and privacy is almost twice as great as in district *B.*

In both these metropolitan areas, the median income of families living in the *C* district was well below that of families in the *B* district.* It is instructive, therefore, to look at the median rents paid in view of the substantial amount of poor quality housing. The last line of Table III-1 calculates median rent as a percentage of median income.** This figure is totally artificial but serves as a useful link between money income and real income.

In SMSA II, the median rent paid in district *C,* despite the amount of overcrowded and inadequate housing, was exactly equal to that in district *B.* Owing to the difference in income, however, this rent represented 21 per cent of the income of the poorer people in district *C,* and only 13 per cent of the median income in district *B.* In SMSA I, the lower income area (district *C*) showed a higher *dollar* median rent which amounted to 28 per cent of median income; in district *B* the median rent was less than half this proportion of median income, amounting to 11.3 per cent.

In the third area the median income of the two districts *B* and *C* was roughly the same: what about housing and real

*Cf. Ch. Two, pp. 39–41
**Since the rents given are for housing *units,* inhabited by both families and individuals, and income is calculated for families excluding single individuals, the percentages will be affected by the rents paid by single individuals whose incomes are not included. One might expect, however, that both family income and rents paid would be higher than the figures for individuals. Therefore if the latter were included, they would tend to reduce the median income and increase the ratios shown.

income? District *B* contains a much smaller fraction of owned homes than does district *C;* on the other hand fewer than two-thirds of that area's housing is sound, compared with 91 per cent in district *B.* The amount of substandard housing is substantial in both areas, but notice that it consists, in district *C,* largely of deteriorating and dilapidated structures, while in district *B* it represents shared baths and other inadequate plumbing facilities. Neither area shows severe crowding and although the bulk of the housing in district *B* is pre-World War II, most of the residents have moved in since that time, as is also true of district *C.* But although the median incomes of the two areas are close, the median rents paid are significantly different. In *C* district, the median rent of $73.40 is almost 25 per cent higher than the median rent in *B* district of $58.40. The first sum amounts to 18 per cent of the median income of the families; the second to 14 per cent.

The inequality of income in these various districts now looks more significant, for the disparity between rich and poor, greatest in each *C* district, evidently reappears in housing. Although we could calculate a Lorenz curve of rents paid, a simpler device serves to check on inequality—merely comparing the percentage of the total population in each district whose rental payment exceeds $100.00. In all three SMSA's, this percentage turns out to be higher in the *C* district than in the *B* district: suggesting strongly that there are more rich people ("rich" meaning distant from the median income) in the former district than the latter. Evidently, then, rich and poor live together in the *C* districts, and shun each other in the *A* and *B* districts.

Although the distribution of income confirms that a few wealthy people do live in these poorest districts, identified as SMSA *C,* it does not explain why rent expenditures are so heavy for almost everyone in the area. We may ask two questions: why do rich people live in these districts and why does everyone pay so much for housing? One answer to both these questions suggests that people *choose* to live in the area. Another answer suggests that people *have* to live in the area because other housing facilities are barred to them for reasons other than their ability to pay. If we now learn that nonwhites

make up less than 2 per cent of the population in each of the
A and *B* districts, the correct answer becomes clear. The *C*
districts have a population more heterogeneous in terms of
economic status than districts *A* or *B,* because they are racially
homogenous. Rich and poor nonwhites live together because
they have to; the other housing facilities are barred to them.

This analysis suggests a complex association between poverty,
especially as reflected in poor quality housing, and the ghetto.
If, within a city or metropolitan area, one district shows a
significantly lower percentage of "sound" housing than another,
it may be a *poverty* area but it is not necessarily involuntarily
segregated. But if the distribution of income within the area
represents substantial inequality, and if housing expenditures
require a greater fraction of income than in another section,
and if a significant degree of crowding takes place, then we
may suspect involuntary segregation and discrimination against
the inhabitants. SMSA II on Table III–1 illustrates this point
fairly well: about two-thirds of the housing in both districts
B and *C* is sound, with a relatively small percentage of totally
dilapidated housing. Yet *C*-district people are more crowded
and pay out more of their income for rent than do the residents of *B* district.

The mere existence of substandard housing does not define
a ghetto because so much substandard housing does not exist
in the city. In 1960 some fourteen million occupied housing
units that were classified substandard, but six million of these
were in rural areas—almost half of all rural housing. In the
small towns and villages and farms that make up our rural
areas, there were dilapidated or ill-equipped housing units providing "shelter" to five million families. Although rural areas
contain only one-third of all housing units, they account for
about 44 per cent of all substandard units.

Nor does the ghetto fit the superficial explanation for an
urban slum, which is supposed to be located in a formerly
high-income urban area where mansions were built by the
wealthy of a previous generation. Waves of immigrants, of
varying origin in various cities, settled in as the wealthy moved
out. Their solid old houses were cut up into flats or turned into
rooming houses, and both the population and the neighborhood

became identified as low-income. In this century, the flight to suburbia was joined by middle-income groups during the twenties and by lower-income families after World War II. The urban areas formerly known as Irish, Jewish, or little Italy—ethnic ghettos of the voluntary sort—have been inundated by new waves of in-migration—Southern Negroes displaced by technological change and Puerto Ricans attempting to work out a cycle of coming North to get rich and going home to live in prosperity for the rest of their lives.

This stereotype does little to explain either ghetto problems or ghetto history: for every large American city that fits the pattern there are many more that do not. Only a few urban slums consist of old mansions cut up into apartments to house ten families where formerly one family and a couple of servants lived. Many more slums consist of the tenements that were built in the early years of this century to house the low-income urban poor of that generation: some consist of public housing poorly designed and constructed only a few years ago. Furthermore, not all of the ethnic groups typifying the city two generations ago have left for the suburbs: many cities have areas with heavy concentrations of second- or even third-generation Americans, who make up Census tracts with a high percentage of residents who have lived in the same house for over twenty years. Finally, the implications of the stereotype—that the present ghettos are merely one more stage in the Americanization process—cannot safely be accepted as long as the involuntary nature of today's segregation appears so clearly evident. If the previous ghetto inhabitants were immigrants who worked hard to better themselves and their children, who found success in moving to a duplex on the outskirts of the city or even to a suburban ranch house, the barriers they faced were economic and social obstacles that could be overcome in one or two generations. Nonwhite Americans, however, have not found the same route out of the ghetto.

The stereotype, valid or not, supports a "trickle down" thesis which has had considerable impact on housing policy. Briefly, this notion suggests that building new and expensive homes for upper income groups augments the supply of housing for *all* income classes. As the rich move into their new homes and

sell their former houses to those less well off, these people
vacate homes which become available to poorer families. So
new construction stimulates trade-ins and the turnover of the
existing housing stock and increases the supply for all. Such a
phenomenon certainly exists in the automobile market: the
supply of second-hand cars allows trading-in and trading-up
by many families for years before they purchase a new car.
For this model to apply to housing requires, first, that families
are free to move in and out of the housing market and, second,
that new and old housing be available on the same terms: the
transactions that would take place would then represent the
purely economic factors of incomes and prices.

But the ghetto exists because neither of these conditions
exist. The majority of new housing units constructed since
World War II has been single-family dwellings located in the
suburbs. The housing that remained to "trickle-down," whether
in the urban core or in older suburbs turned into cities, differed
from new housing in location and tenure.

OWNERS AND RENTERS

If, today, we are a nation of home owners, thirty years ago
we were a nation of renters. The change took place because of
financial and tax policies which represent the chief economic
influences on housing. It is essential to understand these developments, not only to understand the origin of some ghetto
housing, but to decide how to change housing in the future.

The year 1890 marked the turning point of the United States
from an agricultural economy into a country identified as industrial: in that year workers in nonfarm occupations outnumbered those in farm jobs for the first time. Although the
Census did not distinguish between farm and nonfarm *residence,*
the number of occupied dwelling units on farms was 60 per
cent of the nonfarm total. From that year until the decade of
the thirties, while more and more of the country's income and
employment stemmed from factories, utilities, heavy industry,
and service operations, most people lived as tenants. Only a
minority of families (from 30 to 35 per cent) owned their homes.
During the thirties a revolution in financing took place which
put home ownership within range of middle-income families.
After World War II (which practically stopped residential con-

struction), new financial arrangements added millions of lower-income families to the housing market. There follows a simplified example of these arrangements.

Banks and other lending institutions follow rules about writing mortgages which consist partly of state law and partly of "good sound business judgment." Reflecting both these things, the typical mortgage written during the twenties provided half (or less) the appraised value of the home, with interest at 6 per cent (or more), the total to be repaid within five years. Let us assume that a young couple wanted to buy a $10,000 house and applied, therefore, for a loan. The bank would require a down payment of $5,000 plus yearly interest of $300.00 more or less on the mortgage loan. The $5,000 principal was to be repaid at the end of the term; the interest to be repaid monthly or quarterly. The young couple could expect to spend perhaps another $300.00 on taxes and maintenance for their home: their current housing expenditures would therefore run about $600.00 yearly. Such an expenditure for "shelter" suggests that the couple might have a yearly income of between $5,000 and $6,000, if they spent the same proportion of their income on housing that most home owners did. If the young people planned ahead, they would wish to save almost $1,000 a year to pay back the principal of $5,000. And this is approximately the amount of saving that occurred, during the twenties, among families with yearly incomes of $5,000 to $6,000. But they might very well expect to renew the note, with some reduction in amount, for another short-term period so they could use their savings to purchase securities or to expand a small business or to pay for some consumption expense. Of course, any loss of value in the house itself would reduce the chance of renewing the mortgage, and any loss of income would diminish the possibility of reducing the principal owed. Consequently, home-owning tended to be associated not only with a certain income level but also with families whose incomes did not fluctuate from month to month, and were expected to rise in the future.

But only a very few families fitted this overall picture. During the twenties, less than 10 per cent of all families received such incomes; $5,000 to $6,000 in predepression days was a *high* income, well up in the national income distribution. Only a few people could maintain the housing expenditures sketched above: the number who had accumulated savings of $5,000 to make a down payment was even smaller, so prospective buyers did not expand the construction industry. Home-owning was restricted, as suggested by this mundane arithmetic, to upper-income families.

The arithmetic itself, of course, depended on the banking requirements. If, for the same house, down payments had been $2,000 and the repayment term fifteen years, many more potential buyers would have existed. Still others would come forward, had there been a change in the mortgage *terms,* if periodic payments included some reduction in principal as well as current interest. Putting all these changes together provides the following (oversimplified) example of a house priced at $10,000.

With a $2,000 down payment and a fifteen-year loan of $8,000, annual payments might amount to $800.00. In the first year, such a sum would represent $480.00 of interest and $320.00 of principal; in the second year, therefore, the outstanding debt would be not $8,000 but $7,680, on which the interest is not $480.00 but $460.00. The same $800.00 payment would therefore reduce the principal by a larger sum, $340.00, which would mean a smaller share of the total payment going for interest in the next year. By the time five years had passed, the outstanding debt would be about $5,500, and well over half of each payment would go to reducing it, so that both interest and principal would be completely paid at the end of fifteen years. But total expenditures of $800.00 a year (rather than the $1,600 of the previous example) and the much smaller down payment would put home ownership within reach of many more families than those in the high-income brackets.

Just such changes in mortgage financing—one of the most profound innovations of the past half-century—prompted the shift of a nation of renters to a nation of home owners. Banking arrangements began to change in this way when the federal government, through the Federal Housing Agency, provided insurance for approved loans to home buyers and thus reduced the risk to bankers that mortgage terms would not be met. Through the Federal National Mortgage Agency ("Fannie Mae"), a secondary market was established so that bankers could re-

Diagram III-1

Contract Terms of Straight Mortgage Loans Made on Nonfarm Homes 1921–47

————— Life insurance companies   – – – – Commercial banks

•••••• Savings and loan associations

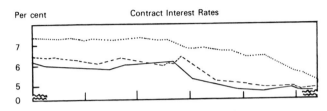

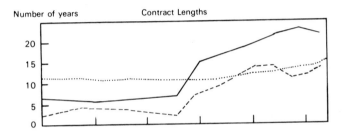

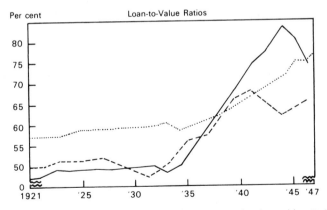

Three-year moving averages of interest rates, contract lengths, and loan-to-value ratios, weighted by three-year moving averages of original loan amounts. Refers to loans secured by one- to four-family homes.

Source: Morton, J. E., *Urban Mortgage Lending: Comparative Markets and Experience* (Princeton: Princeton University Press, 1956), p. 91.

plenish their liquid assets by selling such approved mortgages. The terms of "approval" included the proviso that the borrowers reduce the principal with the regular interest payments, and that the contract period be extended. (Of course, with the reduced risks the banking industry would itself be more willing to extend the life of such loans.) As a result, interest rates dropped, average contract life lengthened, and the ratio of loan-to-value for home mortgages rose.

Diagram III-1 shows all three of these developments, and pinpoints the year of change in 1933. It also shows a significant difference between loans made by life insurance companies, commercial banks, and savings and loan associations. The latter type of institution had provided amortization of loans for home owners prior to the federal government's intervention during the 1930's; after this, the other two types of lenders imitated the approach of the savings and loan associations, and all three showed fairly close agreement by the end of the thirties in length of contract and loan-to-value ratio. Banks and insurance companies, however, made great gains in the number of mortgage loans made, once their safety was assured by the federal government; and savings and loan associations provided a decreasing share of the total funds for home-building.

New changes in contract length, down payment terms, value of insured housing, and other provisions appeared after World War II, when the federal government subsidized returning veterans, and the housing industry boomed once construction restrictions were removed. By the mid-1960's, over half the insured mortgages were written for thirty years or longer, and the median ratio of mortgage loan to house value was over 90 per cent. Although upper-income families are still more likely to own their homes than those with fewer resources, in 1969 at least half the families in every income class owned their homes.

Aside from encouraging home ownership by assisting financial institutions to provide mortgages, the federal government also grants tax advantages to home owners.

As the previous chapter suggested, family income cannot be accurately measured by any sum of dollars, since real income consists of the services and articles which family members buy and use. The real income of a home owner differs from that of a renter in the same dollar income class. Of two families, each with an income of $10,000, the home owner's real income (by whatever "budget list" it is measured) clearly exceeds that of the renter. The federal income tax does not tax this extra, implicit income, but only the $10,000 money income. (Nor does the income go tax-free *because* it is implicit, since other types of income, e.g., board and room given to a nurse, are taxable even though not paid in money.) Dollar for dollar, therefore, the renter pays a higher percentage tax on his real income than does the owner.

It is of course true that home owners pay housing *costs* that renters do not, but the income tax provides for differential (and advantageous) treatment of home owners here as well. In calculating income subject to tax, the home owner may deduct payments for local property taxes and, if he does not own his home outright, the interest paid on mortgage indebtedness. Since in the first years of a mortgage, the monthly payment pays far more on the interest than on the principal, it is possible for new home owners to subtract almost the entire cost of their shelter from their income before figuring taxes, an alternative not open to renters. Such differential tax treatment between renting and owning does not mean that it is always better to buy than to rent, or even that home ownership must necessarily be the preferred form of tenure. It does mean that the present structure of housing reflects a deliberate bias, on government's part, in favor of home ownership.[6]

Government support of home ownership has led to the development of suburbs where home ownership rather than rental property is the rule, and new suburban growth has produced neighborhoods which are extremely homogeneous. Several circumstances seem responsible. Of the families who buy new homes, more are in their late twenties or early thirties, with young children and expectations of rising incomes, than in any other category of family composition. It follows that an area of newly built homes will tend, other things being equal, to have more of such families than any other type of family. It also follows that the income level of such families will determine the kind of houses built: that is, these people represent the biggest market for new homes. The builder who undertakes a substantial housing development plans homes within a given price range, depending on his estimate of the number of such families and their incomes. But he must also consider zoning requirements: most suburbs consist of well-defined areas of "luxury homes" (one acre or more per house), "good neighborhoods" (half-acre lots or swimming pools), or "spacious play areas" (six to ten houses to an acre, but each home with its own front lawn and back yard).

The whole subject of zoning and community planning calls for much more comment than is possible here; within the past two years detailed analyses have been published by The National Commission on Urban Problems,[7] and the Advisory Commission on Intergovernmental Relations,[8] as well as individual experts. At this juncture we may point out that the restrictions on land use and the homogeneity which typifies suburban growth do not wholly stem from the private biases or discriminatory practices of financial institutions or construction firms, but it is not clear that they arise because prospective home owners have deliberately chosen uniformity, either. Consumers' choices in any field are limited to selecting from among what is available, and the availability of housing, to a family or single consumer, reflects many factors beyond individual control.

As the federal government nurtured home ownership, federal housing policy established homogeneity rather than diversity. A famous quotation from the Federal Housing Administration Manual states that "If a neighborhood is to retain stability, it is necessary that properties shall be continued to be occupied by the same social and racial classes." The economist recognizes this as embodying the unproved assumption that mixed neighborhoods lead to a deterioration of value, but notes that such a policy was not devised by FHA in a vacuum, uninfluenced by the opinion of Congress and its constituents. Insofar as it reflects conscious choice, however, it represents a choice by society, not by a particular consumer opting for racial segregation.

Families become eligible to rent public housing by meeting certain standards of income and family composition; these criteria also determine the type of housing units available, the number of rooms and general layout, and so on. A larger proportion of nonwhites than of whites occupies public housing because a larger proportion of poor families is nonwhite. But in the initial stages of the public housing program, almost every local authority planned its projects as either white or nonwhite: although deliberate segregation no longer exists, housing projects do not easily become racially mixed.*

We take it for granted that housing for low-income families in the city *must* be publicly supported, that privately financed investment *cannot* take place. Such a conclusion, of course, merely accepts the tax structure which encourages turning existing housing units into substandard ones and discourages investment in housing for low-income consumers. That living in substandard homes imposes real costs on the family or consumer needs no documentation[9]; but the social costs, that is, the burden on others or on the country as a whole, from maintaining a sizable group of people in such conditions has yet to be fully appreciated. Like the differential between renters and home owners, taxes at both federal and local levels produce a different treatment of landlords and renters, by influencing the net cost of housing.

As in any locality, a city government draws most of its revenue from the local property tax. The amount of the tax on any property owner depends first on the amount of services —schools, police and fire protection, sanitation and traffic control, and the like—and their cost; and second, on the number of taxpayers and their ability to pay. We know that the first has increased steadily, while in most cities the second has not. Although local government expenditures go up, the amount of taxable property may actually go down. Both manufacturing and service industries have shifted to the suburbs, in some cases by moving existing offices and in others by building new plants. And their vacated city premises continue to depreciate in value.

*Recent findings by the U.S. Commission on Civil Rights suggest that government policy continues to promote segregation. Barely one per cent of the suburban homes, built with FHA loans in the past five years, were purchased by black families. A study in St. Louis (declared typical of other housing markets) found that policies of the Department of Housing and Urban Development helped promote and prolong separate housing markets for blacks and whites in suburban areas.

Meanwhile, urban development makes a larger share of property within the city tax exempt. Government offices—federal,
state, county, and municipal agencies—expand with the increase
in government services and payrolls, and the buildings that house
these organizations are not taxable. Public housing and urban
renewal programs occupy land and structures that are either
tax exempt or that pay reduced rates. Finally, as churches,
hospitals, universities, and schools expand their facilities in
urban centers, the amount of land and buildings not taxable
because of ownership by a nonprofit-making institution increases. Although in some cases cities collect excises or contributions in lieu of property taxes, these rarely equal the full
revenue potential from property taxes. It is estimated that about
one-third of the real property in United States cities is tax
exempt: like any other average, this figure includes some cities
with a larger amount of tax-free property and some with a very
small amount.

As the tax base diminishes, the amount of tax paid by an
individual property owner increases (other things being equal).
The property tax is deductible from the federal income tax;
and given its progressive nature, the net effect of local and
federal taxes benefits high-income owners more than low-income
owners. For renters, the net effect of this tax interaction cannot
easily be discerned. We do not know enough about how much
of the total tax burden landlords can shift to tenants; it should
be obvious that claims by landlords that they must absorb a
rise in property taxes or complaints by tenants that the entire
tax is passed along in higher rents are both overstatements.
But however the tax burden is divided between landlord and
tenant, there is no evidence that low-income *tenants* escape
the differential impact of taxes faced by low-income *owners*.

Commercial property owners find that the tax treatment of
depreciation costs and resale-gains tend to favor new investment
in high-income housing and frequent resale. Maintenance or
rehabilitation of existing low-income housing is minimal. The
costs of repair and maintenance represent normal business
expense, deducted to calculate current taxable income. Expenditures for rehabilitation or renovation, on the other hand, constitute capital investment depreciated over a period of time;

they will in all probability raise the building's assessed value, and whether or not the additional expenses of depreciation and taxes can be covered by increased rents does not depend on the individual owner.

Several complex influences exist. Normally the buyer-owner of commercially rented property borrows a substantial portion of the amount paid; profits accrue to him, therefore, from the leverage of his debt as well as from his own investment. Either the original cost or the capital sums devoted to rehabilitation define the *total* amount of depreciation expense deducted over the life of the structure from the owner's profits to compensate for the loss of value in the aging building. But the *yearly* amount of depreciation expense (and hence current profit) depends on the type of calculation used. Accelerated depreciation estimates that a great portion of the building's original value vanishes during the early years of ownership, and allows the owner to reduce his profits and taxes by substantial amounts during these years. Such depreciation charges may exceed the *actual* loss of value (original cost), for in a rising real estate market, resale prices usually exceed the depreciated value and sometimes the original cost. Since gains on resale are taxed at the lower capital gains rate, and since depreciation expenses are not expenditures that require the outlay of cash, these measures operate to provide a "tax shelter" for recurring resales of property. The next owner figures depreciation on the basis of what he paid, not the building's original cost, so the structure therefore continues to provide both cash flow and a deduction from taxable profits. Repair and maintenance costs, on the other hand, require a cash outlay, and hence a specific economic incentive.

In a declining neighborhood (one that contains a significant proportion of deteriorating housing units with perhaps a gradual increase in the number of substandard units), no such incentive exists: keeping the property up will not keep the neighborhood up, and if low-income families move into the homes, middle- or higher-income tenants and owners may wish to move out. If all the landlords acted together and invested in rehabilitation as well as in high standards of maintenance, they might prevent the erosion of quality, but the individual landlord cannot expect to recoup his greater expenses with higher rents. His alternative lies in cutting maintenance and postponing repairs or in enlarging rental income by overcrowding—thus contributing more to the general atmosphere of decay in the area.

No inevitable relationship exists between tenure and type of dwelling unit; condominiums and cooperatives provide ownership rights for multiple-dwelling structures. Nor does any rigid rule require urban housing to mean densely populated highrise structures, or suburban structures to consist of single-family dwellings. So-called "townhouses" and multiple-unit structures represent suburban innovations which show some record of success, while experiments with urban housing of varying density, including five-story walkups and infill single-dwelling structures, have yet to be proved impractical. The *economics* of housing, including the amount of new construction and rehabilitation, the tenure arrangements, and the variety or homogeneity supplied, depend not on any immutable laws of supply and demand but rather on the institutional framework of finance and taxation. This means that housing can be provided, and the nature of housing shaped, according to policy rather than happenstance.

While the entire subject involves extremely complex ramifications, the reader who is not persuaded that government tax and finance measures have helped to create and perpetuate slums may turn to the National Commission on Urban Problems, set up in 1967. Its research reports cover building codes and technology, zoning and land use, federal and local taxes affecting housing and urban growth, housing codes, development standards, and ways to provide housing for low-income families. These make it quite clear that every action to promote the American dream of a home in the suburbs for every family has had its reaction in promoting an urban slum. When these slums are also ghettos, a new dimension to analyzing housing conditions—a new type of standard—must be confronted.

The earlier pages of this chapter showed how a city's ghetto area might be identified by the inequality of income distribution and the high proportion of family housing expenditure to family income, together with the generally poorer quality of housing. These are some of the economic symptoms of involuntary segregation. Some suburban developments should be called ghettos: they contain a homogeneous population whose lives are bounded by the local school or shopping center; where the youngsters are all roughly the same age, and the school bulges in different grades in different years; where the husbands have similar jobs and the wives about the same amount of schooling; where there are few grandparents and no bachelors, and the community is easy to identify because all the houses look alike, too. The President's Commission on Suburban Planning reported in December, 1968, that many of these neighborhoods are in danger of becoming great slum areas. But the population in such districts remains homogeneous partly because when a family's income or outlook changes, it moves. Possibly the young couple, whose first two babies born in the neighborhood are now high school students, buys a more expensive home in keeping with the husband's new executive position, and find their neighbors compatible because most of them have high school children and the men are mostly executives. The new suburb may have as equally limited horizons and uniform makeup as the first, but it will represent some kind of difference to the new residents. This alternative, obtaining variety for the individual family while perpetuating homogeneity for the group, does not exist for the inhabitants of urban ghettos, whose homogeneity is involuntary.

If, therefore, our housing policies as they have developed over the past generation have produced a nation of tight little islands of renters and homeowners, not only polarized into black and white, as the President's Commission on Civil Disorders warned, but fragmented as well (urban neighborhoods and suburban enclaves whose inhabitants share the same characteristics), then we should know about it. Whether variety or sameness should *exist* is a matter of value judgments; there are those who claim that the city's great strength lies in diversity (for a perceptive spokesman, Jane Jacobs[10] can scarcely be equaled). But to decide that variety (or sameness) *should* exist does not give us the right to *impose* variety (or sameness) on a population that has no opportunity to choose. And while various forms of segregation are now illegal, other barriers to movement and free choice are not, but stem from the economic workings of city and suburb.

CHAPTER FOUR

THE ECONOMICS
OF PEOPLE

By using income to describe the microeconomic units of families and individuals, we arrive at two questions. First, what do people *do* with their income—where and how do they spend and save? Second, where do people *get* their income—who receives it and from what source? The answers to these two questions describe people in the *economy,* rather than in society.

PEOPLE AND MARKETS

To an economist, the inhabitants of any given area have two functions, and in our system these functions operate in two markets. First, people supply resources for production and earn wages, or rents, or interest and dividends—the major forms of income. Here, people are sellers in the market for productive services. Second, people demand finished goods and services and assets and purchase all these with the income they receive. Here, people are consumers, or buyers in the market for final output. We may ask, therefore, how the inhabitants of a ghetto fare in carrying out these functions, compared to people living in other areas. Do they have equal access to markets; is there sufficient demand for their productive services to provide a "moderate" income; does the supply of consumer goods and services furnish variety and choice as well as adequate means of day-to-day living?

Next, we must take account of income and consumption which does not involve market transactions. Some nine per cent of the total income received by all the families in this country does not represent current payments for working or for providing capital or land. Pension fund disbursements, Social Security benefits, interest to government bond holders, and welfare payments are all *transfers,* income earned by one set of people and paid in various ways to other people. (Some individuals or families belong to both groups, like the veteran receiving a disability payment who works as a free-lance photographer, or the executive whose interest from government bonds supplements his salary.) Transfer payments differ from earned income in various ways: one significant difference is that the amount of transfer income cannot be determined by the individual or family that receives it. Congress writes laws setting Social Security and veterans' benefits; state and local authorities determine welfare payments; and pension plans provide various arrangements for the recipients of their stipends.

The total amount of income available to a family, therefore, depends partly on the number of earners and the wages or property income they command, and partly on the transfer payments the family members receive. The term "family" is used loosely: specific definitions exist for "the household," "the consuming unit," and "the spending unit," but in general, economists are interested in those small groups of people, living together in one housing unit, who pool most of their incomes ("most" is usually defined as three-quarters of each income) and share certain consumption expenses, principally for housing and food. (The "family" normally implies relationship; the other two terms describe living arrangements where the individuals involved are not necessarily related—for example, four college graduates sharing an apartment in Manhattan, a divorcee with two children and two foster children whom she is caring for under the auspices of a state child guardian arrangement, an elderly widower living with his widowed daughter-in-law and her adult son by a previous marriage, or two unmarried adults who have shared a home throughout their lives.) Consequently the size and composition of the family have much to do with both the sources of income and its total amount.

Elderly people may receive private pensions or monthly checks under Old Age and Survivors' Insurance; they also find it difficult and in some cases uneconomic to take employment and work for wages. Adult males between eighteen and sixty-five are probably part of the labor force, earning wages or salaries from regular employment. The amount of this income of course depends on their occupation and also how "regular" their employment actually proves to be. Four out of ten adult females also work; the average full-time woman worker, however, earns less than half of what the full-time male worker is paid. Almost two-thirds of the working women are married, and they provide almost ten per cent of the income to families in the upper half of the income distribution.

Transfer payments account for a larger share of family incomes in the lower half of the distribution, partly because of the number of old people with incomes below the median who live on Social Security benefits or other old-age pensions. Other low-income families depend on the single largest welfare program, Aid to Families with Dependent Children (AFDC). In most of these cases, the family lacks an adult male member and the welfare mother cannot find employment at high enough wages to provide for child care plus the reduction in her welfare payments. Earnings, therefore, play almost no part in the income of such families; even part-time jobs held by teenagers become uneconomic if the sums earned are deducted from the family's welfare check, so that the teen-ager gets no return at all other than the "satisfaction" of contributing to family needs as determined by the welfare agency. Some men and women are unable to hold jobs because they are physically or mentally disabled, and they also get welfare payments.

All these characteristics account for the finding, when welfare rolls are analyzed, that less than three per cent of the recipients are employable. HEW data as of March 1968 showed that of some 8.4 million people on welfare, fewer than 80,000 were employable adult men.[1] As an example, Henry L. Mc-

Carthy, Chief of the Illinois Department of Public Aid, explained that "contrary to popular belief that the welfare recipient is an able-bodied man who is loafing instead of working [is] this breakdown of the current 400,080 case-load:

  60,000 over 70 years   —unemployable.
  30,000 permanently and total disabled   —unemployable.
   2,580 blind (many others have received vocational training)
                                                    —unemployable.
210,080 children under 18 (average age 10)   —unemployable.
  50,000 ADC mothers taking care of these children
  50,000 to 60,000 on general assistance, including those discharged from mental hospitals and prisons, alcoholics, psychological misfits, all people very hard to place." [2]

Finally, although they are in the labor force, some people are temporarily out of work; whether or not they receive unemployment compensation, which is still another type of transfer payment, depends on whether their former job was included in the unemployment insurance system and on how long they have been jobless.

POVERTY AND POVERTY AREAS

Data showing the sources and amounts of income for families in small sections like the Census tracts would indicate much about the economic functioning of these people, but such information does not exist. We can, however, compare some family characteristics of people living in different areas. How many are married, how many small children there are, what rate of unemployment and what types of occupations for those working, the number of people over sixty-five and the number not in the labor force—each of these characteristics gives a clue to the sources of income outlined above. The education of people in different areas has a special import: the proportion of school-age children presently in school, and the grade level they reach, will of course help shape the future economy, while the education of the adults influences the kinds of jobs, and therefore the income, they can get today. All of these—educa-

tion, employment, size of family, and age of its members—
also affect the ways in which family income is spent and saved.
So we can learn much from a close examination of tract data
for small areas.

Such analyses have been made using two quite different
approaches: one identifies *poor people* and then describes their
characteristics, and the other identifies *poverty characteristics*
and then locates poor neighborhoods. Each of these adds to
our understanding of the ghetto.

It is possible to classify people into poor and nonpoor by
setting some minimum level of income: the technique developed by Mollie Orshanksy and discussed in Chapter Two leads
to "counting the poor," and to describing their characteristics
as people. Such a method shows, for example, that in 1968
about 25 million people lived in households with incomes
below the poverty line, which is a reduction of about 14 million
since 1960 but still amounts to almost 13 per cent of all the
people in the country. This approach helps delineate the macroeconomic picture, the aggregate size of the poverty problem,
or the poverty gap. This is important in deciding how to allocate our national resources because it indicates how big a job
lies ahead in our attack on the causes and symptoms of poverty.

The second approach to counting poor people was developed
at the Bureau of the Census from analyses of tract data. This
method attempts to identify *poverty areas* by measuring certain
quantitative data about the inhabitants of each Census tract
against a so-called "poverty index." The index combines five
variables. Two of these deal with income, like the tables in
the previous two chapters. The first calculates the percentage
of families with 1959 incomes of less than $3,000, the money-
income indicator of poverty used by the Council of Economic
Advisers in 1964. The second determines the per cent of substandard housing units, a real income indicator which is highly
significant. The remaining three deal with family characteristics
which influence the sources of income and its likely disposi-
tion: they are the per cent of adults with less than eight years
of schooling, the per cent of males employed in unskilled jobs,
and the per cent of children not living with both parents. As
suggested earlier, these characteristics have much to do with

the availability of jobs and the earnings they pay, and with the type of transfer income available.

Since these measures exist for every Census tract, the poverty index could be computed for every tract. Each was then placed in a distribution, ranked from high to low, of the 23,000 tracts that exist. About 5,000 tracts showing the highest percentage of poverty by this index were investigated to see what changes (since the 1960 data were collected) might have come about through urban renewal programs. Finally, poverty areas could be mapped. Each area consists of either five or more contiguous Census tracts classified as poor, or a smaller number if they contained at least 4,000 people, or one or two tracts not classified as poor that were surrounded by poor tracts. From the maps of each of the 100 SMSA's studied, we can check on the poverty status of a given neighborhood, or we can locate a given poverty area within its metropolitan surroundings.

This technique establishes a cut-off point, in this case about one-quarter of the total distribution, just as the minimum income technique described earlier does; and it is important to realize that in both cases the cut-off point results from an arbitrary decision and defines poverty in relative terms, that is, by reference to the rest of the distribution. The lowest tenth of an income distribution or the highest quartile of a distribution of poverty indicators will always exist.

We may summarize some significant findings of this evaluation of standard metropolitan statistical areas. First, not all the residents of poverty *areas* are poor *people:* this merely means that some live in sound housing and have incomes well above $3,000. Second, poverty areas within the central cities contain more poor families, and a larger proportion of the city's poor population, than do poverty areas outside the city. Third, and this may surprise some, while the incidence of poverty varies greatly among the SMSA's, the largest cities appear slightly *better* off than the middle-sized cities. That is, the poverty areas of SMSA's whose central cities had a population of over one million contained a smaller proportion of the city's total poor than those with a population between 250,000 and 500,000. The twenty largest cities, including New York, Chicago, Detroit, Cleveland, Washington, D.C., Los Angeles, and others may receive more attention, but the pressure of poverty may be less critical in those metropolitan areas than in places like Albany, Birmingham, Harrisburg, Knoxville, Newark, New Orleans, San Antonio, and others.

Both ways of counting poor people contribute to an understanding of the ghetto, but obviously the second approach, mapping out poverty *areas,* comes closer to identifying any particular location within which people may be confined. Before we pursue this, however, let us look at the characteristics of poor *people* throughout the country, so as to be able to distinguish the characteristics of poor people in the ghetto. Like substandard housing, the incidence of poverty is highest not in the urban slums but in rural areas and small towns outside the SMSA's altogether. Nor are these communities scattered throughout the nation; most are in Appalachia, Southern states, and occasional pockets of poverty like upstate Maine and Vermont, the Indian reservations of Arizona and New Mexico, and portions of Minnesota, Oklahoma, and Texas. The Department of Agriculture has calculated an index of rural poverty similar to that used for SMSA tracts, and lists the top ten per cent, or 306, counties with the largest concentration of rural population with low income, little schooling, poor housing, and a high dependency ratio. Such "pockets" may be the rural equivalent of urban ghettos, but their analysis falls outside the scope of this book.*

The number of poor people differs significantly from the incidence of poverty. Thus, *most* of the poor people live in families headed by an adult under 65, but the *incidence* of poverty is greater among individuals than among families, and is greater among both kinds of households headed by an adult over sixty-five than under sixty-five. Incidence, therefore, refers to the percentage of poor people within any group. Some sixteen per cent of *all* households are poor, but the proportions vary widely for particular groups: seven out of ten of the families living on Eskimo or Indian reservations are poor; one out of three

*Two excellent sources of both data and analysis include *Rural Poverty in the United States,* President's National Advisory Commission on Rural Poverty (Washington, D.C.: U.S. Government Printing Office, 1968), and *Urban and Rural America,* Advisory Commission of Intergovernmental Relations (Washington, D.C.: U.S. Government Printing Office, 1968).

Negro families; over half the single elderly people and one-fifth of the elderly couples are poor; ten per cent of the white children under eighteen years of age, but almost half—43 per cent—of the nonwhite. Some depressing probabilities have been set up: your chances of living below the poverty line are greater than they would otherwise be if your family has five or more children, if you live in the inner city, if you or the head of your family lacks education or training, or if the head of your family is female.

It should be stressed that this type of analysis does not often reveal a causal relationship. To say "he is poor because he is uneducated," may be a useful shorthand expression, but it may also be very misleading. By educating a person, you may improve his chances of earning a good living, but it may not help much if he was born black, or Puerto Rican, or a woman. Demographic associations allow us to identify poverty characteristics and problem areas, but the solutions to the problems do not necessarily lie in removing these characteristics.

With this in mind, let us look at the incidence of poverty within the poverty areas as mapped out by the Census Bureau index. Because of the great number of rural poor, these areas contain only about 42 per cent of all poor persons (1967 data). As a fraction of the total metropolitan population, the people living in poverty areas account for less than one-fifth. But these two figures (aggregate and average) hide a glaring discrepancy between black and white. Over half the nonwhite population of the SMSA's live in poverty areas, while only 11 per cent of the white population does. Nor does this mean that all the people living in poverty areas are poor. It does mean a totally different distribution of the poor, for blacks and whites. A poor family that is white will, in three cases out of four, live *outside* a poverty area; the probability for a poor black family is almost precisely the opposite.

This overwhelming association between poverty areas and nonwhite residence has become strengthened in the past decade. The prolonged prosperity of the 1960's brought a reduction in poverty that has been variously measured. At the aggregate level, the Council of Economic Advisers reported early in 1969 that the total number of poor households was almost twenty-

five per cent less than it had been in 1960. Over this same
period the number of families living in poverty areas fell by
eleven per cent. But most of the improvement represents gains
by white families, especially among those who received higher
earnings as the economy reached full employment. While the
number of white families living in poverty areas dropped by
over 16 per cent, the number of blacks scarcely diminished at
all. And the number of *poor* white families living in poverty
areas decreased even more dramatically, by 36 per cent compared to only 15 per cent for poor nonwhites. These changes
denote the growth of segregation: in 1960 six out of ten families in poverty areas were nonwhite, seven years later they
numbered seven out of ten. In 1960 the poor families living
in poverty areas were half white, half black; seven years later
they were 58 per cent nonwhite.

Actually, these national totals understate the extent to which
this division has taken place. In metropolitan districts of the
Northeast, many more white families moved out of the poverty
areas, while the number of poor nonwhites dropped only slightly.
In 1960 about two out of five poor families in these areas were
nonwhite; in 1967 over half of them were. A few special censuses taken since 1960 reveal even more specific data. In New
Haven, Connecticut, while the total population of the SMSA
grew between 1960 and 1967, the population of the poverty
areas declined by one-fifth. But the Negro population of these
areas increased by 29 per cent, while overall the proportion
of Negroes rose from eight per cent to ten per cent. In the
Providence-Pawtucket (Rhode Island) area, total population
declined, as did the number of people living in poverty areas,
between 1960 and 1965. The Negro population, however, grew
by 24 per cent, and those in poverty areas numbered 27 per
cent more. A similar drastic change occurred in Rochester, New
York, between 1960 and 1966, when the Negro population in
poverty areas soared by 22 per cent, although the area as a
whole had a smaller number of people. On an even smaller
scale, changes in neighborhoods or school districts indicate how
quickly an inner city area can move from white to black. In
a small section of Boston called Mattapan, the situation was
described by a local reporter:

The impending changes first became apparent at the Solomon Lewenberg School, once rated as one of the finest junior high schools in Boston. When the state's racial imbalance law was enacted in 1965, black parents looking for better schools than they could find in their own neighborhoods turned to Lewenberg. The percentage of black students at Lewenberg soared from ten per cent in the 1964–65 school year to 67.5 per cent this school year (1969). As the balance shifted many white Mattapan parents placed their children in still white schools of Hyde Park or Roslindale or in parochial schools. Others simply gave up and moved to the suburbs. . . . Professional real estate speculators last year launched a "block busting" campaign against home owners on Wellington Hill Street. . . . Their traditional pitch: Sell now for a good price before the blacks come in and depreciate the neighborhood. Some frightened whites sold, even for less than market value. The speculators then turned around and sold the properties to black families at inflated prices.[3]

Here, then, we have the meaning of a ghetto—of that state of "involuntary segregation"—as it relates to poverty. The white families whose economic status improves move out—over half a million of them, nationwide, between 1960 and 1967. The nonwhites who climb out of poverty remain—only 27,000 moved out of all the poverty areas between 1960 and 1967. And if we examine the cities more closely, we can find racial ghettos existing *within* some poverty areas, rather than coinciding with their boundaries.

Each of the three cities used in the preceding chapters to illustrate income and housing data contain one or more poverty areas. Table IV-1 calculates the "poverty index" for each of the nine districts previously analyzed, and shows the ethnic and racial makeup of the population. District *B* in each SMSA falls within the boundary lines of a poverty area. The indicators on Table IV-1 show why. In the first two SMSA's, both districts *B* and *C* are in poverty areas, and offer enlightening comparisons. The *B* districts, overwhelmingly white, are, despite their poverty, considerably better off than the *C* districts with their largely nonwhite population. The discrepancy between the two areas shows up most dramatically in the figures for low incomes, unskilled jobs, and one-parent families. Differences between the two groups are less pronounced in education and housing. In the third SMSA, the index shows district *B* as a poverty area but not district *C;* also, district *C* is only 30 per cent nonwhite. But if we look at the indicators for these nonwhite families separately, as in the last column of the table, we discover that they measure poverty. Again, the discrepancy is greatest in the numbers of low-income families, workers with unskilled jobs, and children not living with both parents. Note that the educational level among the nonwhites surpasses that of the whites, and of the total population of *B* district.

Table IV-1

Poverty Index Measures, Selected Areas

	SMSA I			SMSA II			SMSA III			Non whites
Percentage of:	A	B	C	A	B	C	A	B	C	
Families with 1959 incomes under $3,000	8.7	16.3	54.6	7.7	21.1	39.4	4.0	20.5	19.5	21.7
Children under 18 not living with both parents	11.3	18.6	38.4	4.5	18.4	41.2	2.8	18.6	18.8	26.7
Persons over 25 with less than 8 years of school completed	9.0	38.5	53.9	6.4	27.7	35.1	3.2	37.3	21.5	18.1
Unskilled males in the employed civilian labor force	8.1	14.4	24.0	4.6	18.3	38.8	2.2	14.0	16.1	35.1
Substandard housing units	–*	39.2	50.8	–	20.4	29.5	–	23.0	6.2	7.7
Total	37.1	127.0	221.7	22.2	109.7	184.0	12.2	113.4	82.1	99.3
Index	7.4	25.4	44.4	4.4	21.9	36.8	2.4	22.7	16.4	20.0
Whites	99.4	99.7	20.9	99.4	99.4	4.8	99.6	97.4	70.0	–*
Nonwhites	.6	.3	79.1	.6	.6	95.2	.4	2.4	30.0	–
Total foreign stock	46.4	54.4	5.1	11.5	11.2	.1	30.9	45.2	25.0	–
Modal foreign stock	11.0	37.0	–	2.5	4.4	–	6.2	23.4	7.3	
	USSR	Pol		Ger	Can		USSR	Can	Can	

*– less than 1 per cent.

Source: U.S. Census of Population and Housing: 1960. Final Report PHC (1).

It seems obvious that all three C districts contain racial ghettos. By looking at the block data for the Census tracts in the third SMSA we can trace the street boundaries of the non-white area in district C. And the barriers that keep people in and also keep poverty in begin to grow clear.

We know from analyzing income inequality in Chapter Two that the C districts contain some families whose incomes are well above the median level; we know from the survey of housing in Chapter Three that they also contain more crowded families who pay higher rents for worse quarters than do the other districts. We may conclude that these C districts illustrate the general trend described above: that as nonwhite families escape poverty they do not move out of the ghetto as white families do; and that in some areas they cannot move even across the street to more adequate housing. The racial ghettos perpetuate and promote the conditions of poverty summarized by these indicators, yet behind the barriers of discrimination they enclose a wider range of income and social class than do the white ghettos of the city or suburbs.

The association between the different indicators is fairly easy to read. Where a large number of single-parent families exist, a considerable portion of family income represents payments under the Aid to Families with Dependent Children, which means low incomes. Where working fathers help support their families, the large number of unskilled jobs means low and irregular pay. Where a substantial number of adults have not gone to high school, many will not be able to hold skilled jobs. (But note that this relation differs between black and white. In district IIIC, fewer nonwhites have minimal schooling than whites, but the proportion of unskilled nonwhite workers is more than twice that of unskilled white workers.)

The B districts of two of the areas, I and III, suggest an ethnic concentration that may also be a ghetto. The Bureau of the Census collects data on nativity and parentage, defining "native" as:

> persons born in the United States, the Commonwealth of Puerto Rico, or a possession of the United States; persons born in a foreign country or at sea who have at least one native American parent; and persons whose place of birth

was not reported and whose census report contained no contradictory information, such as entry of a language spoken prior to coming to the United States. The category "foreign born" comprises all persons not classified as native.[4]

With this information the Census constructs three categories: native persons of native parentage, native persons of foreign or mixed parentage, and foreign born: the term "foreign stock" combines the latter two categories. Table IV-1 calculates the percentage of such people in each district, and also shows the nationality most frequently reported for the foreign-born. In area I, the percentage of foreign stock is roughly half in both white districts, but the poor district B shows a heavy concentration of one nationality—Polish. In the corresponding poor white district in area III, almost one out of four families is of Canadian stock.

These districts are poor chiefly by contrast with the A district in each area; there are few families that are *very* poor. When we look at the details of the labor force and occupation, we find a significant number of factory operatives and of industries whose employees have long been associated with the two nationalities. To some extent these people represent the "working poor" whose welfare formed part of the administration's family assistance proposals in late 1969; in some cities such groups harbor the antagonisms of discrimination and backlash.[5] Yet if we define the confining nature of a ghetto as that of *involuntary* segregation, then we must differentiate between such ethnic neighborhoods and the areas of black concentration.

Nor should we lay too much emphasis on the data of these tables: they serve only as illustrations, for obviously we cannot draw general conclusions from such limited material. But if we read segregation in these figures on income distribution and housing, we can also read it in summary data that show the occupations of family heads by color, for all the poverty areas in the country. Table IV-2 provides such data, and they are simply analyzed.

Of seven million families headed by professional and managerial executives, six and one-half million are white. Only 4.3 per cent of these families live in poverty areas—perhaps the doctor works at a city hospital, or the urban planner, so-

Table IV-2

Employment and Occupation,

Families in SMSA's, by Poverty Area and Poverty Level, 1967

EMPLOYMENT STATUS AND OCCUPATION	All areas	Poverty Areas					Nonpoverty Areas	
		Total		Below Poverty Level		Total	Below Poverty Level	
	Number	Number	Per cent	Number	Per cent	Total	Number	Per cent
All families	27,092	4,269	15.8	1,015	23.8	22,823	1,584	6.9
Head employed	21,798	3,069	14.1	466	15.2	18,729	647	3.5
Professional and managerial workers	6,819	357	5.2	26	7.3	6,462	136	2.1
Clerical and sales workers	3,346	356	10.6	32	9.0	2,990	93	3.1
Craftsmen and foremen	4,565	550	12.0	38	6.9	4,015	97	2.4
Operatives	4,151	907	21.9	140	15.4	3,244	124	3.8
Service workers incl. private household	1,824	499	27.4	142	28.5	1,325	140	10.6
Nonfarm laborers	937	348	37.1	69	19.8	589	37	6.3
Farmers and farm laborers	156	52	33.3	19	(B)	104	20	19.2
Head unemployed	512	132	25.8	57	43.2	380	62	16.3
Head not in labor force[1]	4,782	1,068	22.3	492	46.1	3,714	875	23.6
White families	23,936	2,517	10.5	427	17.0	21,419	1,342	6.3
Head employed	19,401	1,836	9.5	191	10.4	17,565	527	3.0
Professional and managerial workers	6,513	281	4.3	16	5.7	6,232	125	2.0
Clerical and sales workers	3,056	232	7.6	13	5.6	2,824	84	3.0
Craftsmen and foremen	4,231	392	9.3	19	4.8	3,839	81	2.1
Operatives	3,491	539	15.4	55	10.2	2,952	91	3.1

THE ECONOMICS OF THE GHETTO

Table IV-2 Continued

Employment and Occupation,

Families in SMSA's, by Poverty Area and Poverty Level, 1967

EMPLOYMENT STATUS AND OCCUPATION	All areas	Poverty Areas Total		Poverty Areas Below Poverty Level		Nonpoverty Areas Total	Nonpoverty Areas Below Poverty Level	
		Number	Per cent	Number	Per cent	Total	Number	Per cent
Service workers, incl. private household	1,335	199	14.9	49	24.6	1,136	105	9.2
Nonfarm laborers	636	149	23.4	21	14.1	487	22	4.5
Farmers and farm laborers	139	44	31.7	18	(B)	95	19	20.0
Head unemployed	399	55	13.8	18	(B)	344	43	12.5
Head not in labor force[1]	4,136	626	15.1	218	34.8	3,510	772	22.0
Nonwhite Families	3,156	1,752	55.5	588	33.6	1,404	242	17.2
Head employed	2,397	1,233	51.4	275	22.3	1,164	120	10.3
Professional and managerial workers	306	76	24.8	10	13.2	230	11	4.8
Clerical and sales workers	290	124	42.8	19	15.3	166	9	5.4
Craftsmen and foremen	334	158	47.3	19	12.0	176	16	9.1
Operatives	660	368	55.8	85	23.1	292	33	11.3
Service workers, incl. private household	489	300	61.3	93	31.0	189	35	18.5
Nonfarm laborers	301	199	66.1	48	24.1	102	15	14.7
Farmers and farm laborers	17	8	(B)	1	(B)	9	1	(B)
Head unemployed	113	77	68.1	39	50.6	36	19	(B)
Head not in labor force[1]	646	442	68.4	274	62.0	204	103	50.5

B Base less than 75,000.

[1]Includes families with head in Armed Forces.

Source: U.S. Department of Commerce, Bureau of the Census, Current Population Reports, Consumer Income, Series P-60, No. 61 (June 30, 1969).

cial worker, or teacher lives among the people for whom he works. But more than 95 per cent of these families live in nonpoverty areas, if they are white. Such professional and managerial jobs occur very rarely among nonwhites, but unlike their white colleagues, one-quarter of these executive families who are nonwhite live in poverty areas. The next most prestigious occupations, those of clerical and sales workers, craftsmen, and foremen, follow the same pattern. Nonwhites hold a larger share of these jobs—eight per cent as opposed to the five per cent for managers and professionals. But these families and their homes are not divided between poverty and nonpoverty areas like those of whites. Fewer than one out of ten white families headed by such workers live in poverty areas; more than four out of ten nonwhite families with like occupations live in poverty areas.

Involuntary segregation means, in economic terms, that people are denied access to certain markets: that this is true of the housing market is obvious. But ghetto residents may also face other market barriers which prevent them from carrying out their economic functions. The income a family receives depends only partly on the ability and willingness to work of its individual members, for the market for labor determines wages. The real income a family enjoys depends only partly on the skill with which the adults shop and keep house and the thriftiness of the children: it also reflects the market for consumables —not only available housing but the supply of other goods and services. In the next two chapters we shall look at each of these economic conditions of the ghetto: employment in the labor market and consumption in the retail market.

Before doing so, one demographic characteristic needs more mention, and that is the educational background of the individual. The value of labor depends only remotely on willingness to work or physical strength: far more important in today's economy is intellectual competence and willingness to learn. The economist credits a large part of increased productivity (and hence income) in the country to the growth of basic skills and human knowledge. Less obvious, perhaps, is that skillful consuming can also increase real income. But education has a critically important role in both areas.

THE MARKET FOR EDUCATION

This book began with a look at the well-known correlation between education and income: the more education, the higher the future income. Evidence for the correlation relies on data for white males: the relation between education and income is not as close for black males and for women. The Miller data cited in Chapter One were used in an exhaustive study by Gary Becker[6] calculating the rates of return to college and high school education, based on lifetime *earnings* for men and lifetime *income* for women.* This excellent study is one of a number of recent attempts by economists to come to grips with education as a form of investment—in human beings rather than in physical capital goods. Becker assumes, for analytical purposes, that expected returns induce people to invest, and therefore that those people for whom college produces a high return will tend to invest more in college, and so on. To move from this sort of analysis to a social policy advocating more education requires considerable caution.

First, we need to know what makes the *individual* decide to invest in education. At present, our system requires an investment of both time and money from the individual involved: "money" at least in the sense of the income foregone by not working. It would be possible to remove this problem by paying students; such compensation exists in some countries and has been suggested for ours. This would not, however, relieve the individual of necessarily committing his time and energies for a given period. Such an investment, by the person concerned,

---

*Becker's analysis is perhaps not more antifeminist than the basic data with which he deals: information on women's occupations, earnings, and income simply does not exist in the detail that it does for men. On the other hand, Becker begins his book with a revealing quotation from Marshall's *Principles of Economics:* "The most valuable of all capital is that invested in human beings." In the original, the next line reads "and of that capital the most precious part is the result of the care and influence of the mother, so long as she retains her tender and unselfish instincts, and has not been hardened by the strain and stress of unfeminine work."[7] Although Becker omits this conclusion, he suggests that few women invest in education for any expected increase in earnings. "Many women drop out of college after marriage, and college women are more likely to marry educated and wealthy men. These well-known facts suggest that women go to college partly to increase the probability of marrying a more desirable man."[8]

would be required regardless of any system of compensation. Now few, if any, *individual* decisions to get more education represent the marginal calculation of costs and benefits—the return on investment—which an individual could make according to tables of lifetime earning. For one thing, education also has consumption gains not disclosed by lifetime earnings. We live differently, consume differently, and enjoy life in a different way if we are educated, whether or not we earn more money. For another, the process of education itself is a positive good to many people—learning can be fun and is sometimes intensely exciting. So one's decision to become educated does *not* mean merely calculating the impact of education on one's productivity in the labor market. The individual recognizes, however subconsciously or inarticulately, that his education will affect the rest of his life, and in particular his economic roles as a consumer (which is not simply a matter of buying things and making some kind of "wise choice").

More important, the individual most concerned frequently takes little part in the actual decision-making. Of the number of persons enrolled in school, how many are there because of deliberate decisions *they* have made about their schooling? Education (or at least time put in) is legally required for most of one's minority, and even a college education is usually a matter of family decision, rather than that of the college-bound student. And family decisions to "buy" education for the children can be analyzed by data that, for once, show remarkable unanimity on a straightforward proposition. Whether or not a person goes to college depends more on the level of his parents' education than on any other factor. Education as a form of consumption is a notable exception to the general law that consumption is a function of income, for educated parents at low-income levels will spend more on education than noneducated parents at higher income levels.

This relation had been suspected for a long time before adequate data existed. Alfred Marshall, who was very proeducation as befitted a college professor, pointed out in his *Principles of Economics* that better-educated parents—or those whom he forthrightly called the "higher grades of society"—"exert themselves much to select the best careers for their sons, and the best trainings for those careers."[9] Many consumption surveys provide further evidence of this relation between parents' education and spending for children's education. Finally, the Michigan team of James Morgan, Martin David, Wilbur Cohen, and Harvey Brazer, in their book *Income and Welfare in the United States,* applied multivariate analysis to data on the average completed education of children and various family characteristics. These included income, occupation, number of children, race, age, urban-rural location and origin, and education of both parents. To quote the conclusion, "education of the spending unit head proved to be the most important factor influencing the education of children."[10]

The significance of this finding is hard to overemphasize. What it means, first, is another vicious circle: educated people do get higher incomes, therefore they are *able* to provide more education than people with lower incomes, and therefore their children will be more highly educated. This was pointed up recently by more dramatic data from Project Talent showing that the group of high school graduates in the lowest-ranking quartile by ability had more college-bound students from families with high incomes than the group of students who ranked highest in ability but lowest in income.[11] So it remains true that income does influence the ability to provide education, particularly higher education, to children. Hence low-income people, whose incomes are low *because* they lack education, may lack either income or motivation to provide education for their youngsters.

Second, this finding suggests a way out of the vicious circle, by providing motivation to young people whose parents lack education. If education is a "good thing," let it be a remedy for ghetto inhabitants. But here great caution is needed, for it may be that people lack income rather than motivation.[12] In fact, there is no clear indication that the nonwhite population with its generally lower level of education sets a lesser value on educating its children than does the white population, and some data suggest quite the opposite.

For example, one out of four white adults, compared to only one out of ten nonwhites, has some college education: it might be thought, therefore, that a similar discrepancy might exist among the present generation. Although a larger percentage of white young people are in college than of nonwhites, the gap has narrowed significantly: in October 1968, 46 per cent of the whites, aged eighteen to twenty-one, were enrolled in college, and 21 per cent of the Negroes in that age group. Similar conclusions can be drawn by comparing the level of education among adult males to that among their fathers. The present generation is better educated, but the improvement—the gains of sons over their fathers' attainments—is distinctly more marked among nonwhites than among whites.

The economist will leave such speculation about motivation and family influence to those in other fields, in favor of looking at the educational process itself and the quality of its various institutions before advocating education as a remedy for ghetto problems.* A given investment in education, by society, can take place at a number of levels and in new or existing facilities: more scholarships to college students, more books and equipment for high school libraries and laboratories, more training for teachers in the grade schools, more counseling for families and students, continuing education in the summer or in adult life, providing day care centers and nursery training for infants, and so on. To invest in education for ghetto inhabitants requires more than a choice among such alternatives: it means ensuring that the investment will in fact pay off. If a school does a poor job at educating its pupils, they may be more productive as drop-outs;[13] if a trained technician can find employment only as a window washer, the resources devoted to his schooling have been wasted.

Finally, the economist will realize the limits to the notion that education *is* investment. A survey of children's attitudes toward school reveals two quite different kinds of aspirations, corresponding to differences in the family background, in the children's own comments. One group typically says, "When I *go to college,* I will . . ." in contrast to the others who state "As soon as I *quit school,* I will. . . ."[14] A recent survey in *Fortune*[15] suggests that a very similar attitude exists on the part of college students and their families, reminiscent of Marshall's distinction between the "higher grades of society" and

*Cf. Chapter Nine.

the lower ranks. In one group of undergraduates, the reasoning goes: "With a college education I can earn more money, have a more interesting career, and enjoy a better position in society." But another group exists, whose members use different words. Such a student explains "I'm not really concerned with the practical benefits of college. I suppose I take them for granted. College for me means something more intangible, perhaps the opportunity to change things rather than make out well within the existing system." The *Fortune* article describes the characteristics of the students within these two categories and points out the numerical superiority of the first, who account for 58 per cent of the total. Their *economic* significance needs to be explored.

Members of the first group, the ones who say, "With a college education I can earn more money," and so on, are really considering an investment opportunity and its yield in terms of lifetime earnings: they know why they want to be educated and they are seeing to it that their investment in education is going to pay off. They major in accounting, business administration, (home economics or education if they're girls), engineering, or perhaps agriculture, and they will earn higher incomes than their parents in accounting, business administration, agriculture, or home economics. What kind of careers should we design for the children of the ghetto, and how can we make it true that "With a college education they can earn better money, have a more interesting career, and enjoy a better position in society?" And how do we get them out of the ghetto into that rarified atmosphere where students can say "I'm not really concerned with the practical benefits of college—I suppose I take all that for granted?"

CHAPTER FIVE _

EMPLOYMENT
AND THE LABOR MARKET

To SEE if ghetto-dwellers differ from the rest of the population in their means of producing and consuming, we need to examine ghetto markets.

People earn income chiefly in the market for labor; while some individuals do command land and property which yield income for them and their families, they are in the minority. For most people, wages and salaries provide over three-quarters of total family income (62 per cent earned by the husband, 9 per cent by the wife, and less that 5 per cent by other family members) although of course these proportions vary at different income levels. Only six per cent of total family income represents dividends, interest, rents, and trust fund disbursements—all strictly property income. Some eleven per cent stems from mixed labor and capital sources like farms or unincorporated business.[1] To state it another way, although almost one-third of all families own some kind of investment assets (publicly traded stock, investment real estate, or business equity) the income they receive from these sources adds little to their wage and salary income. Over half of all such income-producing assets belong to families in the top ten per cent of the income distribution; if people are ranked by the size of their wealth, the top two per cent (whose wealth exceeds $200,000) hold 54 per cent of such property.[2]

Nevertheless, *some* families below the poverty line do own property—could they use it to supplement their low incomes? One analysis has calculated the results from liquidating all the assets that are owned by the poor, except their homes, and figuring a four per cent return on the value of a home as additional income. The results of this exercise show that if such a scheme were enforced, only 9 per cent of the families and 19 per cent of the individuals would find their incomes raised above the poverty level, defined by the measures discussed in Chapter Two. Dorothy S. Projector and Gertrude S. Weiss spell out the obvious implications of such a program, and they are worth serious consideration:

> As a practicable program for raising consumption levels of units with incomes below poverty criteria, use of accumulated savings has limits. Young people might be expected to rely on their assets to tide them over temporary periods of low income, but young families with incomes below poverty levels have little wealth. Units with head aged 65 and over comprise about half of those who . . . have implied returns on their home equities and sufficient liquid and investment assets to bridge the gap between their incomes and the poverty income standard for at least five years. And if these older units used their assets, they would have difficulties in replacing them. Assuming that wealth accumulated over a lifetime is used to supplement retirement incomes, a program for such use of these assets would need to take into account individual uncertainties as to life expectancy and emergencies.[3]

For poor people as for most Americans, wages and salaries constitute the chief way income can be earned. Contrary to a widespread opinion, a substantial number of poor families depends entirely on such earnings: 35 per cent of the poor families in poverty areas and 30 per cent of these in nonpoverty areas derive their total income from wages and salaries. The proportions are higher for nonwhites: 38 per cent of nonwhite poor families in poverty areas and 45 per cent of those living elsewhere live *only* on earnings from their jobs. A significant number of these, of course, live in rural areas and on the out-skirts of Southern metropolitan centers rather than in the ghettos of Northern inner cities.

EMPLOYMENT AND UNEMPLOYMENT

Labor income depends on the amount of employment and the type of occupation: each of these deserves comment. We may look at employment and unemployment rates for different groups of people, at the regularity of work and the amount of moonlighting, at the extent to which job opportunities exist and are publicized in different regions of the country or different parts of the metropolitan area. Each of these helps determine "the amount" of employment. Occupational distributions reveal income differences; educational achievement is related to the type of job held and so are various restrictions and regulations, especially for working mothers.

In the aggregate, a given rate of unemployment is usually cited either to indicate a nation's level of prosperity or to set a national goal. But any aggregate rate of unemployment, like figures for average income, hides disturbing differences in unemployment by age and race and location. For example, in 1967 the annual average showed 3.8 per cent of the total labor force out of work—but this meant unemployment for 2.3 per cent of the men, 4.2 per cent of the women (twenty years and older) and 12.9 per cent of the teenagers. Among white workers, 3.4 per cent were without jobs compared to the 7.4 per cent of nonwhites who were unemployed, 1.8 per cent of the married men but 4.4 per cent of the blue-collar workers were jobless, and so on. Averages also hide the *duration* of unemployment: in good times people go without work only temporarily, and so from 1960 to 1967 the number of those who had been unemployed for as long as fifteen weeks dropped from 0.7 per cent to 0.4 per cent of the total labor force.

This link between employment and prosperity has also produced the notion of an inverse relation between the rate of unemployment and the rate at which prices go up. Diagram V-1 plots data for the past fifteen years showing this association (first described by A. W. Phillips[4] and now known as a

Diagram V-1

Price Changes, Total Unemployment, and Nonwhite Unemployment, 1954–68

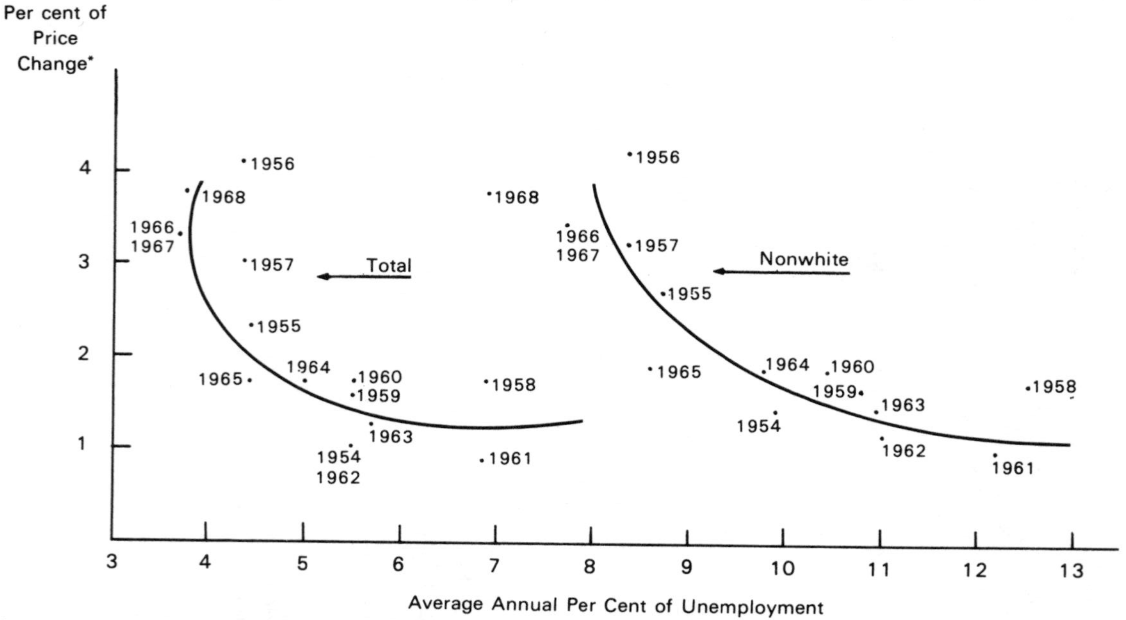

Average Per Cent of Unemployment

*Change in the implicit GNP price deflator during the year, calculated from end of year and first quarter of a given year deflators derived by averaging the fourth quarter of a given year and first quarter of the subsequent year.

Source: Economic Report of the President, January, 1969 (Washington D.C.: U.S. Government Printing Office). p. 95, Chart 8, and p. 255, Table B-24.

Phillips Curve). Two curves are shown: one the rate of total unemployment in the country and the other the rate of unemployment among nonwhites. Both suggest that increased unemployment necessarily (and unpleasantly) accompanies any reduction in inflationary price rises. But the right-hand curve emphasizes how much more heavily the burden of such unemployment falls on minority groups.

We expect all such figures to translate to the local level with greater impact—for example, in poverty areas within SMSA's where black families predominate. And in 1967, when the national unemployment rate was 3.8 per cent and less than half that in urban areas, the rate among Negro men in poverty neighborhoods was 5.1 per cent—higher than that for poor white men, or for nonwhites outside the poverty area. People living in poverty areas go without jobs for longer periods than do the rest of the unemployed—12.8 weeks in poverty areas, 10.2 weeks elsewhere in 1967. Poverty area residents work sporadically rather than regularly: while only 3.5 per cent of the urban employed men worked less than thirty-five hours a week, 7.1 per cent of the nonwhites in poverty neighborhoods did so. Furthermore, in the first group most people worked short-time at their own choice; in the second group most of the short-time was involuntary. At the other end of the scale, opportunities for overtime and increased income are fewer for nonwhites, and even less in the poverty areas than elsewhere.

For those ghetto residents who *do* hold jobs, the wages earned frequently provide only poverty level incomes. More than half the employed nonwhites in poverty areas work as laborers or service workers—dishwashers, porters, car-washers, sweepers, and the like. We have already seen data suggesting that lack of education is not the reason why black adult men predominate in such jobs. A major cause of the concentration of poor jobs in poor areas stems from the recent growth of employment opportunities in areas outside the urban centers.

EMPLOYMENT OPPORTUNITIES

During the nineteenth century, when the United States shifted from a largely agricultural economy to an industrial nation, the growth of manufacturing occurred within cities, and the rail transportation system provided efficient intercity carriage of both materials and finished goods. The technology of railroads makes them extremely efficient for carrying large quantities of goods long distances (and extremely inefficient for carrying small numbers of people very short distances). Some considerable inducement therefore existed for factories to locate as close to freight terminals as possible, for easy access to incoming raw materials and for shipping out finished goods. In small cities and towns, company housing put workers within walking distance of the plant; as cities grew larger, the sites near freight yards and railways shifted to industrial use, and a system of interurban transportation for people developed. Tenements and working-class housing spread out along the streetcar lines as the further growth of the city produced specialized districts. One area contained shops; another the financial activities of banking and brokering; still others separated the merchandising functions from the industrial sections that remained clustered around the freight terminals, since handling goods within the city was relatively costly. The ugliness of cities that ensued, the smoke and smells from factory chimneys, the soot and noise from freight yards, and the congestion of manufacturing areas encouraged this specialization and also initiated the flight to the suburbs for the select few.

What changed all this was, of course, the internal combustion engine: during the 1920's, the automobile accelerated the flight to suburbia as a place to live, but it later spelled the financial doom of interurban transportation and, gradually, of railroad commuting. As far as carrying people was concerned, automobiles became synonymous with transportation. A massive shift of production from the public or quasi-public sector to the private sector followed, as many local transportation systems, municipally owned or regulated, disappeared while individual owner-drivers perfected the traffic jam. A transportation system is essential to economic development, and neither socialism or government ownership need accompany a responsible national policy for transportation, one which coordinates the planning of roads, airlines, mass transport systems, and the like. In this country, the infrastructure of transportation has been almost totally turned over to private operation, with a substantial part of this infrastructure owned and managed not by private business but by private individuals. Only recently has the dramatic rise in pollution, traffic dangers, and time spent in getting from one place to another made the public aware that social costs not only exist but may outweigh the private benefits of the existing system.

As for carrying goods, beginning in the decade after World War II, the new transportation technology perfected long-distance trucking, which provided industry with substantial economies in locating outside the city. A shift of employment and production from the urban core to the outer ring followed the earlier shift in residence patterns. Raw materials could go over the roads in tank cars, refrigerated trailers, and special-purpose vans that were designed to deliver almost anything anywhere. The advantages of locating a factory near the railroad freight terminal within the city disappeared. If goods could be brought in and out of the factory by truck, workers could go to and from in their own private cars. Meanwhile new construction materials and designs were developed to make the one-story factory building economical (e.g., by using the fork-lift truck rather than gravity). The spatial requirements of some industries changed completely and firms abandoned their inner-city locations, where the value of land was measured by its proximity to rail transportation facilities and there was a clear incentive to build upwards, in favor of cheaper and more readily available land for a sprawling building, surrounded by acres of parking lots, good access roads, and a railway spur track for weeds to grow up through.

As manufacturing industries moved out, and new firms built outside rather than in the inner city, urban industrial growth slowed dramatically in a self-perpetuating way. Some service facilities began to move out, such as the headquarters of large companies, the office buildings of financial and communications firms,* and the retail stores (after the invention of the suburban shopping center). The changing technology of transportation proves to have been responsible for much of the contemporary crisis called "the problem of our cities." We cannot here attempt to analyze or answer what is perhaps the most basic question of all—is urban renewal worth it?—do we want a city these days? But this all-too-brief summary of some urban history shows, once again, the complexity of the economics of the ghetto.

The interaction between city and transportation contributed two types of impetus to developing ghettos. First, as city dwellers moved to the suburbs, their urban residences—older, less desirable, and therefore cheaper—became available to the new in-migrants with low incomes. But, second, the interurban transportation system provided less and less access to jobs. The street railways and buses sufficed when the railroads handled most of the goods traffic, and the public transportation system took people from their city flats or tenements to their city jobs and home again. But it could not take people from their city dwellings to suburban jobs. Even those systems that connected city and suburb were ineffective, for they had been built to run mostly to dormitory suburbs, residential areas from which the financial men and business executives traveled downtown to work and home again in the evening.

By the 1950's and 1960's, such suburban areas had been fully built up, and the new industrial growth appeared elsewhere, in abandoned farm areas or what had been wasteland on the outskirts of both city and suburb. The phenomenon of "urban sprawl" meant that development pushed out into open spaces, not into the residential areas. So no public transit systems existed between the new, scattered factories and the city quarters where new populations moved into the newly available cheap housing. Ghetto restrictions prevented the in-migrant Negroes and Puerto Ricans from moving to where the job opportunities lay; public transportation to and from did not exist; and poverty precluded these workers from commuting in the American fashion—by private automobile. The supply of labor remained separate from the demand.

The prevailing pattern of job opportunities in central cities offers less and less escape from either poverty or the ghetto. Low-paid, temporary, unskilled, and service jobs remain for the inhabitants of poverty areas. The new industries, employing

*Thereby contributing to the loss of taxable property, discussed in Chapter Three.

higher percentages of technical and skilled employees, locate in outlying districts, often beyond the reach of public transportation, and in neighborhoods where housing is strictly segregated. Two brief summary statements are worth remembering. First, between 1960 and 1965 suburban construction accounted for almost two-thirds (62 per cent) of all the industrial buildings and over half (52 per cent) of the commercial buildings in the country. The trend away from the inner city accelerated in the latter part of the decade.[5] Second, during the same time-period figures for four metropolitan areas show an overall gain of half a million new jobs, of which only five per cent were in the city; in New York, only one-quarter of the jobs provided by an equal gain in employment were city openings.[6] Such figures do not exist for all metropolitan areas, but there is every reason to think these patterns occur elsewhere; some cities have reported an absolute decline in employment opportunities over the past few years.

The interaction between employment and transportation appears dramatically in specific examples, rather than in the aggregates quoted above:

> Employment has been expanding rapidly in suburban areas of Philadelphia . . . while the City of Philadelphia, at least since the early fifties, has suffered an absolute decline in employment. The worst loss . . . has been in manufacturing activities where employment has plummeted nearly 20 per cent . . . Since 1950, the Negro proportion of the population of Philadelphia has nearly doubled . . . the city has a smaller number of appropriate jobs to offer to its citizens . . . Employers with the greatest number of job openings were too far away . . . As one businessman who signed up a hundred workers from North Philadelphia complained, the expense and inconvenience of the two-hour bus and trolley ride to his suburban electronics plant caused most of the new employees to quit within a few weeks.[7]

In Baltimore, the trip by public transportation from the inner core to a suburban job ranges from a 40-minute ride each way at approximately $4.00 per week to an hour's ride each way at a cost of $25.00 a week. . . . In St. Louis, there is no public transportation to many of the suburban areas to which jobs have moved; to other large employment centers, such as the McDonnell Aircraft Corporation, the trip from the St. Louis ghetto would cost some $6.50 each week and total travel time each day would range from three to four hours. . . .[8]

The public transit systems in most metropolitan areas carry few city residents to jobs outside. The term "commuter" means one whose employment is within the city; the incoming train cannot take a load of workers (except for household help) back to the outlying areas. If the present trend toward increasing reliance on private automobiles continues, highway development will intensify the housing crisis in the cities by taking away land and demolishing structures, at the same time that it intensifies the employment crisis of city-dwellers.

OCCUPATIONS

Before turning to the illustrative data of the nine districts met previously, one other aggregate employment trend must be mentioned. While industrial jobs are shifting to outlying areas, employment gains within the city occur largely in white-collar occupations. Most of the new job openings are with firms in communications; insurance; banking or finance; certain types of mercantile operations; medical, technical, or educational institutions; and business services of all kinds. When we look at data about the employment of ghetto residents, therefore, we should be concerned with the number holding white-collar jobs, as well as the number able to get industrial jobs in the suburbs. And since people commonly work in areas other than where they live, this kind of information requires looking at the three metropolitan areas in toto.

Table V–1 shows one kind of employment analysis. It lists for each of the three SMSA's those industries which provide at least five per cent of the total employment and which also are among the fifteen largest employers. Comparing the percentage of Negro employees in these industries to the fraction of total employment represented by Negroes shows how this racial group is concentrated in certain industries with few if any jobs in others. There is some implication that Negro em-

Table V-1

Percentage of Negro Employment
Selected Industries, 1966

Industry	SMSA I	SMSA II	SMSA III
All industries	13.5	8.9	4.1
Electric machinery, equipment, and supplies	13	6	11.1
Machinery not electric	7.8	4.3*	1.4
Food and kindred products	22.1	12.9	—
Transportation equipment	15.3*	7.5	—
Paper and like products	—	—	1.6
Miscellaneous manufacturing	—	—	6.9
Primary metal industries	21.9*	12.4*	
Retail trade general merchandise	16.9	5.7	2.1
Wholesale trade	7.5	3.7	1.1*
Medical services, etc.	19.7*	26.4*	8.4
Insurance carriers	4.7*	1.6	2.2

— not among the top fifteen industries.
* industry total employment amounts to less than 5 per cent of total SMSA employment.

Source: U.S. Equal Employment Opportunities Commission, Report No. 1, *Job Patterns for Minorities and Women in Private Industry 1966,* Part I, pp. D45, D121, D222.

Table V-2

Percentage of Negro Employment
Selected Occupations, 1966

	SMSA I	SMSA II	SMSA III
Total employment	13.5	8.9	4.1
White-collar, all industries	4.6	2.1	1.1
Officials, managers	1.3	0.7	0.4
Professionals	2.0	1.9	0.9
Technical	5.0	6.6	2.3
Sales workers	3.1	1.1	1.0
Clerical	7.3	2.4	1.2
Blue-collar, all industries	20.6	14.3	5.8
Craftsmen	7.0	4.1	2.0
Operatives	20.2	11.9	5.6
Laborers	31.2	18.9	9.2
Service workers	30.4	32.0	8.3

Source: U.S. Equal Employment Opportunities Commission, Report No. 1, *Job Patterns for Minorities and Women in Private Industry 1966,* Part I, pp. D46, D122, and D223.

ployment consists of unskilled and laborers' jobs: for example, medical service employment accounts for two to three times the average number of jobs for Negroes, but Negro employment with insurance carriers or in wholesale trade falls well below the average number of jobs. Table V–2 confirms this impression of restriction: it shows the percentage of Negroes in white-collar and blue-collar jobs throughout the industries of each SMSA. Not only is Negro employment in white-collar jobs from one-fourth to one-third that of total Negro employment, but such jobholders are largely concentrated in the low-paying clerical or technical occupations. Among blue-collar employees, the ratio of skilled Negro craftsmen is less than that of total Negro employment, with a heavy concentration of laborers and service workers.

AREA ANALYSIS

With Table V–3, we take the analysis to an even smaller area: the nine districts we have examined in other contexts. These data refer to people rather than to jobs; they tell how many men and women of working age live in each district; what proportion of them are in the labor force; and what types of jobs, if any, they hold. Looking first at the males fourteen years of age and over, unemployment rates indicate clearly that districts *B* and *C* are much worse off than the districts *A*. Also, the poorer areas show substantial numbers of low-paying, unskilled occupations among those employed. In the first two SMSA's, the proportion of skilled craftsmen is highest in the *B* districts: these are poor but largely white. The percentage of semiskilled jobs in these districts ("operatives," etc.) is several times the number in the wealthy districts *A,* and also higher than those held by residents of the largely nonwhite districts *C.* Clerical and sales jobs include both high- and low-paying positions: the residents of district *A* outnumber the others in these occupations, but it is safe to assume that an industrial sales engineer would live in district *A,* while his file clerk would live in district *B.* The most striking contrast, of course, occurs with executive positions—in the white suburbs of II and III (the *A* districts) roughly half the employed males work as managers,

Table V-3
Employment and Occupation
Three SMSA's, Selected Census Tracts

	SMSA I			SMSA II			SMSA III			Non white
	A	B	C	A	B	C	A	B	C	
Total population (thousands)	19.5	19.1	19.6	12.0	13.0	12.1	10.6	14.1	14.0	6.2
Males, 14 years old and over (thousands)	7.5	7.3	6.1	3.9	4.6	3.7	3.5	4.8	4.6	1.7
Per cent in labor force	81.8	79.1	65.9	83.4	78.1	74.7	79.7	79.6	73.9	82.8
Per cent unemployed	1.8	6.8	9.3	1.9	6.9	7.9	1.2	6.5	7.3	5.1
Per cent employed as professional and managerial	38.3	7.6	2.6	43.5	7.9	2.6	57.0	6.4	9.5	3.0
Clerical and sales	29.4	12.2	6.2	26.6	15.2	7.7	25.2	10.9	18.9	6.5
Craftsmen, etc.	11	18.9	10.4	14.1	22.1	8.9	9.3	18.3	17.9	13.9
Operatives, etc.	7.0	37.5	32.9	8.4	29.4	18.1	3.9	42.6	28.1	34.9
Private household	.1	.7	.5	—	.0	1.1	.0	.1	.5	.9
Other service	6.7	7.8	14.6	2.5	8.9	20.9	1.3	5.7	7.7	8.8
Laborers	1	6.8	15.4	2.1	9.3	8.8	0.9	8.0	12.6	18.2
Females, 14 years old and over (thousands)	9.1	6.7	5.7	4.5	5.4	42.5	4.1	5.8	5.5	2.0
Per cent in labor force	50.1	46.6	27.7	33.5	42.2	51.6	25.1	41.9	38.6	42.0
Per cent of labor force married with husband present	42.7	53.7	41.5	28.5	48.7	46.3	17.8	31.8	44.3	33.7
Per cent of these with children under 6 years of age	7.9	25.2	33.7	15.0	20.2	21.5	8.8	22.5	21.8	32.5
Per cent employed as professional and managerial	6.6	4.5	3.0	25.2	8.4	2.6	29.6	8.5	10.8	7.2
Clerical and sales	44.5	32.2	17.1	51.5	45.8	6.7	32.2	15.7	33.5	19.4
Craftsmen, etc.	.6	1.6	2.0	1.9	2.5	.4	1.5	2.7	1.6	.5
Operatives, etc.	4.6	35.8	26.6	6.6	23.8	13.8	2.6	42.9	23.1	27.2
Private household	1.6	.3	8.8	2.8	1.4	18.8	2.6	2.1	8.8	17.8
Other service	5.6	14.6	14.5	6.8	10.9	14.7	4.4	13.8	14.0	17.2
Laborers	.4	1.1	3.2	—	.9	.8	.0	.5	.8	1.0
Per cent unemployed	1.4	9.2	16.8	1.4	4.9	2.3	0.8	8.4	8.2	?

Source: U.S. Census of Population and Housing, 1960.

officials, professionals, and the like; in the predominantly black areas of the C districts, fewer than 3 per cent of the nonwhites hold such positions. "Laborers" are almost unknown in the high-income white districts, but together with service jobs they employ 25 to 30 per cent of the nonwhite workers in the ghetto areas.

What is particularly disheartening about this recital of differentials in job opportunities, employment, and consequent earnings, is its effect on the supply of labor in ghetto areas. Economists measure the "labor force participation" of different groups in the population by the number of people who are employed as civilians, unemployed, or in the armed forces: other civilians fourteen years old and over are then defined as "not in the labor force." These include five groups: those "engaged in own home housework," "in school," "unable to work" because of long-term physical or mental illness, "doing only incidental unpaid family work (less than fifteen hours)," and "other." The last category consists of retired workers or people too old to work, seasonal workers in their off season, and those who are "voluntarily idle." As Table V-3 makes clear, a much higher proportion of labor force participation exists among men in the highest income areas than in the poverty districts C, where substantial numbers of Negroes live.

SMSA III is something of an exception: here the lowest rate of labor force participation is among the white males living in district C, and the nonwhites show the highest rate. Their numbers, however, are fairly small for this type of analysis; furthermore district C contains a disproportionate number of older white men who have retired from the labor force. But in SMSA I, for example, more than three out of ten males in district C are not in the labor force; coupled with the high unemployment rate, this means that only just over half the adult males are working. Nor does this low rate of labor force participation mean that many young men are in school —the percentage in high school and college is significantly smaller than in the wealthier districts. On a national basis, only 57 per cent of the males over fourteen living in poor areas are in the labor force. In those local areas where black participation runs slightly above that of white, like district C in SMSA III, it is because poor white men tend to be older.[9]

A survey by the Department of Labor[10] found that in 1968 over twelve million men were not in the labor force. Significantly, only seven per cent of the whites said they wanted jobs, compared to eighteen per cent of the nonwhites who wanted jobs. Most of the twelve million men were, of course, either students or retired, while those who were ill or disabled accounted for sixteen per cent of the whites and almost three out of ten nonwhites. But the potential labor force members number almost one million. Yet few have any plans for the future; most are discouraged dropouts from the labor market. In an atmosphere of enforced idleness, underemployment at dead-end jobs, sporadic employment followed by unexpected layoffs, a situation where jobs are scarce and people are surplus—in such an atmosphere the drive to keep looking and keep trying, to think of oneself as a worker rather than a drifter takes remarkable motivation. Such men may fall into the Labor Department's classification of "voluntarily idle" because they do not belong in the other categories. But how appropriate is the term "voluntary"?

THE EMPLOYMENT OF WOMEN

The total supply of labor consists of both men and women: for poor families the woman's position as earner can be crucial. Some thirty-five per cent of the poor families have no male head: more than half the nonwhite families rely on a woman as mainstay.* Whether or not these women hold jobs depends largely on whether there are children at home. About eighteen per cent of the poor families have two income earners and in most cases this means husband and wife. Working wives are more common, however, among families who are better off. About 40 per cent of *all* wives work, and they contribute more of the total income at higher income levels than at low levels. Again, this merely reflects the presence or absence of children: mothers who have school-aged children can more readily take full-time jobs; their earnings will therefore form a larger share

*Among the single individuals who are poor, women are even more numerous; 71 per cent of the total although only 62 per cent of the nonwhites.

of the total income and will frequently put the family into a higher income class than otherwise.

Whether or not a woman works also depends on her color: the labor force includes 40 per cent of the white females eighteen years and older, but 45 per cent of the nonwhites. And black families contain working wives much more frequently than do whites—in more than half of all the Negro families with both husband and wife present, the wife is employed. In the nine SMSA districts we have analyzed, the proportion of married women (with husbands present) in the labor force varies from about 18 per cent to 28 per cent in the A districts, but from 33 per cent to 36 per cent in the C districts. Negro women who work also contribute a larger proportion of their family's income than do white working wives. One estimate suggests that about 42 per cent of all nonwhite couples (with or without children) would have been living in poverty if they had depended solely on the husband's income; adding the wife's earnings meant that only 19 per cent of the families were below poverty levels.[11] The number of black women whose earnings spell the difference, for their families, between subsistence and comfortable living far exceeds the similar group of white working wives.

Working women do not, of course, earn as much as working men—partly because many high-paying occupations have been restricted to male entrants. But the differential between the sexes—that is, the extent to which women's incomes fall short of men's—is smaller for nonwhites than for whites. Figures for 1967 earnings of year-round full-time workers appear in Table V-4.

For the most part, this reflects the fact that black women attain somewhat higher levels of education than do black men, and have also made gains in traditionally female occupations like clerical and sales work, while other occupations, particularly the skilled trades, have been closed to both women and nonwhite men. But jobs in retailing have been dwindling in urban centers; and the problems of getting out to work, from the ghetto to the cross-roads shopping center or industrial complex, loom even larger for the women with home and family responsibilities than they do for the man.

Table V-4
Annual Earnings, Full-time Workers, 1967

	Median Income
Male, white	$7,518
Male, Negro	$4,837
Female, white	$4,383
Female, Negro	$3,269
Ratio, white female to white male	58.3
Ratio, Negro female to Negro male	67.8
Ratio, Negro male to white male	64.2
Ratio, Negro female to white female	74.5

Source: Current Population Reports, *Consumer Income, Series P-60,* No. 64 (Oct. 6, 1969), U.S. Department of Commerce, Bureau of the Census.

Like the dead-end jobs of unskilled and casual labor so prevalent among nonwhite males, service work provides the largest amount of employment for nonwhite women, especially those living in poverty areas. Because household service offers so many job opportunities to black women, the average duration of unemployment is comparatively short. The percentage of unemployment, however, exceeds that for nonwhite men, or for either men or women who are white. As jobs in other areas besides housecleaning and janitorial work open up, we may expect that earned incomes will rise, but so will the average length of time between jobs when unemployment does occur.

All of this discussion merely postpones the truly critical question about female employment—in the ghetto or in the suburbs, among whites or blacks or Puerto Ricans—whether to continue the remarkable waste of productivity and effort represented by the existing arrangements for household and child care. Most analysts of female employment use marital status, number of children, and the presence of preschool children in the home as variables or explanatory factors. This usage of course takes for granted the established arrangements that require a woman's presence in the home with her children. (Much the same built-in bias occurs, on the male side, when labor force participation rates are calculated for males between eighteen and sixty-five, thus taking for granted the established arrangements which make retirement at sixty-five so prevalent.) It is not only possible, but fruitful, to turn the analysis completely around and ask whether these arrangements make the best use of economic resources or whether something else should be devised.

Household care (including a large part of the economic function of spending the family income, to be discussed in the next chapter) has been associated with the woman's role in family life almost from the beginning of a market economy. In the early days of the industrial system when labor had to be sold outside the home, instead of being devoted to home production, working hours and conditions made it almost physically impossible for one individual to earn an income, and also to consume or dispose of that income. The division of function between the sexes left a large share of home production as well as consumption to the wife and daughters as men went outside the home. In the United States, home production has dwindled steadily for the last seventy years, and although household servants have been the prerogative of the upper-income classes, technology and appliances have rapidly lessened the physical burden of household labor as well as its requirements of time and skill. The chief household function that has not yet been replaced or even much diminished is child care, from birth to six years of age.

A survey of working mothers (not confined to those in low-income groups) found that in 1965 some 22 per cent of all the children under fourteen had a mother who worked. Nearly half of them (48.9 per cent) were cared for at home while their mother worked: the chances were one out of three that their father provided care, but about one out of ten that another child (under sixteen) took the responsibility. Relatives in other homes looked after 16 per cent of the children, and the remaining 35 per cent enjoyed various arrangements—including having the mother work only during the child's school hours or having the mother combine her work with caring for the child. Group care centers accounted for 2.9 per cent of the cases: 3.7 per cent for full-time working mothers within SMSA's, and less frequently elsewhere.[12]

The same survey found that nine out of ten women, when

asked, said the reasons they worked were economic: "Money! What else?" "To support my family. I am too proud to ask for welfare help. I have pride!" "Need money for glasses for the children. Also braces for their teeth."[13] Table V–3 shows that married women whose husbands are present do not make up a larger share of the female working force in the poor *B* and *C* districts than in the *A* districts. But the working *mothers* ("in labor force, married with husband present, with children under six") drop to half or less the number of working wives, in the *A* and *B* districts. Only in the *C* districts, where incomes are lowest and the percentage of nonwhites highest, do mothers with pre-school children form a significant share of the labor force.

Census data contain no information on their arrangements for the children, but the connections between such arrangements and employment can be complex, as illustrated by the following exchange. Mr. Wiley is executive director of the National Welfare Rights Organization; Representative Griffiths, Congresswoman from Michigan, is the Chairman of the Joint Economic Committee's Subcommittee on Fiscal Policy:

Mr. Wiley: . . . Of the female-headed family, 69 per cent in 1966 were not in the labor force. Our feeling is that a good number . . . of the welfare recipients should not be in the labor force because they have other important responsibilities at home, to take care of their families. . . . It is an important question for many people that they find jobs. But the important thing is that the men, that the people who are able to be heads of households or ought to be legitimate heads of households be the ones that get those jobs. . . .

Representative Griffiths: . . . You say that this work incentive program will be used to force mothers to work. . . . After we went through all of this in the Ways and Means Committee, Mr. Cohen called me and told me that they were quite surprised. They had run a survey in New York City and they discovered that 70 per cent of the women drawing welfare in New York City who had families, 70 per cent of them wanted to work if they had a place to put their children.

And I said to him, well, Mr. Cohen, the other 30 per cent did not understand the question or they would have wanted to work, too. Who would not prefer to have a job?[14]

EMPLOYMENT ELIGIBILITY

Along with the physical difficulties of finding and keeping employment when residence and work lie in separate areas, and the conventional difficulties of home and child care, a further barrier to the employment of ghetto residents (particularly to those with incomplete education or to members of minority groups), exists in the network of regulations, tests, requirements for recommendations or background references surrounding the apprenticeship or the training for entry into many labor unions. These have been customary practices for decades, with the result that Negroes were effectively excluded from union membership and therefore from employment in many trades. The story of this development, which of course mirrors the American tradition of racial discrimination, has been documented by Herbert Hill and Ray Marshall.[15] The total situation at present can be summarized by the announcement, in October of 1968, that Negro participation in union apprenticeship programs had almost doubled over the previous eighteen months. In the middle of the year, there were 8,100 black apprentices who accounted for 3.6 per cent of the total enrolled in such programs. Nor is it wholly correct to single out unions as solely responsible for this state of affairs: the apprenticeship programs cited, for example, are certified by the United States Department of Labor.

This problem involves the economics of discrimination, a larger question for a later chapter. We note here only two cases where such occupational barriers play a strategic role in the economics of the ghetto. The first is the restriction of employment opportunities, to ghetto dwellers, stemming from the so-called "referral unions," those which provide applicants for specific job openings. Although some twelve per cent of their total membership appears to be Negro, this consists chiefly of workers in the lesser-skilled, low-paying categories. Furthermore, in most cities the Negro membership in such unions is less than half the percentage of Negroes in the city population, as suggested by Table V–5. The table also illustrates the second problem, the dearth of minority group workers in the building trades.

Table V-5

Negroes in Labor Force and Negro Membership In Referral Unions, 1967 Percentage of Total, United States and Selected Cities, 1967

Area	Labor Force	Building Trades		Nonbuilding Trades
		All Construction Trades	**Mechanical Trades**	
Albuquerque	–	1.3	0.0	5.9
Atlanta	–	22.8	0.1	.3
Birmingham	–	16.3	0.0	
Chicago	24	4.6	0.4	37.6
Cleveland	36	4.6	0.4	37.6
Detroit	34	14.7	0.5	4.3
Houston	28	18.1	0.0	40.9
Kansas City	–	10.8	0.0	10.2
Los Angeles	20	8.2	0.5	9.4
Memphis	–	16.6	0.9	.7
New Orleans	–	21.7	0.3	18.7
New York	17	12.3	8.2	17.9
San Francisco	30	13.2	4.5	10.0
Washington, D.C.	71	10.7	3.4	40.5
United States	16	8.4	0.8	12.0

Source: Equal Employment Opportunity Commission, 1970, and U.S. Department of Labor, *Manpower Report of the President, 1969, Supplement* (Washington, D.C.: U.S. Government Printing Office, 1969), p. 74–5.

Much of the physical decay of the streets and buildings in ghetto areas will require new construction to replace or rehabilitate the surroundings, and the construction industry can therefore provide new jobs for workers in the various building trades. These have historically required fairly long periods of apprenticeship and training; and they also have been severely criticized for discrimination against minority groups.

Again, the detailed figures for the metropolitan areas we

have been examining reinforce this general picture. Table V-6 presents data for the number and type of jobs held by Negroes in firms engaged in contract construction for SMSA I and SMSA II. In the first area, where Negroes make up 13 per cent of total employment in the industry, they account for less than one per cent of the white-collar jobs, but almost half of the laborers' jobs. Craft occupations engage about half the workers in the industry, but the percentage of Negroes in these jobs is less than five per cent in one area and less than two in the other. Some of the figures can be compared to those in Table V-2 (p. 113) to show that the general characteristics of restriction are intensified in the construction industry. For ex-

Table V-6
Employment in Contract Construction,
Selected Standard Metropolitan Statistical Areas, 1966

	SMSA I	SMSA II
Total employment, SIC 15, 16, and 17	16,045	3,593
Percentage Negro	13	7.4
White-collar employment, per cent of total	22	21.0
Percentage Negro	.8	.4
Officials and managers, per cent of total	6.8	11.6
Percentage Negro	.0	.7
Professionals	6.1	3.9
Percentage Negro	.5	.0
Technicians	4.6	2.0
Percentage Negro	1.9	.0
Sales workers	.9	1.1
Percentage Negro	2.0	.0
Office and clerical	3.7	2.3
Percentage Negro	1.2	.0
Blue-collar employment	77.5	78.7
Percentage Negro	16.3	9.0
Craftsmen	49.3	53.9
Percentage Negro	4.6	1.7
Operatives	8.4	10.8
Percentage Negro	11.6	6.4
Laborers	19.8	14.0
Percentage Negro	47.5	39.2
Service workers	.5	.4
Percentage Negro	37.5	69.2

Source: U.S. Equal Employment Opportunity Commission, *Job Patterns for Minorities and Women in Private Industry 1966,* Part III, pp. 47, 177.

ample, in SMSA I, seven per cent of all craftsmen are Negroes, and this in itself is a small percentage. But only 4.5 per cent of the craftsmen in the building trades are Negro. Or, in SMSA II where Negroes account for almost nine per cent of the total employment tabulated, 6.6 per cent of the white-collar technical jobs were held by Negroes, but none of these was in contract construction.

The barriers to employment in the labor market that confront the ghetto resident include his lack of information, ability, transportation, and training. Most of these can be summed up by the term "lack of opportunity." Most of them, also, consist of barriers which are not deeply rooted in *economic* circumstances or require long-term efforts to change. We shall return to this subject in a later chapter, after surveying next the other market in which any individual deals, the consumer's market of things to buy for himself and his household.

CHAPTER SIX

CONSUMERS AND MARKETS

For people to function as consumers, two economic activities must occur. The family or individual must decide how to divide income among different goods and services and sort out the many ways of spending and saving. But then, having chosen what to consume, someone must go out and buy it. Although economists generally concentrate on the first topic, we must deal with both, for we buy most of what we consume. It takes marketing facilities to get the goods and services into stores for us, and it takes transportation facilities to carry us and our purchases. What of the facilities available in the ghetto? Do ghetto residents face obstacles when buying things? Restrictions on their consumption choices?

Consumption Patterns

Before analyzing this question in terms of neighborhoods and localities, let us look briefly at the first topic—consumer choice, or how income is divided among goods and services and assets. Clearly income, more than any other factor, accounts for the chief differences in how families and individuals spend their money, and we know that ghettos contain many people with very low incomes. But what about racial or ethnic differences in buying patterns and living habits? Will two families *of the same size and income* choose to spend their money in the same way, if one is black and one is white? This subject has recently attracted a great deal of interest, especially among business firms suddenly aware of the substantial market among black people. One of the few specialists[1] remarks:

> One of the consistently amazing things about the modern view of the Negro consumer is that an entire mythology of "marketing insights" has been developed to describe the Negro in the almost total absence of factual information. Even more amazing is the fact that as new, reliable information comes to light, many of the myths are found to be reasonable approximations of the truth, although often for the wrong reasons.
>
> One of the greatest lacks in the presentation of the Negro consumer market in the United States has been the absence of reliable research. In an age where "linear programming" and "Q-sorting" have become advertising catchwords, the Negro market remains almost—but not quite—as impenetrable as it has ever been.

Reliable data about consumption differences—or preferences —require much more intensive analysis than looking at broad categories of expenditure, as any market research analyst knows. In this country such data exist from about 1875 on, although the more recent surveys provide both more detail and more reliability. Beginning in 1903, the U.S. Department of Labor, in what is now the Bureau of Labor Statistics, conducted nationwide studies at irregular intervals—most recently in 1960. (The findings help to measure price changes; they have also been used to compile budgets, as explained in Chapter Two.) Two observations keep recurring in every survey made. First, there is the familiar fact that saving amounts to a larger sum of dollars and also to a larger *share* of family or household income at high-income levels than at low-income levels.* Second, what may not be so familiar is that at every income level Negro families save a larger proportion of their income than do white families.

Let us be exact about what this means. Since, overall, the incomes of black people average only about one-half to sixty per cent of those of whites, the amount of saving by black families is of course less than that of whites, whether measured

*Cf. Chapter Two.

by the number of savers, the dollar sums, or the average saving-to-income ratio. But when families are grouped by income class, and then by race *within* each income class, quite different results appear. The survey data let us measure savings in relation to income by three different methods. First, we can calculate the number (or percentage) of savers in each income class: in 1960, for instance, families who drew down their savings outnumbered those who increased their savings at all incomes below $4,000. Next, we can calculate an average, for all the families within each income class, by adding the savings of some to the dissavings of the rest and then dividing by the total number of families in the group. In every income class below $5,000, such an average figure turns out to be negative—that is, the saving by some families was outweighed by the dissaving of the rest. Finally, we can calculate for each family the percentage of income it saves (or dissaves) and compare the number of families, at different income levels, with large or small ratios of saving to income. For various reasons, the dollar figures used for saving contain some unavoidable errors and it is useful to have these different approaches to the subject.

In 1960–61 those families and single consumers with incomes between $6,000 and $15,000 who saved ranged from 75 to 95 per cent among Negroes but only 60 to 67 per cent among whites. At lower income levels, families who could save anything at all were fewer in number, and those who dissaved (spent more than current income) were about as frequent in both racial groups. But the average saving of Negro families was larger and their dissaving smaller than that of white families in the same income bracket. Finally, the average saving-to-income ratio also showed this difference between the races.

Table VI-1 summarizes these findings, and a brief reference to previous data may reinforce the point. A survey taken during the 1930's contained data for the break-even point—where families neither save nor go into debt—in different cities: In Columbus, Ohio, this income level for white families was $1,300, for Negro families $900; in New York City white families with $2,300 broke even but Negro families with $1,600 did so.

Table VI-1

Family Saving By Income and Race, Urban Areas, 1960–61

	$1,000 to $1,999	$2,000 to $2,999	$3,000 to $3,999	$4,000 to $4,999	$5,000 to $5,999	$6,000 to $7,499	$7,500 to $9,999	$10,000 to $14,999
Av. saving white	−$259	−$232	−$290	−$61	$14	$118	$414	$878
Av. saving Negro	−$72	−$64	−$123	−$36	−$39	$298	$681	$694
S/Y ratio, white	−17.0	−9.3	−8.2	−1.3	.2	1.6	4.7	7.5
S/Y ratio, Negro	−4.8	−2.5	−3.5	−.8	−.7	4.5	8.0	6.0
% dissavers, white	55	47	51	45	41	38	33	32
% dissavers, Negro	32	54	50	46	42	28	20	40

Source: Bureau of Labor Statistics, *Survey of Consumer Expenditures,* 1960–61.

The data, of course, consist of observations, not explanations. But clearly this major choice in allocating income—the division between spending and saving—has differed significantly between the races. The next obvious question is, what about other choices? Does spending for food, clothing, shelter, education, and everything else differ, significantly, between black and white families? Comparisons *must* be made between households at the same income level, and comparisons *should* be made between households of the same size and composition. An even more stringent analysis has been demanded[2]:

> Differences in consumption patterns are caused by many factors, among which one's station in life, his opinion of himself, availability of credit, income expectation, age, dependents, education, location, and financial resources, to mention only a few. To date, no study has explained the effect of all these variables on consumption patterns. . . . Before any realistic comparisons are made between the amount spent on consumption by Negroes and Whites, adjustments should be made for the difference in such factors. Once these adjustments are made, differences attributed to race may find their origin in other factors.

Table VI-2

Consumption and Income, by Income Level and Race, 1960-61

Family Income, before Taxes, Urban Families and Single Consumers

	$2,000–$2,999		$3,000–$3,999		$4,000–$4,999		$5,000–$5,999		$6,000–$7,499		$7,500–$9,999		$10,000–$14,999	
	W	N	W	N	W	N	W	N	W	N	W	N	W	N
Average family size	2.1	3.0	2.5	3.5	2.9	3.8	3.4	4.0	3.5	4.0	3.8	3.7	4.0	5.0
Per cent homeowners, all year	41	23	39	27	43	31	53	34	66	50	71	51	78	62
Per cent auto owners, end of year	44	25	66	42	78	63	88	67	91	76	94	85	96	95
Per cent with children under 18	22	50	36	60	51	56	61	67	65	58	66	61	63	73
Money income after taxes, average	$2,505	$2,511	$3,523	$3,492	$4,506	$4,455	$5,500	$5,448	$6,715	$6,658	$8,579	$8,457	$11,733	$11,544
Income per capita	$1,193	$837	$1,409	$997	$1,554	$1,172	$1,618	$1,362	$1,910	$1,660	$2,255	$2,286	$2,683	$2,309
Per cent total expenditures for food, per capita	11	7.6	9.2	6.2	7	5.5	6.1	4.9	5.6	4.7	4.9	4.5	4.1	2.9
House furnishings	3.6	4.4	4.6	5.4	4.9	4.5	5.2	5.4	5.5	6.3	5.3	6.6	5.3	7.8
Alcoholic beverages	1.1	1.7	1.4	2.0	1.6	1.9	1.6	1.5	1.6	3.1	1.7	2.4	1.9	2.5
Average dollar expenditures for personal insurance	86	108	148	181	240	234	303	296	389	392	512	542	696	701
Other shelter	9	–	16	4	21	4	25	14	42	15	54	16	110	33
Recreation	70	81	122	119	167	130	193	182	260	254	337	337	487	399
Food away from home	139	142	194	177	226	158	222	186	292	296	403	292	565	514
Clothing, etc., per capita	$90	$95	$117	$125	$147	$138	$146	$175	$181	$198	$220	$271	$283	$355
Auto by owners	$427	$508	$676	$676	$801	$919	$848	$1,072	$976	$721	$1,169	$1,070	$1,460	$1,294

Source: Bureau of Labor Statistics, Survey of Consumer Expenditures, 1960–61.

On the other hand, with survey data cross-classified by three or four variables, the chances of empty cells (an inadequate number of cases to supply valid data) increase mightily. Table VI-2 gives some highlights of spending on certain broad categories, by white and Negro urban families and single consumers with incomes between $2,000 and $25,000, from the 1960-61 survey.

Because data for Negro families show an average income after taxes that is smaller and an average family size that is larger than the white families, per capita figures have been calculated for income and for expenditures on food and clothing. Expenditures on house furnishings, alcoholic beverages, and automobile transportation were not adjusted in this way, although the dollar figures for the last item represent average expenditures of only the automobile owners, not all the families in a given income class. The table shows that differences between spending patterns do exist, and that they are consistent.

The share of total expenditures given to food is higher, at every income class, for white families than for Negroes. (Applying Engel's law might suggest that blacks were *better* off, at every income level, than whites.) In general, house furnishings, alcoholic beverages, and clothing take larger shares of total expenditure by families at higher-income levels; and for each of these items the average amounts spend by black families exceed those spent by whites. In most income classes, both dollar and percentage amounts for personal insurance expenditures by Negro families are higher than those by white families. On the other hand, except for families with incomes between $5,000 and $6,000, spending for automobiles puts Negroes ahead of whites at low-income levels and reverses the position at high-income levels. Many other comparisons can be drawn, but the basic concern of economists studying questions of social policy is to understand these comparisons, and their implications.

First, do differences really exist and what are they? Second, if distinct consumption patterns do exist, are they dependable —can we use them to predict the future choices of blacks and whites? Finally, do these different consumption patterns reflect a real freedom of choice?

This last point deserves amplification; it concerns a value judgment which is shared by most Americans, but which is rarely made explicit. The economist analyzes market demand as a derivative of consumers' choice. Consumers confront a myriad of alternative goods and services, each with a finite price, among which the family or individual must allocate a limited income. The economist's model of consumer choice contains three "givens": prices, income, and the tastes and preferences of the consumer doing the choosing. The economist sometimes represents these tastes and preferences by means of indifference curves, and he depicts an elegant solution where the consumption-possibility line dictated by the amount of income falls tangent to the highest possible indifference curve, such that the ratio of prices is equal to the marginal rate of substitution.

A rarely drawn solution is shown in Diagram VI-1. Here, A and B represent two consumers. With the same income, (CC = C'C') and with commodities X and Y available, Mr. A and Mr. B choose quite different quantities of each. Mr. A buys about equal amounts of both X and Y (OM, ON); Mr. B, however, splurges on Y and uses about half as much X as does Mr. A (OM' and ON'). One conclusion is that these choices reveal the preferences of the two consumers—their decisions to buy are different because the set of indifference curves representing A's likes and dislikes is different from the set of curves picturing B's. Furthermore, both A and B are as well off—as satisfied—as they could hope to be. They can buy no other combination of X and Y that will give them greater satisfaction.

We may, and both economists and market researchers do, spend a good bit of time examining these different choices. We may find that many consumers are like Mr. A—and, furthermore, that they are all between the ages of eighteen and twenty-five. Or we may find that many consumers are like Mr. B—and that they are all stockbrokers, or doctors, or high school teachers. Such investigations provide very useful information to firms making and selling goods and services, and to economists hoping to predict the future course of business activity by predicting what consumers will buy. But suppose we find

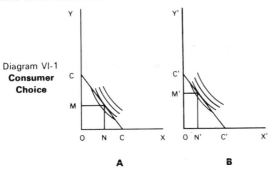

Diagram VI-1
**Consumer
Choice**

that many consumers—and Mr. *B*—choose to spend most of their income on *Y* because they believe *Y* will add ten years to their life, while other consumers, like Mr. *A,* know perfectly well this is nonsense, but they do like the taste of *Y* so they buy some of it. In such a circumstance, it can be argued that the diagram does *not* picture the best solution for the Mr. *B*'s of this world, for his choice does not maximize satisfaction or utility. It can also be argued that some means should be found to prevent deception (or maybe just ignorance) on the part of these consumers.

Or suppose we discover that Mr. *B*'s apparent preference for *Y* over *X* is due to his unfamiliarity with *X*—he doesn't know where to buy it and he feels shy about investigating; none of the stores around his home stock it, and other stores won't sell to him, because people sneer at the thought of the *B*'s of this world consuming as much *X* as the *A*'s do, since everyone knows that only the *A*'s are the big *X*-users. In this case also, the economist would doubt whether consumer's choice—the so-called "revealed preference"—represented maximum satisfaction for *B*. Both cases impose restrictions on Mr. *B*'s choice: the first limits his freedom of action through ignorance or lack of information, and the second limits his access to the market. We are not obliged, therefore, to accept *B*'s choices as representing his tastes and preferences, because we doubt that they represent his *free* choice.

So, when we investigate the apparent differences in consumption patterns between ethnic groups, we are also concerned to find out if any differences that exist truly represent tastes and preference, i.e., free choice. Or, to turn the question around, the economist must analyze the market to see whether or not the market imposes restrictions on consumer choice. This, of course, provides the link to the economics of the ghetto: the term ghetto has a strong association with restrictions, so we may ask whether consumption and marketing in the ghetto are restricted.

Now the answer to this is not simple. Let us return for a moment to the facts about Negro-white differentials in the savings function. James Duesenberry used these data in testing his hypothesis about consumption (or saving) as a function of rank in the income distribution.[3] His argument ran like this: Because black families live quite separately from whites and because there is little association between the two, black families and white families cannot be ranked in the same income distribution. Because income among black people is generally lower than among whites, the same dollar sum may represent a *high* income within a distribution of black families but a *lower* income within a white distribution. For example, a family with a $10,000 income would be richer than 97 per cent of all families, if they were black; but a white family with the same $10,000 would find that only 89 per cent of the whites were below them in the income distribution. Therefore, argued Duesenberry, if saving among the top ranks of an income *distribution* is higher than saving at a lower rank, the black family with $10,000 would save more than the white family with the same income—and such a disparity does exist.

Duesenberry's stress on the income distribution rather than absolute dollar income as a determinant of consumption choice stems from his hypothesis that people learn new ways to spend money by observing those slightly richer or better off than they are. And such demonstrations of higher standards of living presumably take place within fairly small groups of people— in neighborhoods, for example. The entire thesis seems to require the existence of a ghetto, or something like it, for separate income distributions and separate consumption patterns to exist; and we may well be tempted to argue that if the ghetto does exist, then the rest of the thesis follows. Certainly it is easy to interpret some of the expenditure patterns—food, clothing, alcoholic beverages, and so forth—by saying that a black family with a $7,500 income is relatively more prosperous than a white family at this level.

But in this day of mass communication, mobility, and awareness, the notion that we learn our tastes and preferences from a small group of people immediately around us lacks convincing strength. Even the notion that all goods can be ranked, that there is universal agreement on what is "better," and that everyone strives to ascend this ladder of ranked products as his income rises can be questioned. After all, television sets did not "trickle down" from the upper classes to poorer families, and most national manufacturers cater to the mass market in their innovations rather than to a taste-setting elite. Finally, of course, there are other interpretations to give to the data of Table VI–2.

A simple but significant rule, frequently overlooked in analysis, is that percentages of a total must sum to 100, or the total. What this means is that *if* black families spend more than whites on one expenditure category, they *must* spend less than whites on some other category. If now we investigate a category where rich people spend considerably more of their income than poor people, namely recreation, we find that white families spend more than Negroes in the same income class. The same holds true for "other shelter," which means chiefly hotels and motels, although it also includes vacation homes, rented or owned—in short, all shelter away from home. Next we note that the absolute dollar spending on food away from home shows a differential of up to 40 per cent between white and Negro families in the same income class, and we may remember the similar differential on automobile expenditures in the upper income classes. At lower-income levels, automobile expense represents chiefly purchase and maintenance; richer families spend more on their automobiles partly because they buy more expensive models, but partly because they go places more often. All these figures that show what kinds of things Negro families spend *less* for than whites might be summarized by saying that Negro families stay home more than white families; and this may help account for the fact that black families spend more on furnishings and household equipment.

This last point gains reinforcement from another set of comparative data that shows income and expenditures by race and tenure of family. We know that owners spend more than renters on outfitting and running their homes, and that people who move spend more on these items than either. We know also that people at higher-income levels spend more on these items than people at lower-income levels, and finally, that Negro family income is about half that of whites, so that there is less money to spend on the family home among blacks than whites. Yet Table VI-3 shows explicitly that Negro families spend *more* of their smaller incomes in this way.

Table VI-3
Income and Expenditures, by Tenure and Race, 1960–61

	Average money income after taxes	Percentage of Total Expenditure on		
		Average family size	household operations	house furnishings and equipment
Owners all year, white	$7,056	3.3	5.9	5.0
Owners all year, Negro	$4,519	3.2	6.1	5.8
Renter all year, white	$4,885	2.7	5.9	4.8
Renter all year, Negro	$3,465	3.2	6.2	5.0
Moved during year, white	$6,570	3.6	6.0	8.3
Moved during year, Negro	$5,202	3.8	5.1	10.6

Source: U.S. Department of Labor, *Survey of Consumer Expenditures, 1960–61,* Supplement 2, Part A, to BLS Report 237–38 (July, 1964), Table 23.

Do these data reveal that the different races have different preferences? And do these preferences represent free choice? The answer, of course, must be no. The survey, taken in 1960–61, recorded the result of discrimination against Negro families in hotels, restaurants, vacation resorts, theaters, tennis and golf clubs, and all the other places summarized in the formal terminology of the expenditure categories: when there are few places to go, obviously a family does not spend much on travel and does spend by adding to the comforts of home.

When you ask a Negro, "Where are you going on vacation?" you don't think of going to the Gulf of Mexico in Mississippi. By the same token, you don't think about going fishing up in the Minnesota lakes. You don't think of going to many areas for golfing. You don't say you're going to Sun Valley for skiing, or to Arizona. Because whether discrimination is real or imagined, it is there. . . . The American Negro is nothing less, nothing more, than a human being, subject to precisely the same variations in vacation tastes, in utilization of vacation hours, in patterns of behavior. And . . . he is not different with respect to his discretionary spending.[4]

This explanation of the difference in travel and household expenditures between whites and Negroes cannot, of course, be "proved" correct either by the data or the quotation above: at most they do not contradict the hypothesis, which we know to be reasonable from other evidence. The point of outlining this possible explanation is to show the ambiguity that lies in the entire notion of racial differences or preferences, once we insist that freedom of choice must be a desideratum.[5]

Analysts of food consumption patterns used to devote considerable attention to a variable known as "regional tastes and preferences," exhibited, for example, in the North-South differential for beef and pork purchases, and to another variable known as "ethnic preferences," that account for such specialized stores as kosher meat markets or Italian grocers. Today both these types of preferences (if indeed they still exist) have been swamped in their impact on food consumption and marketing by still another variable which the analyst may, if he wishes, call "changes in tastes and preferences." But it is not without significance that World War II, which caused American families to move all over the country and also upset normal patterns of food distribution, marked the end of some regional or ethnic preferences and greatly accelerated the disappearance of others. It does not seem unreasonable to hypothesize that, as families gained access to different markets, they bought things there; so that Northerners now eat more pork, and supermarkets distribute kosher products. It may be inferred that not until *all* families have equal access to *all* markets with the only limitation on·their demand being the market limitations of prices and incomes, can we draw any firm conclusion about different "preferences" among families.

MARKETING PATTERNS

We turn now to examine neighborhoods and localities, the places where consumers live and go shopping, the ways in which they spend their incomes as well as the ways they make their choices. Like the subject of racial or ethnic preferences, the area of marketing facilities is fraught with misinformation and superficial judgments. Ghetto merchants—chiefly white— have been accused of exploiting the poor families—chiefly black—with high prices, shoddy merchandise, and stringent credit terms. In rebuttal, some retailers have cited their high costs of insurance, pilferage, breakage, and credit losses. The economist will try to remove the denunciatory aspect of both charges to see whether, how, and why the poor pay more.

To collect valid data on this question for any specific area requires solving some technical problems. "Paying more" can mean a number of quite different things. First, obviously, it is possible for the same item—a five-pound bag of Gold Medal All-Purpose flour—to sell for two different prices in two different supermarkets. Second, it can mean that the range of substitutes (Gold Medal, Pillsbury's, Robin Hood, and private brands of flour) includes low-priced items in one store but not in another, so that the *average* price paid differs. But unless the *majority* of goods in one supermarket have higher prices (in either of these two ways) than in another, few people will be really concerned. Determining whether the "majority of items" are priced differently is itself a formidable task: supermarkets normally carry thousands of items. Fortunately only a few hundred make up the bulk of sales, or of what most people buy. (The Bureau of Labor Statistics, in collecting food price data for computing the monthly *Consumer's Price Index*, lists about sixty products; some of these are foods almost everyone uses, like sugar and bread and chicken, while some represent a group of foods whose prices tend to move together, like layer cake or cinnamon rolls for fancy breads, and chicken or bean soup for a wide variety of canned condensed soups.)

But comparing prices of food items in two different areas is not a simple matter of writing out a detailed specification ("bean soup, condensed, made with white Navy or pea beans, and flavored with bacon, ham, or smoked pork. Eleven or 11½ ounce can. Exclude vegetarian bean soup")[6] and then visiting two different stores. The woman shopping for food does not buy merely the canned soup or cinnamon rolls or bag of sugar she comes home with. Part of what she pays for is the display of thousands of items that offers her variety and choice, the quality of fresh meat or produce, the dependability of the store's offerings, the cleanliness and convenience of the surroundings which can make it easy or difficult for her to find what she is looking for and to check prices and quality, the care with which her purchases are packed and loaded, and many other intangibles. These characteristics of her shopping process* depend on the operation of the particular store, which cannot be identical to any other store, even an outlet in the same chain. Other differences also exist: the hours during which the store is open, what days of the week it runs "specials," whether it gives credit or provides check-cashing facilities without charge, the speed of its checkout and bagging operation, the size of its parking lot (if any), and the whole host of factors which some economists have labeled "services," but which cannot be provided without the consumer's shopping effort. Consequently, one should investigate prices in two different areas only by comparing two stores that operate in the same way.

But this, of course, raises still another problem. Consumers may pay more in one section of town than another because only high-priced stores exist in one section of town. The small independent grocery store or specialty food shop sells higher-priced goods not to exploit its customers but to recoup its higher costs. And if such high-cost stores are predominant in ghetto areas, then ghetto residents pay more either in high prices or else in the added time and transportation costs they require to shop elsewhere.

Finally, consumers may "pay more" in what looks like an uneconomical form of choice. Buying small packages rather

*Cf. the author's *Consumer Choice in the American Economy* (New York: Random House, Inc., 1967), Chs. 5 and 6.

than the large economy sizes, ground round steak rather than chuck roast, prepared "convenience" foods rather than the ingredients for home cooking, buying sporadically rather than taking advantage of sales and specials—all these have been criticized as wasteful practices on the part of the poor. Some have advocated extensive programs to educate homemakers (and to revise the "domestic science" or "home economics" offerings in the public school), but the economist will ask about the other requisites to efficiency in buying and managing.

Buying the large economy size or stocking up when canned goods or staples are on "special" takes more money than buying sporadically in small quantities. The consumer's capital represented by a well-stocked pantry is not insignificant, and may be more than the poverty level family can easily amass. Aside from the original investment, the family with a substantial inventory needs storage capacity—to have a bulging cupboard takes not only money and wise buying but also the cupboard space. Using pudding mix and canned spaghetti may in fact be cheaper than making a pudding with sugar and eggs and milk, or preparing spaghetti from the basic ingredients, if roaches or rats or other vermin can infest food supplies in the home.

As well as storage space, most food economies call for fairly extensive preparation at home; and this requires cooking equipment and space. The long slow simmer that turns a chuck roast into a nourishing casserole takes a heavy pot and a stove that can be adjusted to slow, even heat: if the kitchen provides living and play space for the family with small children, preparing such a dish may be far more costly, perhaps even in terms of safety, than frying up a quick meat pattie. As we have seen before, the interrelationships of economics at the household or family level become intricate: low income means not only poor levels of current consumption, but little investment in consumers' capital which could raise future levels. Substandard housing conditions detract from consumption efficiency in both buying and home management. Inadequate levels of nutrition, whether from ignorance or the inability to devote care and attention to preparing meals, make for inattention and loss of energy; children do not perform well at school nor do adults on the job. And with low productivity, no worker can earn higher incomes.

No counterpart to the details of the Census tracts previously quoted exists for consumption and marketing data. A number of specific surveys in particular neighborhoods have been made which substantiate the general picture drawn above. Thus, on the general difficulty of comparing prices, a Bureau of Labor Statistics study in 1966 "found no significant differences in prices charged by food stores located in low-income areas v.v. those charged by stores in higher-income areas, when the same types of store (chains, large independents, small independents), the same qualities of foods, and the same sizes of packages are compared."[7] But the report goes on to note that the volume selling item tended to be a smaller package in low-income areas than in high, e.g., "for flour, CPI quotations related to a 5-lb. sack; outlets in low-income areas frequently report a 2-lb. sack to be the volume seller, but a few in Atlanta reported a 1-lb sack as the more popular. The price per pound ranged from 14 per cent higher in N.Y. City to 35 per cent higher in Chicago, when purchased in 2-lb sacks rather than in 5-lb. sacks."[8]

Next, the same report points out that the *type* of store differs sharply between high- and low-income areas: "Based on the observations of the BLS agents who collected the data in this study, there are relatively few grocery chains in the very low income areas, especially in the larger cities. Many of the stores listed in the grocery route lists were not full-line grocery stores, but were beer parlors or pool halls that sold a few food items, or delicatessens. If the major volume of purchases of the low-income families is made in the small neighborhood grocery stores, and the major volume of purchases of higher-income families is made in large grocery stores, price differences for the same quality goods appear to be associated with the size of the store in which purchases are made rather than with differences in the geographic location of the stores."[9] And aside from the organizational difference between stores (delicatessen versus supermarket), this report also quotes the investigators' opinions of the inventory carried and the surroundings of the store: "Stores located in low-income areas tend to be somewhat less orderly and clean than those located in higher-income areas, and meats and produce do not appear as fresh."[10]

This first study was heavily criticized because the Bureau had advised the management of each store, some two weeks prior to visiting, of the project and asked for cooperation: it was therefore open to charges that special prices had been set for the Bureau's investigators to find. Later surveys looked into other problems: price hikes on the day that welfare checks were distributed, damaged goods sold with no price reduction, the unavailability of advertised specials, or a discrepancy between the advertised price and the actual price charged. Community organizations in a number of cities gathered data to present to a traveling congressional committee which held hearings in Washington, St. Louis, and New York, and officials of the largest grocery chains testified about their pricing practices.

The most recent analysis by the Federal Trade Commission stresses the lack of competition among food retailers in low-income, inner city areas. From the consumer's point of view, this had already been noted as one of the chief reasons why the poor pay more:

> The consumer who is able to shop near his home in chain stores in low-income neighborhoods in Washington, D.C., generally pays comparable prices for comparable items to those sold in medium income areas. . . . Large numbers of poor families have no supermarkets near them and can exercise no choice: they are obliged to buy in stores with limited supplies and high prices.[11]

> For reasons which are unknown to us, many inner city supermarkets have closed in the past few years—to be replaced in many instances by independent stores. . . . In our survey of major chain supermarkets only, there is no significant pattern of discrimination in terms of prices, quality, or sanitation based on race, income level, or geographic location.[12]

On the other hand, Professor Charles S. Goodman surveyed food buying in a low-income, urban renewal area of Philadelphia to find that none of the three dozen stores within the area were supermarkets. Confronted with this lack of choice, almost 90 per cent of the residents shop outside the area at supermarkets or large independents, and do not, therefore, "pay more."[13]

Clearly, therefore, where competition provides variety in store types and retailing practices, consumers have a wider choice. The FTC report points out that supermarkets in upper-income areas compete not only in pricing but in maintaining high standards of quality, cleanliness, personal service, and in offering more specials and promotional campaigns. In many inner city areas without supermarkets, the consumer's shopping process lacks all these benefits. Competition can also stem from consumer-organized efforts, like the buying clubs and cooperatives which offer families quality merchandise at very low cost. But a good general summary of the entire problem comes from the FTC report: "The distribution system performs less satisfactorily in low-income areas of our inner cities than in suburban areas. Many foodstores serving low-income, inner city areas are small, less efficient, and have higher prices. Consumers in these areas are frequently sold lower quality merchandise and are provided fewer services than in other areas. Moreover, the retail facilities of low-income areas are often old and in a shabby state of upkeep."[14]

The emphasis so far given to food merely reflects a similar concern on the part of government agencies, congressional committees, and consumers themselves, organized or not. It is reminiscent of the early years when consumer expenditures surveys first began, and analysts of the "cost of living" stressed the importance of food. And, of course, this is due to the fact that food expenditures take the largest share of low-income family spending. Another type of retailing which has gained considerable attention is sales of appliances and furniture: there are the same complaints of overcharging and exploitation on the part of the retailer, the same defense of extra pilferage and breakage, high insurance rates, and high costs on the part of the storekeeper. But a special problem with these goods concerns the use of credit.

There are many indications that appliances and furniture mean more to ghetto families than to other households. Earlier in this chapter we discussed the higher proportion of family income given to household furnishings and operations among

Negroes; now we should state explicitly that the difference between rich and poor in this country does not mean two different lists of household furnishings. Washing machines, vacuum cleaners, refrigerators, and television sets are all purchased by rich families and by those just above the poverty level: and the dollar expenditures are not dramatically different. Thus in 1960–61, 46 per cent of low-income families bought TV sets, for which they paid an average of $65.00; at higher incomes 61 per cent of the families bought TV's, spending on the average $70.00. Similarly, 7 per cent of the low-income and 9 per cent of the higher-income families purchased washing machines: prices paid averaged $140.00 and $197.00; 6 per cent of the low-income and 8 per cent of the high-income families bought refrigerators with average prices of $175 and $265; 32 per cent of the low-income and half the high-income families spent $32 and $56 for pets and their care. Of course for the low-income families, these prices represent a larger proportion of their total spending. A national survey in 1968 showed that 43 per cent of all consumers purchased at least one appliance and 20 per cent of those with less than $3,000 annual income did so.[15] The average amount spent by these low-income families was $230 compared to $460 for all families: it is likely, however, that more of the upper-income families bought two or more appliances. Using credit for such purchases has become commonplace: 40 per cent of all families, and 36 per cent of the lowest income families borrowed to make their purchases.

The terms of such credit can have a substantial impact on the consumption patterns of ghetto residents. Credit spells the difference between buying and not buying a given appliance and imposes substantial financial burdens on a low income. If we now recall the demographic characteristics of many inner city residents described in the previous chapters, one conclusion appears obvious: these families are not good credit risks, by conventional standards. Their low income, uncertain employment experience, unstable family circumstances, and substandard housing mean that any potential lender would treat them as marginal customers. It follows, therefore, that they are extremely dependent on the isolated sources that *will* grant credit—the neighborhood merchants. Banks and personal finance companies exclude these families from their market; department stores "downtown" and discount houses in suburban shopping areas do not number most ghetto residents among their regular customers. To establish credit or a credit reference may mean surmounting prejudice: women have more difficulty than men (and women are commonly household heads of inner city families), old people than middle-aged, and blacks than whites. Not surprisingly, ghetto residents most frequently buy their appliances and furniture from ghetto stores, where markups may be two to three times higher than those of conventional retailers; and the finance charges also exceed those of retailers in other markets.

That credit is the key to the problem appears obvious from a sample of purchases by low-income customers reported in a study of Washington, D.C.[16] Typical of the burden assumed is that of the three-person family, headed by a female, with a monthly income of $240, who purchased a standard single-door electric refrigerator, paying $18.00 monthly for twenty-one months. The price of the refrigerator was $360.00; among retailers in other markets most refrigerators sold for between $200 and $250, with a number of models priced below $200. Another family of nine people living on welfare payments of $194 monthly purchased a TV set for $308.95, contracting for payments of $40 a month; among general market retailers, prices on TV sets ranged from 50 per cent to 60 per cent of those in low-income areas. These families, and others like them, not only pay more for their purchases in the first place but pay a substantially larger fraction of their income for interest and debt repayment. They do so not necessarily out of ignorance, or wastefulness, or stupidity, but because they lack the cash to buy these items and can get credit only on these terms.

Three different approaches to the problem have been suggested. The first calls for more legislation to protect the consumer from being victimized by fraud and deception. But much of the legislation that now exists, from municipal requirements for sanitation or safety to the federal truth-in-lending law, does not provide a remedy, either because enforcement funds and staff are inadequate or because it does not touch the real difficulty. A summary of legal aid cases showed that consumer sale contracts accounted for less than six per cent of the total. More significant was the finding that "Forty per cent of the cases that came to the legal services offices during fiscal 1967 received only advice, and 15 per cent were ineligible for services. Many times there is simply nothing that can be done—no fraud, no overreaching—just wretched poor judgment on the part of the individual."[17]

Accordingly, a second approach stresses consumer education of the most basic kind, how to read labels and calculate prices, what credit costs consist of, and where a wider choice can be obtained.

> The poor must learn how to cope with the marketplace before they can hope to extricate themselves from poverty. . . . As part of the course of instruction in consumer education, we have discussed the shopping habits of limited-income people within their own communities. . . . In Project Moneywise, our aim is to educate the poor in the ways of assessing merchandise and credit costs so they will have enough information available to make the best choice for themselves.[18]

But another way of widening the opportunities for choice, so the consumer can buy with the certain knowledge that more than one retailer is eager for the trade, seeks to alter the existing marketing arrangements.

For example, if other sources of credit than ghetto stores or peddlers were available, then families could shop anywhere in the city. Credit unions represent a kind of cooperative arrangement, similar to buying clubs for food, and forming such groups is the goal of some community organizations. Other groups have demanded that large retailers change their credit rules, so as to enable families receiving welfare payments to buy now and pay later. Sears, Roebuck has been the primary target of the effort by the National Welfare Rights Organization; but other chains, including Gimbel's and Lane Bryant, have agreed to extend credit, and some purely local arrangements are being worked out with welfare groups. Such a program seeks to change the established standards for granting credit, by emphasizing the reliability and security of welfare income. It is undoubtedly true that a mother with two preschool children can depend on regular monthly AFDC payments with more assurance than the skilled auto worker can count on his high monthly wage in a time of declining sales. On the other hand, denying credit to welfare recipients reinforces the notion that credit is a "luxury" or even a status symbol. Neither argument has much to do with the primary function of making credit available, which is to widen consumer's choices and therefore competition.

Again, since the type of retail operation now existing differs substantially between the suburban shopping center and the crowded ghetto, there is a case for encouraging new stores, especially if they can be managed by residents of the community. Their primary function—whether independents, cooperatives, or branches of established retailers—is to offer competition to the small-volume specialty store with its typically high costs.

These three approaches to the problems of consumption and marketing in the ghetto are not the only ones: another, more general remedy would change the position of the buyers by giving them more income and therefore a wider consumption choice. But before considering specific proposals along these lines, we should review the whole question of policy and the economist's contribution to policy-making for the ghetto.

INTRODUCTION
TO PART TWO

THE PRECEDING CHAPTERS dealt with various dimensions of the ghetto, and with methods of quantifying both its conditions and those of its inhabitants. Most of the data have been illustrative rather than conclusive: any reader can collect and interpret material along similar lines for any specific neighborhood. Nowhere in these chapters has it been explicitly stated that "these conditions are bad," or that "people should not live this way," yet probably most readers feel that such value judgments or normative conclusions are implicit—if only from the selection of topics discussed. Turning now to policy proposals—programs for doing something about the ghetto—we may ask about the economist's approach. If we use economic analysis to study a situation, can we use economic analysis to study policies to deal with that situation or plans to change that situation? Do economists have a general answer to the impassioned question that began this book: "What about values; what about the justice of distributing national resources?"

Economics is not a science of ethics, of "good" and "bad" or "should" and "should not." Yet economists cannot, anymore than anyone else, avoid such ethical judgments. One of the chief contributions of economic analysis, however, is to delineate *what* value judgments have to be made, what decisions confront us about good and bad or should and should not.

The economist's role often lies in distinguishing means from ends. For example, most people would agree that no child in this country should be left hungry and cold, and this is a value judgment about which economists have little to say (except perhaps by pointing out the economic effects of having cold and hungry people about). But most people would not agree on how to prevent hunger and cold, for many different means exist to achieve this end. We might give all the children at school two meals a day, or we might turn public schools into boarding dormitories to house and feed children, and dress them warmly as well; we might send families direct shipments of food and clothing; we might subsidize research and production so that disposable clothing is available for the asking; we might sponsor powerful advertising campaigns to teach people efficiency in budgeting and buying, and so on. What frequently happens is that a program which should be regarded as merely one alternative comes to be thought of as an end in itself.[1] For example, school lunch programs have aroused controversy at many levels: school boards, citizens, and congressmen alike regard the decision of whether or not to introduce, continue, or expand such programs as a difficult policy problem. In this as in other cases, the economist performs an extremely useful service if he inquires about the purpose of school lunch programs. Providing a noon meal to children in school buildings cannot be a goal in itself: it is a means to an end. What is the goal of this program? Why do we want to serve these meals? Distinguishing means from ends is the beginning of the economist's approach to policy proposals.

Such questioning must precede another contribution of the economist—his insistence that all the alternative ways of reaching a given goal be considered, and that their costs be calculated, so far as possible, so as to compare one with another. The economist lays much stress upon identifying the least-cost method, but we should be clear about the reasons for doing so. Costs determine productivity: if school lunches cost less than, say, food stamps, then the resources available will feed more hungry people if they are devoted to school lunches rather than to food stamps. In matters of social policy, no country or people possesses enough resources to do all that is needed, let alone what may be desired, so it is essential to do the most that can be done, by selecting the least-cost, or most productive, means to a given end.

Perhaps the most extensive attempt at such a review of programs, which identifies their goals or benefits and lists their costs, appears in the report on federal poverty programs of the Comptroller General. Congress authorized the General Accounting Office to determine:

> (1) The efficiency of the administration of such programs and activities by the Office of Economic Opportunity and by local public and private agencies carrying out such programs and activities; and

> (2) The extent to which such programs and activities achieve the objectives set forth in the relevant part or title of the Economic Opportunity Act of 1964 authorizing such programs or activities.[2]

But the report did not precisely follow this mandate; as its authors say, "The methods of evaluating social programs such as these and the indicators of progress of accomplishment are not well developed or understood." Less restricted in its viewpoint and considerably more outspoken in its style is a recent appraisal by Sar A. Levitan, who has this to say about cost-benefit analysis[3]:

> The bases for calculating benefits and the assumptions necessary for placing price tags on the presumed benefits are arbitrary, so that almost any cost-benefit ratio can be fabricated. Only when two programs have the same type of benefits, and when their cost-benefit ratios can be calculated under the same assumptions, are the comparative ratios likely to be meaningful.

Despite this demurrer, both these reports present data which allow far more objective appraisals than the usual outpouring of approval or condemnation by interested parties. They may be contrasted with the following attempt to evaluate the results of social work[4]:

> Does the generally negative outcome of the project indicate that social casework should be abandoned as having no effect? We do not think so . . . if people feel that good has been done, who is to say that this feeling itself is not

> beneficial? In this project, for instance, both the caseworkers, as well as the Director of Social Services, conscientiously feel that a great deal of good was done in some cases, whatever our attempted measures might show.

This statement comes perilously close to saying that caseworkers should be paid for doing whatever they think they should do. An economist would argue that society has not yet established such a goal; and if society does, it would probably be cheaper and easier to give caseworkers' clients money to do what *they* think they should do. The quotation illustrates the confusion of means with ends, and the abandonment of any attempt to measure costs.

It remains true, however, that some costs cannot be calculated without a value judgment. The Phillips curve shown in Chapter Five is a good example. If unemployment is the "cost" of inflation, no economist can identify the "least-cost" position. It is up to society to choose the trade-off position; it is up to people themselves to determine how much unemployment and how much inflation are tolerable. But even where such "non-economic" reasoning is required, the economist can at least set up the terms of the trade-off, and urge that the people most affected be consulted: in this case, those most likely to be hurt by inflation and those most likely to suffer from unemployment.[5]

The remainder of this book will follow these precepts in discussing policy proposals for the ghetto. We turn first to analyzing specific programs for remedying the condition of ghetto inhabitants—income and welfare, employment and training, education and housing—and last to the economics of discrimination, and of the ghetto as a separate economy.

CHAPTER SEVEN

INCOME
AND WELFARE PROGRAMS

THE ECONOMICS of the ghetto is not synonymous with the economics of poverty, yet poverty occurs more frequently and is more firmly entrenched within the ghetto than elsewhere. Some ghetto conditions—substandard housing and the lack of transportation to markets—could obviously be remedied by the people living there, if they were rich enough to buy houses and remodel them, or to buy cars to work and shop elsewhere. So the policies to combat or relieve poverty apply to many ghetto residents.

The value judgment that everyone in this country should have some minimum level of living has been part of the American ethic for generations; the difficulties have arisen in determining this minimum level and in devising programs by which the minimum standard can be implemented, because the objectives of these programs have not always been clear. An economist might see the problem as how to allocate resources to keep people above a subsistence level. But some ways of supporting people seem "better" or at least preferable on grounds other than whether they make the most efficient use of resources. Primarily, therefore, the problem is one of untangling means and ends, and discerning social goals and the roads open to them. Such is the content of this chapter.

FREEDOM OF CHOICE

Most of the existing welfare programs providing income payments share one characteristic with more novel proposals for a guaranteed minimum income, a family or children's allowance, a negative income tax, or the Nixon Administration's family assistance program. That is, they all operate on the principle that if people are poor, they should get money. This is not true of programs for public housing, food stamps, clinics, or Medicaid which resemble the poor relief of earlier centuries in that this earlier form of welfare provided goods and services rather than money. This difference is more than casual: it goes to the heart of the controversy over how to support the poor.

The first national program of public assistance to the needy, enacted in 1935 along with old age and survivor's insurance (better known as OASI, with the whole package termed "Social Security"), stressed this difference between the old approach and the new[1]:

> The Social Security Act defines assistance, for example, as money payments to, or medical care payments on behalf of, needy persons. This provision has been interpreted as preventing any restrictions on the recipient's use of his money payment. The person receiving aid is given responsibility for deciding how best to use his income, as others do in the community. This provision enables a needy individual to have in his possession the money necessary to purchase the essentials of living and to continue to live in his own home without interruption of family life because of economic need alone. In contrast, under poor relief, congregate care was usual; the "poorhouse" sheltered the aged, the unemployed, the disabled, the abandoned child, the deserted mother and her children, the unmarried mother and her infant, as well as the senile person and the feeble-minded. Food, clothing, and medical care and other services were usually inadequate. Aid given to the poor in their own homes was meager and usually in the form of vouchers for groceries, clothing, or fuel, which not only limited the aid to certain items at a

specified store but also identified the needy person as a "pauper."

To the founders of the Social Security system, which was inaugurated in the depths of a depression that had made "paupers" of the most worthy, hardworking, thrifty citizens, money payments also enabled the individual to maintain a decent respect for himself[2]:

> The act affirmed the dignity and responsibility of recipients by specifying that aid was to be given in the form of money, which the receiver was free to spend as he or she deemed best, rather than as aid in kind, such as orders for groceries or fuel, which too often reflected condescension and unwarranted suspicion in past relief administrations.

The difficulty with this attempt to preserve dignity and freedom of choice for the welfare recipient appeared almost instantly, as states grappled with the question, What is "needy"? This question had two parts: who was "needy" enough to be eligible for aid; and how much money assistance would relieve his "need." Not surprisingly, the several states worked out quite different answers to these questions along with other differences in administrative procedure. Both questions were usually answered in money terms; that is, the definition of "needy" depended on one's dollar income and, in some cases, one's assets, while the benefit "needed" consisted of a money payment. But this did not mean that recipients had, or now have, the freedom implied in the statements quoted above.

For a simple example, the welfare payment to a mother with three children of twelve, seven, and two-and-one-half years old (paid in Massachusetts in the fall of 1968) amounted to $64.40 per week. This sum was calculated by allowing $26.35 for food, $8.78 for clothing, $17.63 for rent, $7.93 for heat and utilities, $1.83 for household supplies, and $1.88 for personal care. To say that the mother "is given responsibility for deciding how best to use income, as others do in the community," seems scarcely correct: the responsibility belongs to the social worker who devised the budget applicable to the particular family and who could also determine whether or not the family received additional benefits. Supplements to the regular budget illustrate more clearly how far the welfare system has departed from the notion of "preventing any restrictions on the recipient's use of his money payments." This family could receive money to buy furniture, pay a telephone bill, or meet an emergency need for clothing only if the social worker approved. In most cases, approval specifies the type of item to be purchased and the price to be paid.

A similar system exists in other states, and its effects can best be understood from first-hand experience, like that of a witness before the Joint Economic Committee of Congress:

> A lot of our people can sew . . . they can make things that would help themselves. We cannot get sewing machines because the department says you have to go to the store, tell the man that you are on welfare, get a statement from him that he has a machine for a certain amount of money. The department is not going to give you but a certain amount anyway. They have it written in their book, anyway. They are only going to give you a certain amount. Yet you have to put your life on the line, go to the store, get the statement, bring it back, and give it to your caseworker to show that you went to the store and that they have a machine for a certain amount.
>
> You do the same thing with the washing machine, which does not make sense. They are only going to give you $125.00. Why should I go and get a statement for $175.00, when they are only going to give me $125.00 anyway? Why not give me the $125.00 and let me use it to get the machine the best way I possibly can, because they are not going to give me the rest of it?[3]

In earlier chapters we have seen how expenditures for one item (for example, housing) restrict the total spending pattern, and how "freedom of consumer choice" depends not only on money income but on the marketing resources available. It seems quite clear that the welfare system does not, in fact, provide income which the receiver is "free to spend as he or she deemed best, rather than aid in kind."

This conflict between allowing freedom of choice and assuring the "essentials of life" or an "adequate income"* is partly

*Cf. the discussion of this problem in Chapter Two, p. 45.

responsible for the wide variation, among the states, in the amount of money they provide and the number of people eligible. In general, welfare recipients in Northern states get three to seven times the amounts available in Southern states, and to some unknown extent this has induced poor people—especially displaced workers from mechanized agriculture—to migrate from Southern states to the North. It is probably correct to say that by allowing disparate answers to the question "How much does a needy person need?" the welfare system has helped to create ghettoes in Northern cities. Nixon's family assistance program, however, proposes a totally new answer by defining a national minimum, one standard of need for families everywhere in the United States.

WHO NEEDS WELFARE?

At this point we may ask the economist's question about means and ends, specifically, what is the objective of providing a minimum level of income? Is it to guarantee a minimum level of consumption to everyone, or to help certain people? Do we designate these people in terms of their need?** or in terms of their merit? Do we assist *all* poor people or only the deserving poor? And this, of course, restates the earlier question, "Who is needy?"

**The concerned reader may also wonder about other forms of assistance to prevent or repair the conditions that make people needy. This raises a host of questions about the entire field of social work, which lies well beyond the bounds of this book. One reference, however, seems particularly appropriate because of some comments on the problem of minimum income: "When only 'budgets of despair' exist, when there are only inadequate medical services to which clients can go, or services extremely difficult to get at, where there is no homemaker service, or child care center, where there is nothing but a dreadful kind of reform school in the old tradition—the expectation that casework can substitute for these essential resources is one that we ought to banish quickly. . . . I believe the cure for poverty is money, not casework. . . . We certainly need to fight for higher standards of assistance so we do not further pauperize these people. The standard of assistance granted today is well below what the country has determined as the minimum income a family should have. There is an awkward inconsistency when we talk about a war on poverty and yet hold people down to the poverty we are trying to fight. . . . In many cases the provision of adequate income may be the only service needed and . . . there must be distinctions in patterns of service geared to the various needs and requests of individuals and families who come to public agencies for help."[4]

The original 1935 act made old people, blind persons, and dependent children eligible (if they were "needy"), and in 1950 those who were permanently and totally disabled were added. A later amendment broadened the aid to include the families of dependent children (AFDC). Implicit in these categories is the probability that such people are incapable of working to earn sufficient income to meet their needs: our system of public assistance seems to identify the "deserving" poor as those who cannot be *producers.*

Such an identification would account for other features of the public assistance programs. The blind and disabled deserve vocational training and rehabilitation along with financial assistance, so they can eventually contribute to production and, incidentally, become self-supporting. The aged, excluded from the labor market by laws and institutions, must be stripped of any productive resources they may own, like houses or land or financial assets, before they can be called "deserving." Eligibility criteria, therefore, focus on the individual's economic role of producing: if he is unable to produce, then he will not be able to consume unless society helps. (And, perhaps, *because* he is unable to produce and earn his income, then he no longer is entitled to spend that income freely, like others in the community.)

Much of this reasoning obviously applies to children, who are "incapable" of earning income in the labor market either because they are physically immature or because society has decreed that they spend a certain number of years in school rather than at work. All children normally depend on some adult to produce income so that they can consume; even infant heiresses rely on trustees and guardians to manage their productive resources. The welfare system attempts to maintain consumption for a child who lacks productive adults. But, like encouraging the migration from South to North and from rural areas to urban centers which has so multiplied total welfare costs, the system itself has encouraged a rise in the number of dependent children, with a consequent increase in welfare costs. And this, oddly enough, is a result of the system's focus on the family as a unit.

To quote again from the original philosophy[5]:

> The social security program has given increasing recognition to the significance of the family unit. The public assistance provisions in the original law affirmed the importance of family life by limiting use of federal funds . . . for needy children to those who were living in family homes in the care of one of a number of specified relatives. . . . In countless homes, therefore, insurance or assistance payments mean . . . that children in families broken by death or separation or impoverished by the breadwinner's disability can continue to receive their mothers' care instead of being parceled out among relatives or left without supervision or placed in foster homes while the mother takes outside work.

Like their definitions of need and eligibility, the various states have produced rules and regulations that prevent AFDC aid from reaching the objective set forth in this quotation. Many states do not give aid to families with an unemployed father; and the social worker's responsibility for drawing up a budget of "needs" may extend from advising (or urging or even requiring) that the mother work or sue her husband for nonsupport, to encouraging a teenager to get a job and support his family, to discouraging a husband from returning to his family. From recognizing the family as the primary unit in our society (rather than the individual or the community), the welfare system seems to have moved to defining the particular kind of family that may exist.

One result of defining the family as the primary *economic* unit is that if an individual family fails to perform successfully, the individuals within it are affected since they are not economically independent. So we have a new term for the children of such families, who are called "social orphans," meaning that although their parents may be living, they are not functioning members of society. As Robert Lampman puts it, "Over a third of the 35 million poor are children whose misfortune arises out of the chance assignment to poor parents. In some cases this poverty comes out of being members of unusually large families."[6]

Presumably, society's goal in setting up a welfare system of aid to dependent children is to maintain consumption for these children, so they need not suffer because of inadequate family income. But the system does not measure need in terms of the consumption levels of these children; it determines eligibility for welfare on the basis of the adults' inability to produce. As a result, it is entirely possible for poor children to live and grow up in poverty, with no social assistance.

The notion that people do not "deserve" welfare if they are able to work but are not working embodies the basic conflict of our public assistance programs, which are *both* needs-related and work-related. The problem is often posed in simplistic and value-loaded terms; the following letter rather neatly expresses two complaints, that of the taxpayer that people will "get on welfare" rather than work, and that of the welfare mother that the system will not let her be self-supporting:[7]

I have been working quite a while now and I really enjoy my job. I was just as happy as you when I was able to reduce the welfare cost over a hundred dollars a month. Even though I received a small grant from AFDC, I still carried the brunt of my children's support. I glowed with new independence and the sense of accomplishment I felt.

When other nonworking AFDC mothers marched on the Public Assistance office for Easter clothes for their children and for furniture for their homes, I sat back and tish-tished, I looked down on the proceedings and elevated my working nose. I was just as indignant as the rest of the taxpayers. Welfare unfair and unjust: Ridiculous!

Well, last month welfare came up with a new way of computing the AFDC working mother's income on a monthly basis. We are given the first $30.00, then one-third of the remainder, plus $11.00 per month for work-related expenses. Our babysitters have to fill out vendor licenses and send a bill in triplicate to the Welfare Department, and if they are lucky, they will get paid six months after the bill is submitted.

Of course my babysitter quit!

My clothes, cleaning bills, lunches, and transportation cost far beyond the $30.00, one-third, and $11.00 now allowed for the month. I cannot afford my job.

So Taxpayer, as much as I hate to say it, I am going to have to give up my job and go back on straight AFDC and once more increase the welfare rolls. The next time you read of AFDC mothers marching on the Public Assistance office, telling of the injustices in the welfare system, I will be one of those mothers, having found out the hard way, the have-nots will never be allowed to have, no matter how hard they work.

Yes indeed, I have been very nicely put back in my place where society feels I belong: on the AFDC rolls.

The basic conflict between work and welfare includes at least three disputed areas: one, that people who get welfare should be required to work if they are able; two, that the welfare system should improve the recipient's working ability; and three, that if people are working they don't need welfare. All three of these have been given explicit recognition in the proposals set forth by President Nixon in August of 1969 for a sweeping overhaul of present welfare arrangements.

These proposals for a system to be known as family assistance accept the first two provisos and reject the third: it is not at all clear, however, that the new system will wholly resolve the dilemma of work and welfare. At this writing, many of the details of administration have yet to be worked out, and congressional action will probably not occur before the middle of 1970, but no one doubts that the existing welfare system will be overhauled, along these or similar lines, if only because the present system is almost universally condemned—by recipients, administrators, and the general public.*

Three parts of the program speak directly to the provisos listed. First, any family receiving aid must have its able-bodied members accept suitable training or employment, if transportation exists and if working mothers can depend on day-care centers for their children. Exempted from this provision are mothers with children under six. Second, existing manpower programs would be coordinated and expanded to enhance the productivity of the poor. Finally, the "working poor" have been

*In September, 1969, the Harris Survey found only 16 per cent of a national cross-section of people disagreeing with the statement, "Up to now, welfare has been a colossal failure."

acknowledged by the plan that helps families with employed adults who do not earn enough to keep the family out of poverty. Two sliding scales (uniform throughout the country) define poverty level incomes for different sizes of families and allow decreasing amounts of assistance as earned income increases.

Aside from its general impact on work and welfare, the program will tend to reduce income differentials among the states. The nationwide minimum specified ($1,600.00 for a family of four) amounts to much more than present welfare payments in many Southern states. This may lessen the incentive of poor families to migrate, as half the federal expenditures proposed will be channeled to Southern states. Northern urban areas, where welfare payments significantly exceed the minimum, will face increasing difficulty with finances.

THE WORK ETHIC

The work requirement—that anyone able to work register for jobs or for training—endorses the definition of "need" as the inability to produce, equates eligibility with the readiness to accept paid employment, and concludes that anyone unwilling to work should not receive income, even at minimum levels. This reasoning implicitly argues that economic deprivation acts as an incentive and that guaranteed family income would lure people away from their jobs to idleness. The validity of this argument can be neither proved nor disproved. It has not been fully tested, and opinion varies widely, as can be seen from two statements by respected and competent scholars:

> Most economists have long since given up the idea that a progressive society needs the threat of poverty to induce work and sobriety in the lower classes.[8]

> Anyone who prefers a minimum income without work to a higher one with work can still escape work, and unless the minimum is very low—below what most of us would consider a decent level—it is likely that many would choose not to work.[9]

An experiment to produce data revealing the effects of income guarantees on work incentive began in September, 1968, in Trenton, New Jersey; three other urban areas and two rural areas were added later. In each project, selected families receive monthly payments calculated in terms of their present income and family size; the families report monthly on their financial status and how they are getting on as producers and consumers. By following these families over a significant time period (three years in some cases) the Institute for Research on Poverty hopes to collect useful answers to questions about income and incentive.[10] Do people "prefer a minimum income without work to a higher one with work?" With income security, do people take more risks by embarking on training programs or trying new jobs or moving to other places with more opportunities? Does the level of family income or its security affect the children's performance in school or the parents' marital arrangements? What happens to patterns of saving and spending as incomes increase or as earned income increases? The experiments may also help to quantify some answers: by paying different amounts to families of equal size and economic status, the Institute can test the relation between economic deprivation and incentive. If people do prefer idleness on welfare to working for an income, what is the minimum level required to get people into the job market? If income is assured (whether from a steady job, welfare payments, or a trust fund), what is the trade-off between working to get more income and not working to get more leisure?

Some of these questions have been studied in connection with tax policy: how much do income taxes deter people from working? Most investigations have found very little impact; most people choose to work even when their earnings are subject to very high tax rates. Whether we can argue from this evidence that potential welfare recipients would also prefer to work is not entirely clear: although the rewards of working can consist of personal satisfaction and even enjoyment as well as wages and salaries, such additional benefits are probably more common among high-salaried positions than with the low-wage jobs available to low-income families.

Useful as the experiments with work incentives may be, no results were available during the period when the family assistance program was being designed. A preliminary report of early experience with the New Jersey program found no evidence that income assistance substituted for earnings: more families receiving benefits reported increased earnings than did those not assisted. But the work *requirement* is, of course, not being tested.

If we agree that work is unpleasant, that no one would work if he didn't have to, that everyone faces an *economic* work requirement, and that therefore denying welfare to anyone who refuses training or employment is only logical and consistent, —if we accept all these premises, we arrive at a major question of freedom. The program planned will not require the welfare recipient to take any job, only one that is "suitable," and then only if transportation exists (and there are child-care centers for working mothers). But the decision on suitability, as well as the availability of transportation, will be made not by the prospective worker but by the welfare administration. Although federal guidelines will be set out, state and local officials will do the interpreting in any specific case, and inequity or inconsistency cannot be ruled out. Quite aside from that, a decision made by government officials denies freedom of choice to the individual. The present welfare system allows little, if any, freedom of choice to the consumer; a welfare mother cannot decide where she will buy or what to spend. The proposed welfare system allows little, if any, freedom of choice to workers; the welfare mother cannot decide whether a job is suitable or how she will get there.

Removing the freedom of choice in working amounts to repudiating the American economic system, which relies on the economic incentives of prices and wages operating in relatively free markets. Some people now depend on welfare because barriers to their employment exist, and the new program proposes to remove these—to give people training, find them job opportunities, develop transportation and child-care facilities. If, after their access to the market is assured, people must be coerced into working, then the viability of the entire market system can be questioned. If welfare recipients will not work unless they are required to, how much productive effort will they contribute to the job? What employer will hire an unwilling worker, or continue to pay an employee merely for being present? Welfare officials may indeed force an individual to report for work, but how will they control his performance on the job? United States history contains considerable data on the efficiency of forced labor, compared to that of free labor; and previous experience suggests that the costs of a work requirement may outweigh the benefits.

The new family assistance proposals also represent a complete reversal of the "work ethic" as it applies to women with families. Up until 1969, the notion that people should work and not rely on welfare to support themselves and their families was adamantly opposed as far as working mothers were concerned. Welfare policy ruled that mothers should *not* work to support their children, and welfare arrangements in effect tied a mother to her home by subjecting her earnings to a one hundred per cent tax. (If a woman whose family income consisted of AFDC payments took a job, the entire amount of her wages would be subtracted from the AFDC benefits.) Since most jobs require some additional expenses for transportation or lunches or even stockings or hairnets, the working mother would clearly be worse off unless she could find a job paying well above welfare benefits. In 1968 some states introduced a sliding-scale system that allowed a mother to keep $30.00 monthly of her earnings, and a fraction of what she earned over that sum. But the 1969 proposals include the *requirement* that mothers accept suitable employment or register for training, provided that transportation and child-care arrangements exist. Mothers with children under six will be exempted from this requirement.* Three separate issues arise from this requirement.

One concerns the nature of the family unit. For a mother, the question of working or not working is not the simple alternative between employment and leisure that it is for a single woman or for a man. The alternatives are those of employment at a paid job or employment at home caring for the children. Allowing the mother to choose whether or not to work recognizes her dual role, as part of the labor supply and as a mother in the family. Presumably she will choose according to what she thinks best for her family. The mother who participates in the family assistance program gives up her right to consider

*Cf. the discussion in Chapter Five, pp. 117–22.

the needs of her family: she must work, or she must work if someone else decides that she should, despite her role as the mother of children. Other mothers, whose incomes do not depend on welfare payments, remain in control of their status: they may choose whether to work or not, and they are free to consider the best interests of their family.

We are describing, of course, the institutional arrangements which exist in the United States in 1970, not the preferred or wisest or most efficient arrangement. Whether or not a mother should work could be settled not by the mother but by the children, or by trained experts in child care, or by society as a whole. But there is no a priori reason why this question should be settled by congress for one group of mothers and not for all mothers. The proposed work requirement discriminates not by making one group of women work, but by depriving them of their status as mothers. To quote one economist:

> Given the high labor force participation of mothers in general, what is so special about mothers on welfare? . . . One of these answers is that the caseworker, rather than the welfare mother, may decide whether the mother is needed at home. . . . If adequate incentives were present, . . . I submit the decision whether to work could safely be entrusted to the mother herself.
>
> Let me hasten to add that I do not favor child neglect or oppose day-care centers. But I do not see why society should enforce higher standards of child care for welfare mothers than for self-employed waitresses or beauticians, whose arrangements for child care are a matter of public concern only when they are flagrantly inadequate. We do not really believe that waitresses are by and large better mothers—we simply do not have a set of institutions that scrutinizes their behavior so closely.[11]

The new program envisions setting up a substantial number of day-care centers for children, and this raises the next issue. The working mother's employment opportunities are sharply limited by the need to find substitute care for the children. It may be that she can accept only a job that pays well enough to cover the costs of a full-time babysitter, and not all women are sufficiently trained or able to fill such high-paying positions. It may be that she can work only part-time, and not all industries offer work on other than the normal work schedule. It may be that she can go out only when a relative or neighbor cares for the children, and such arrangements tend to be impermanent and not always reliable. Providing organized day-care centers will, therefore, greatly widen the opportunities for a working mother to find employment, to escape the limited number of part-time or temporary or low-paying jobs available, and to increase her productivity. But only if she is a welfare mother: the day-care centers will be set up to take care of children whose mothers are required to work, not children in other families whose income lies above the poverty level.

The economic implication is clear: the country can no longer afford individual or family child care among low-income groups; the "wife and mother" role will be preserved, like other luxuries, for the upper-income classes. Day-care centers and group arrangements for children can be provided by society and even imposed on families supported by society, while remaining as private purchases for everyone above the poverty level. Again, it may or may not be a good thing to enable mothers to widen their employment opportunities, or to improve their child-care arrangements, but there is no a priori reason why Congress should take action for one group of women and not for another.

Finally, the work requirement as it applies to women raises another question about the "suitability" of employment. The differential between women's and men's incomes is roughly equivalent to the disparity between black and white incomes: even among full-time, year-round workers the average income for a woman amounts to about 60 per cent of a man's income. "Women's jobs" are mostly low-wage occupations (retailing, clerical work, and service occupations) and women are virtually excluded from other occupations by custom, tradition, and accepted practice. Women who participate in the family assistance program will commit themselves to taking "suitable" employment, but will training programs or placement services accept the definition of "suitable" implied in the existing employment practices?

The *Wall Street Journal* of August 21, 1969, reports:

Republic Steel Corporation said it is hiring women to work

in its Buffalo steel mill because of a critical shortage of male job applicants. It is the first time since World War II, when the plant had 400 female mill workers, that women have been hired for production jobs. . . . The women would be recruited through the State Employment Service. . . . Bethlehem Steel Corporation . . . said it did not plan to follow Republic's lead, even though it also has problems getting and retaining employees. A Bethlehem spokesman said the manpower situation was so critical that for the first time in its history the plant soon may have to base its production on the number of employees available rather than how many orders it has.[12]

This item prompts some questions: Why have women been excluded from production jobs since 1945? Will the State Employment Service list jobs in steel mills as "suitable" employment for women welfare recipients to fill? If a woman production worker at Republic is later laid off, will she be able to refuse a clerical job on the grounds that it is not "suitable"? Should training programs exist in Buffalo for male "hard-core unemployed" to take steel jobs, if women are available? What other shortage areas exist where women are not employed?

The Working Poor

Despite the fact that the work requirement raises all these difficulties, it is firmly grounded in the accepted American ethic that values work as a means of self-support and self-respect. There is a corollary which suggests that anyone who works hard enough can escape poverty, but this has been decisively rejected by the new program's recognition of the "working poor." These men and women may be currently employed, but they do not earn enough to bring their family income above the poverty level. By providing income supplements on a sliding-scale, the family assistance program in effect lets society help where individual effort is not enough. It is estimated that the number of people receiving assistance will almost double as those who are presently ineligible for welfare because they have jobs become eligible for welfare because their jobs provide insufficient income. Aside from income, the program will give training to the working poor, so they can take better jobs with higher pay and work themselves out of welfare by becoming more productive. And this part of the program also raises the problem of conflicting goals, of work versus welfare, of whether we want to secure adequate consumption levels for people or whether we want to make people more productive.

At the moment, a significant number of families have incomes above poverty levels because two adults are working. Since most women receive low wages, the promise of supplemental assistance to families with incomes below a certain level may very well induce some working wives to leave the labor force and bring their family's income down to "poverty" levels, hence making it eligible for aid. The alternative between working and not working must be measured differently for women and men; it also differs between single-earner families and those with two or more family members at work. Finally, the proposals for the "working poor" will inevitably affect the economic role of women, both in the labor market and at home.

For those of the working poor who accept training along with their income supplements, there is a strong implication that jobs will be available at the end of such training schemes. Existing government manpower programs have been criticized for their inadequate placement activities, and it is not clear how the new programs would escape this criticism. Nor is there any guarantee that the overall level of economic activity will be maintained with a high level of job opportunity. Finally, it is very likely that at least some people will not benefit from training, which cannot always compensate for limited abilities. Individuals vary in their productiveness, and the number of jobs calling for limited productivity diminishes, year by year. It may be, in short, that the working poor will remain dependent on government assistance to maintain an adequate consumption level.

But this requires another look at the meaning of an adequate consumption level, and at the fact that the new family assistance proposals for the first time recognize family size as a factor in determining poverty level incomes. Much of the mounting criticism of present welfare arrangements comes from the working poor, and race prejudice contributes to the resentment of welfare recipients in city ghettos who are black. (They are, of course, less likely to find work, more likely to have only one parent present, and to have an income much below the poverty line.) Many of the poor white families who would receive assistance under the new proposals will be eligible, however, because they have large families. It follows that two ways exist of preventing families from becoming poor and needing government assistance: one, ensuring adequate training and productive employment and two, limiting the size of the family.

Poverty and Population

Every budget standard consists of a list of items—whether these are drawn up for welfare payments, for determining a "luxury" level of living, or for setting out a nutritious meal plan. The quantities and sometimes the type of items included must be adjusted for family size. This procedure takes the number of people in a family as given and measures consumption accordingly. It is tantamount to defining children as exogenous factors that are not subject to any economic influences like income or employment. But in fact the association between size of family and size of income has been extensively studied, and it can be quite correct to consider having children as one kind of consumption. People can have a small family and live at a high standard, or have a large family and live in less affluent circumstances. Consequently we may ask about minimum standards of consumption with respect to having children.

Such standards could be derived in exactly the same way that other budget quantities have been calculated: by recording the actual choices of actual families. The BLS budget for a moderate standard of living includes a radio (replaced every three years) and a used car (replaced every four years), because most American families consider these items and quantities reasonable or customary. One might expect a similar determination of the customary or accepted number of children for a moderate living standard, with perhaps one or two more at the "higher level." No such standards exist, nor do the budgets contain any explicit discussion of the consumption choices involved in having children.

Such discussion may become inevitable if future welfare

programs provide automatically higher incomes for larger families, and equate "need" with family size. In recent years the working poor have protested some welfare budget allowances—the allotments to welfare mothers for new clothing and furniture, for example—on the grounds that poor families make do with hand-me-downs and second-hand furniture, while working and paying taxes to help support the nonworking welfare recipients. Low-income families accuse welfare recipients of being lazy and improvident, or expecting others to pay for their way of life. In the years ahead, a similar protest may be voiced by small families, ineligible for assistance, who will be working and paying taxes to help support the populous poor. In April, 1970, the Supreme Court upheld the Maryland law limiting to $250 monthly the amount of welfare payments a single family may receive. This law, however, was passed to implement the present welfare system which does not, as the proposed one will, legislate income assistance in terms of family size.

The new program will pay supplementary benefits in cases where income is insufficient *because* there is a large family. Ostensibly, the family assistance program will adjust welfare payments to consumption levels, first by measuring need in terms of the kind of consumption budget discussed in earlier chapters, and second by varying this budget for families of different size in order to secure some kind of per capita consumption minimum. But the program ignores one important form of consumption, expenditures for children, presumably because to do this would be to open a Pandora's box of ethical and moral questions. Yet to the familiar goals of maintaining consumption and improving people's earning capacity, the planned program implicitly adds a third—subsidizing procreation by the poor or near-poor. The welfare families of the future may be charged with being lazy and improvident for their failure to control child-bearing; and we may eventually have some discussion of how many children a family "needs."

These considerations remind the economist that all welfare programs constitute transfer payments: that is, income earned by one set of persons and transferred to another set who supply no productive services to earn this income.* At present, Social Security benefits transfer income from young to old, Veterans' benefits transfer resources from all taxpayers to men and women who have had military service, aid to the blind and disabled provides income transferred from active earners to the incapacitated. Quite obviously there is some limit to the amount of income, or fraction of the total, that can be transferred: the proposed expansion of welfare to a family assistance program prompts a close look at such a limit.

Transfer payments to the poor (the simplest description of the new program) can accomplish two things: a general redistribution of income or a once-and-for-all investment effort to lift people out of poverty. Most advocates of the program emphasize the latter: if we spend massively *now* on income maintenance, employment, and training, if we seek to remove the environmental conditions of poverty with direct aid, *future* spending will be less. This is the viewpoint expressed by Representative Martha W. Griffiths:[13]

> The economics of programs are questions of objectives and the best way to achieve them. In one view, the objective of welfare programs is to alter the distribution of income through transfers from those who have to those who have not. The economic way to effect these transfers is that way which entails a minimum of distortions in resource allocations—that is to say, the least interference with free choice by households in consumption and labor supply. However, to my mind, there is a better view of the primary objective of the welfare system. In this view, the end of the welfare system is to go out of business. Unless welfare is a self-liquidating enterprise, it is a failure. Insofar as possible, welfare programs should reinforce individual responsibility and human resource development programs. They should seek to move people into a dignified and rewarding participation in the economic life of the nation and to give people the opportunity and incentive to make personal provision for contingencies which all families must anticipate.

The argument is, in effect, one for investment in human re-

*Cf. pp. 83–85.

sources so as to achieve a rise in the rate of economic growth; it gains added meaning from realizing, as Robert Lampman points out, that "Few children, even those of below average ability, who are not born and raised in poverty actually end up in poverty as adults. This suggests that poverty is to some extent an inherited disease."[14] By getting rid of the disease, we not only relieve the poverty in consumption of those who are presently poor, but we ensure greater productivity and hence less poverty for future generations. The pay-off, therefore, from transfer payments that will bring about such changes is quite different from the benefits of transfer payments that merely redistribute income and that must appeal to human feelings of concern for others.

To make this point clear, consider the implications of the new welfare plan for Puerto Rico and other offshore United States areas, vis-à-vis the fifty states. Income in these islands falls far below that within the country; half the families in Puerto Rico, for example, receive less than the $3700.00 designated as the poverty line income level; federal welfare expenditures there have always been a fraction of those provided to state governments. If the minimum incomes set out in the new plan and its provisions for assisting working families were applied to all these areas, it is estimated that federal expenditures would increase five-fold. The fact that no one seriously contemplates such an action means, in effect, that it would exceed the limit to transfer payments, that neither congress nor the American people wishes to redistribute income on such a scale to the inhabitants of these islands.

Conclusions

Evidently the new program for income and welfare, like previous ones, suffers from ambiguity in its objectives. To make the most efficient use of scarce resources—to do the most with what we have—means first of all that we agree about what we are trying to do. Such an agreement requires a clear statement of policy goals, and of the way in which any specific program will help achieve these goals. Everything about the new program demands scrutiny in these terms.

What is the goal of the program—to assure that people have

enough to eat and decent living conditions, or to insure that everyone is working who is able to? Does welfare seek to help children or the adults on whom they depend? What does society see as the proper role for women, the proper definition of the family unit, and its economic function? How much of the family assistance program represents wholesale income redistribution, and how much represents investment in future production from those assisted? The knotty questions of work versus welfare must be faced directly: the dilemma may be insoluble but it cannot long be evaded by describing the new program as "workfare."

CHAPTER EIGHT

EMPLOYMENT
AND TRAINING

WHETHER OR NOT it is tied to welfare, a manpower policy is emerging that calls for conscious effort to improve job training and job placement for ghetto inhabitants. Such a policy offers the hope of escape from the constraints of low income (meaning low earnings) because of low productivity. It also implies less unemployment, and fewer jobs offering only sporadic or part-time employment. What programs have been designed to fulfill these policy objectives, and how well do they work?

One chapter does not allow a review of the plethora of existing manpower activities run by government agencies,* private business, community organizations, academic institutions, and autonomous organizations formed by cooperation among these groups. But we can identify three major types of programs and their particular costs and benefits. Some projects seek to put people into jobs that already exist, some to train prospective employees, and some to establish new job opportunities. All three types should be susceptible to market analysis: we are used to thinking of labor in terms of supply and demand.

*A useful compendium of federal government programs exists in the *Catalogue of Federal Assistance Programs, June 1, 1967,* published by the Office of Economic Opportunity. Although the new administration that took office in 1969 has revised some of these programs, the book still gives an excellent picture of the scope and complexity of federal activities.

EMPLOYMENT

Turning first to programs that attempt to widen employment, let us define the problem. Unemployment exists, yet there is a labor shortage. The so-called "hard-core unemployed" reside mostly in the inner city, and many of them are nonwhite. On the books, they may appear as casual workers, temporarily unemployed, out of work for more than twenty-six weeks, or not in the labor force at all.*

How to account for such pockets of unemployment in areas where all the symptoms of tight labor exist—employers advertising heavily, calling employment agencies, offering higher wages and fringe benefits to make jobs more attractive—except by passing harsh judgments? It is said that the unemployed are lazy and don't want the jobs that are going begging, or it is more patronizingly said that the unemployed are incapable, and know better than to apply for jobs they can't handle anyway.

But another explanation which disallows such conclusions is that the market—the meeting place of the supply of potential workers with the demand of potential employers—does not function properly. In economist's terms, an imperfect market allows a labor shortage to coexist with unemployment because the supply of labor available to employers is less than the supply of labor offered by workers. Two conditions make this true: the methods used to recruit labor and the way in which individuals are placed. Changing either or both of these conditions, therefore, may heighten productivity and income for people who find jobs or better jobs.

For a highly sophisticated economy like that of the United States, the technology of recruiting remains remarkably primitive. Employers use classified advertising and more selective media, like spot announcements on local radio stations or notices in union halls, transit advertising, billboards or posters, and signs outside the plant gates. These techniques consist, basically, of informing people that job vacancies exist: although some advertisements contain elements of persuasion, normally the employer waits for positive action on the part of the prospective employee. Small employers with only one or two

---

*Cf. Chapter Five, pp. 105–07.

occasional openings may rely completely on word-of-mouth
information, where people currently at work bring job applicants from among their circle of friends or relatives. Employment agencies, both private and state, perform both the information function and a certain amount of positive placement.
A recent survey of workers who shifted from one labor market
to another analyzed the relative importance of these sources of
information; the findings are summarized in Table VIII–1. The
authors conclude:

Table VIII-1
Sources of Job Information, by Occupational Categories and Usefulness

Percentage of Movers Using

Source of information about jobs	White Collar Jobholders	Blue Collar Jobholders	Percentage of Users Finding Helpful
Friends, relatives	38	58	85
Special trip	43	28	76
Employer or his representative	27	6	85
Newspaper ads	16	10	51
Private employment agency	11	6	63
State employment agency	6	7	43
Union	1	8	50
Other	26	13	

Source: John B. Lansing and Eva Mueller, *Geographic Mobility of Labor*, (Ann Arbor,
Michigan: Institute of Social Research, 1967), pp. 225, 228.

Heavy reliance is often place on friends and relatives for
information, especially by blue-collar workers and those
with lower levels of education. . . . On the fact of it, a
program and increase and make more readily accessible
information about job opportunities . . . would be of assistance in directing more economically efficient mobility—
particularly for blue-collar and less educated workers. . . .
At present, people seem to consider only a narrow range
of choices[1]

It follows that one of the simplest ways to improve the labor market has turned out to be communicating news about job vacancies to more people. New programs have developed more specialized means of communication. For example:

The company is now using minority contacts far broader than the usual doctors, lawyers, ministers, social workers, teachers, to get to the grass roots: PTA officers, block club presidents, rulers of Elk Lodges, scout leaders, barbers and beauticians. (The Negro beautician is a prime social center and reaches many women regularly.) Beauticians' clubs have been taken on plant tours, showing them kinds of jobs, telling them of the qualifications needed.[2]

Many residents of ghetto areas . . . were unaware that employment opportunities existed for them in our bank. I personally called on leaders of the Negro community to explain our position and to solicit their referral of employment applicants.

We initiated a program of advertising, designed to reach minority groups. Concurrently, we worked with many agencies and community groups, and now work closely with more than 50. We produce a monthly employment bulletin, listing job openings, which is mailed to 100 anti-poverty agencies. We visit these agencies and invite their staff members to visit us, so as to gain first-hand knowledge of our needs and the environment within the bank.[3]

My job is to make contact with . . . city residents, find out their problems, and their needs and try to convince them to come into our neighborhood employment center to further our discussions.

I'm out in the neighborhood say half of the day. Normally, in the morning or afternoon to do my recruiting—I'm knocking on doors, talking to people in the streets, pool rooms, stores, barber shops, etc.

There's many, many places we could find the unemployed and hard core, just by simply walking in your neighborhood. I usually find them in front of pool halls or either in front of bars, streets, and by door to door knocking.[4]

These examples illustrate one type of program, that which seeks to remedy the inadequacy of existing methods of hiring. From the economist's point of view, the firm improves its buying efficiency by changing its purchasing practices, that is, its behavior in the market for the productive factors called labor. From the firm's point of view, the personnel department rather than the purchasing office handles recruitment, so that changing existing practices usually calls for a change in personnel policy. (Clearly every firm has a personnel policy: even the absence of any explicit recruitment program or "personnel officer" is itself a policy.) Either way of looking at it leads to the same conclusion: this particular change in the existing situation can result from a purely *managerial* decision. It does not take a government program at any level—federal, state, or local—to bring about such change. Nor is there proof that such managerial decisions are justified only by government pressure of either the carrot of tax relief or the stick of withholding federal contracts. The changes make sound economic and business sense: if recruiting in a different way increases the number of applicants for a given job, the firm is better off since it has a wider choice. And at least some changes of practice (such as calling guidance officers at ghetto schools rather than private employment agencies, revising a mailing list, or placing ads in different newspapers) require no additional costs.

So we may ask: if management *can* improve its hiring techniques, why hasn't this happened before? To some extent the answer reveals deliberate or disguised discrimination. Firms which employ no members of a minority group can insist that they do not discriminate but that no qualified applicants have turned up. The situation can be perpetuated by the simple, but quite common, recruitment practice of using the present staff to round up prospective employees. Hiring the friends of employees in a firm with no minority group workers to begin with will not result in actively reducing discrimination. (Interestingly enough, however, the same technique can be highly useful, once the payroll includes *some* members of a group formerly unrepresented, in enlarging the number of applicants from the group.)

A managerial decision is not only sufficient to implement such programs, it turns out to be necessary. Data collected in the late 1950's and early 1960's emphasize not only active recruitment, but the need for a clear-cut corporate policy, determined at the top,[5] which prohibits discrimination. Later studies conclude that top management must enunciate company policy clearly and, more important, set up systems for following through, so that policy statements are effectively carried out. Significantly, most of the spokesmen quoted earlier referred to a "credibility gap," and reported that when they tried to publicize job opportunities in a company, or industry, "people just don't believe what we're talking about."[6]

Many firms have also changed their application and placement procedures with some success. Like hiring practices, these techniques have not kept pace with technological change, even while that has radically altered the nature of employment. Application forms or placement tests may offer little opportunity for the would-be worker to demonstrate or discover his potential productivity, and they may stress achievements or background data that discourage a potential employee. Although the skills required for a job may differ substantially from firm to firm, or from what they were two decades ago, the accomplishments required of applicants for that job frequently show little, if any, revision. Some job requirements, such as a high school diploma, for example, exist simply because of inertia, and these will continue until someone suggests that they be dropped or asks what purpose they serve.

While adopting a new policy for recruiting enlarges the number of *people* available to fill jobs, changing a policy of placement increases the number of *jobs* available to people. Again, the best illustrations come from company experience:[7]

> Gerald Davis is 30 years old . . . black and, until last year
> . . . considered useless for technical work by traditional
> industrial standards. New Jersey Bell Telephone Co. broke
> tradition to hire and train Mr. Davis and others. He finished high school at night, was made a technician and sent
> to the company's Newark office, and has already been
> promoted. . . . "Look, I took a test when I came here and

I failed it, but they hired me anyway," he said. "Since then, I've finished school, but they won't let me retake that test. They said, " 'Forget about it—you're in.' "

In some cases, firms themselves have reevaluated the usefulness of long-standing internal procedures, as described in this interchange between a personnel executive and a member of the Equal Employment Opportunities Commission[8]:

Miss McWilliams: . . . We have many, many job categories. The primary jobs that you're recruiting for, of course are your secretaries, your clerks, and your messengers.

Commissioner Jackson: . . . Well, what are the general requirements for those jobs?

Miss McWilliams: . . . Well, typing, shorthand; we no longer adhere to a policy of high school diploma. . . .

Commissioner Jackson: . . . What tests do you administer?

Miss McWilliams: . . . We use the typing, shorthand, and the Wonderlic test and some arithmetic tests. . . . I seriously question and am considering dropping the Wonderlic test. You know, that's probably given by every company in New York City, and you can almost memorize it, as an applicant. . . . We would never make a judgment based on the results of that test.

In other cases, an outside agency trying to place unemployed people has urged firms to reconsider their requirements:

We asked the gas company what the requirements were for their meter reader jobs. They said, "They have to know mathematics." We said, "Wait a minute. Mathematics? What do you mean?" "Well, you know. Arithmetic?" "That is a little better. They do not need to know algebra? How about multiplication and division?" "They don't do any multiplication and division." "All right. You are talking about addition and subtraction, aren't you?" "Yes." "Let them get multiplication and division in night school later."[9]

Analyzing a particular job to find out precisely what skills are involved not only provides more opportunities for the available supply of labor but tends to increase the productivity of the jobholder:

The key to it has been this approach of taking entry-level

jobs apart and examining them in terms of what fundamental aptitudes and abilities are required to do the job. And to then examine applicants on the basis of the possession of those aptitudes and those skills and on no other basis. Since we've been better able to match people and jobs, productivity has increased.[10]

Tri-Faith hired as a project director a Chicago Transit Authority night policeman "who had spent the previous 13 years walking up and down elevated trains at night. He does not write too well, but we were impressed by the fact that while living in public housing he had helped to organize a credit union and was in the process of organizing a cooperative laundromat. We put him in an employment office which had been producing zero, and in three months he is now making well over 60 placements a week at a cost of about $14 per placement. Here is a man with enormous management talent. He knows how to manage staff. He comes up with creative ideas. He knows how to get jobs from business." But his former employer had found him only suited for policing subway trains at night.[11]

While most attention has been focused on the so-called "entry-level" job (the employment opportunity open to a person with no previous experience), future programs must take the next step, that of upgrading and training for promotion. After all, once a firm accepts a commitment to recruit and place minority group workers—whether they are Spanish-speaking, deaf, female, or black—*some* immediate jobs open up for the Spanish-speaking, deaf, females, blacks, or whatever, in interviewing applicants and helping to administer the program. Productivity will not increase indefinitely simply because the company now lists a Director for Community Relations or a Special Assistant to the Vice-President for Personnel. But if market imperfections are totally removed, then *all* positions, not merely those at "entry-level" or in special programs, will benefit from the rethinking of "aptitudes and abilities required." For the employer as well as the employee, the widening of employment channels may produce substantial benefits at minimal cost.

TRAINING

A second area of manpower policy attributes higher income to greater productivity, and seeks more effective performance through specialized training programs. These programs are plentiful and varied: sponsors include employers, government and social agencies, voluntary groups, and community organizations. While the type of education and skills offered may seem similar, business programs differ from the rest in their approach to training and its expected benefits. There is some evidence that costs per trainee also vary substantially among the different types of administering authorities.

It seems obvious that job-related training is more efficient in that it turns out more productive workers with fewer resources devoted to their preparation, than systems which offer vocational courses with no specific placement for the graduate of such courses. If programs can be tied to recruitment and placement efforts, specific training can be designed to meet the requirements of a particular job or the needs of workers brought in by unorthodox recruitment. A company's previous experience with training gives a built-in advantage: facilities and personnel and programs already exist, rather than having to be established as a totally new organization. These arguments suggest that training programs devised and executed by employers, who in this country consist chiefly of private business, may be preferable to those run by government agencies.

The Comptroller General's report* on federal antipoverty programs found that most employment and training activities were costly, fell short of their goals, or achieved little, if any, advancement for the participants. The costs of these programs reflect primarily their newness: some have required wholly new agencies to be established while others have been carried out by subcontractors, who in turn have needed either to expand or establish new organizations. Launching the training program, therefore, requires both time and the considerable start-up costs associated with any new activity. The inadequate achievement of government programs is due primarily to a gap between training and placement. Recurring criticisms cite courses that train beauty operators in a city in which the number of barbershops and beauty salons is dwindling; that teach clerical skills in a market where mechanics are scarce; or that train people to be factory operatives who can find only custodial or service jobs little different from those held by nonparticipants. The record of the United States Employment Service on job evaluation, counseling, or even referral and follow-up evokes little optimism about expanded efforts to place those who may be newly trained but were formerly unemployed or unemployable.

The best known, and largest, effort by private business consists of the National Alliance of Businessmen and its JOBS program. A listing of benefits includes the 380,000 "hard-core unemployed" hired between early 1968, and June, 1969; the pledge to expand that number to half a million by 1971; and the continued employment of about 200,000 of these new workers, after one year. The turnover rate compares favorably with that among the existing work force. Other benefits, less easily quantified, include the gains to the companies by improving their training courses and reshaping job requirements. The public relations aspect of the program cannot be readily evaluated: its organization, with acknowledged business leaders as prime movers, has presumably put considerable pressure on firms to participate. In some communities, notably cities where violence in the ghetto has either occurred or is threatened, a firm's efforts to hire and train the hard-core unemployed have improved its image and spared it from attack: the program brings benefits. In other contexts, the "do-gooder" label means considerable criticism from stockholders or from an existing work force that for one reason or another feels threatened by the program: these are costs.

More specific costs consist of the subsidy paid to firms by the Department of Labor: the average sum during 1968–69 was about $3,000 per trainee, with a drop to $2,500 during the latter part of 1969. It can be argued that costs will drop farther, because firms have gained experience and know-how in operating the program; but it can equally be argued that costs will rise in the future, as people who are less easily trained come into the program. Like all averages, the costs and benefits suggested vary widely among firms and industries: for the

*Cf. Introduction to Part Two, p. 148.

most part, however, small firms have so far been almost untouched by the JOBS program. To secure their participation requires intensive effort on the part of those working for the National Alliance of Businessmen; whether it would also require generally high subsidies, per trainee, is not clear.*

In some cases, job-related skills must be supplemented (or preceded) by coaching about on-the-job behavior, local geography and transportation, how to handle checks and tax forms, personal hygiene, and good grooming. In other cases, job skills depend on teaching people how to read and write, do simple arithmetic, follow instructions, fill out forms, and so on. This kind of training requires very special attention to the individuals enrolled and attempts to make up for the failure of public schools. Business firms offer such instruction in the so-called "vestibule" system or in some arrangement for part-time working and part-time learning.

In the vestibule system, formerly unemployable workers go through a training course in a shop, office, or plant separated from the regular operations of the firm, and learn specific skills as well as orientation to working life:

> Hard-core refers not to those without steady jobs, but to those who are not equipped for any job . . . Whatever training is required to make them able to work . . . doesn't mean instruction in operating a lathe or a drilling tool. It comes right down to blackboard drills, teaching the letters that spell common colors, so they can read the instruction card that tells them what color seat belt or steering wheel to put on a car as it comes down the assembly line. It entails teaching people addition, so that they can count boxes of parts they take off a supplier's truck. . . . We showed those people, one by one, how to recognize the right bus to take, and in some cases how and when to transfer to another necessary route. . . . In addition to bus routes and alarm clocks, we have had to overcome fear and resentment, hostility, and a history of failure. We are allotted twenty-three weeks to train these hard-core people

---

*A recent study suggests that fear of government sanctions and of adverse publicity accounts for many firms' activities in the program.

for useful work. . . . But the first group was ready for regular employment in only eight weeks. . . .[12]

The course of instruction, interspersed with personal counseling, varied from six to twenty-five weeks depending upon the job objective. Included were basic communication arts, specialized trade skills, and a course in social survival. This course, which was well received by the trainees, included civics and organization of society, personal hygiene and public health, interpersonal relationships, money management and competitive shopping, and the setting of attainable personal goals. . . . The training center resembled an actual work location and environment as realistically as possible. The students became accustomed to the personal discipline of leaving their home area each morning on schedule and traveling ten miles to the school. This made it easier for them to accept the prospect of mobility in the job market and the need to commute for better jobs.[13]

Instruction offered while people are working may be after hours with voluntary attendance, or it may be in-plant training with the employee attending sessions as part of his regular work schedule. For young people, work-study programs combine a part-time school day or instruction within the firm with regular employment.

All the various business arrangements for training and education suggest two questions for the economist: can private industry educate more efficiently than the existing public school system? and, should people be paid to learn? The first question is not confined to vocational education, where obviously both schools and local employers gain from close cooperation. It refers rather to those cases where business programs exist because the local schools have failed. Explicit statements to this effect are common:

We try to hire as many people from the Negro and Puerto Rican group as we can. We have been very, very disappointed at the schools' failure to turn out high school graduates who can even read and spell, and we have a training program to raise their levels of literacy. We have sat in one meeting with school people, but they just set up their committees and do their studies.

One very large corporation reported to us through its personnel department that it had to interview 10,000 applicants to find 1,700 who were qualified for the lower level white-collar jobs it had available. All kinds of businesses are suffering in this city as a result of not being able to get people to fill these positions.[14]

If business must provide remedies for the failures of tax-supported schools, cost-benefit analysis may argue for subsidizing business programs at government expense; but it may with equal force argue for fundamental change in the existing arrangement of government, i.e. public schools.

Such a fundamental change could take place if the American system of education shifted from its present socialized nature to one of competition and free enterprise. This does not, of course, mean that education be competitively *marketed* (so that those with most money to spend get the best), but only that education be competitively *produced.* The programs now being designed and executed by business firms for the "disadvantaged" and ghetto residents, for example, may prove superior to those designed for other students by the public schools. A notable experiment along these lines is developing in Texarkana, Arkansas, where business firms bid on a contract for basic remedial education in the fall of 1969. The school system, in effect, subcontracted part of its responsibilities to private enterprise, with significant implications. Unlike the school system, the firm will not be paid if it does not succeed: the contract specifies that the school children demonstrate achievement by objective tests. On the other hand, the firm has much greater freedom than the school system in the methods it uses to teach children and in the means of getting children to learn. Whether or not this particular experiment succeeds, similar efforts will occur in the future; and what firms are now doing, in evolving training and educational programs for their new employees, may prove to be a kind of pilot plant run or market research project.

The other question, should people be paid to learn, finds an affirmative response in most business training programs. Since paying wages to trainees clearly adds a cost, what are the benefits, aside from encouraging attendance or attention by the students? For the hard-core unemployed, of course, such wages substitute for welfare payments, and a net gain therefore occurs whenever any employment at all results from the education or training. Paying wages also changes, literally, the nature of the education offered: public schools may fail partly because no price is charged and no wages paid for the instruction given, so that it is easy for students to conclude that such instruction is "worthless." This is not merely a semantic conclusion: most data show that school dropouts believe that little or nothing can be gained by continuing their education. In an economic system where the most common source of income consists of earnings from employment (wages or salaries paid for doing something), putting trainees or students among the earners reinforces the economic gains from education.

On the other hand, some nonbusiness sponsors argue that providing a training allowance detracts from the chief goal of learning and using skills. One of the best known agencies with such a philosophy of self-help is the group of Opportunities Industrialization Centers, known as OIC, whose motto is "We help ourselves." Originated by the Reverend Leon Sullivan in Philadelphia, over one hundred centers now exist in cities throughout the country, each relying heavily on community organizations and local firms. The program offers a variety of vocational courses: machine tool operation, electronics, cooks' training, sheet metal work, laboratory technician training, drafting, power sewing machine operating, teletype operating, and keypunch operations, restaurant practices, offset printing, and secretarial and office skills. But the organization lays equal stress on personal counseling and "feeder courses designed to encourage esteem, motivation, and good working habits."[15] The courses include the basic skills of good writing, speaking, simple computation, job strategy, consumer education, minority history, and community affairs. The counseling includes aptitude tests, guidance into an appropriate training course, placement at the end of training, and on-the-job coaching if necessary. Because personal motivation plays such a large role, payment for participants would detract from the success of the program, which has been designed and is managed by ghetto residents for ghetto residents.

THE ECONOMICS OF EMPLOYMENT AND TRAINING

If recent efforts to provide new employment and training opportunities are to have any significant impact on the ghetto, they must continue and expand: what economic policies will sustain such efforts?

Their very existence requires that the overriding economic goal of the country be to secure and maintain a high level of employment. No training program, however cheap, will show any pay-off without providing a job that allows the trainee to use his newly acquired skill. Some of the willingness by businessmen to take on less productive workers and embark on costly (if subsidized) training programs was due to a labor shortage, and these programs have been cut back or abolished in cases where demand slackens and the pace of output slows. The first fears that the "hard-core unemployed" were also unemployable and would not remain as steady workers have been replaced by the fear that, being the last hired, they would be the first to be laid off at the threat of recession.

These programs require first, therefore, that the federal government recommit the country to a policy of securing full employment; some have specified that the commitment include the federal government's acting as employer of last resort. That this appears only elementary wisdom is glaringly obvious to some. For example:[16]

> You forget that it's the tax dollar that keeps white America affluent. Thousands of kids are graduating from Harvard and M.I.T. with their engineering degrees every year. So we put them to work in the NASA program and they can make top dollars there. Same thing with defense work and highway construction and the oil-depletion allowance and the farm subsidies. That's all tax money. Only the white folks don't look at their hustle that way. They don't see that the multi-million-dollar programs that pay their rent and send their kids to school and buy their homes in suburbia are really a welfare program on the grandest scale. Now if white folks could see our jobs-in-housing program as a small Government program for black folks who need it most desperately, then maybe they wouldn't feel threatened by it.

Second, even a booming economy may not affect all areas or industries. The extension of these programs for job opportunities may therefore require specific economic incentive. In some cases, business efforts to take on hard-core employees have come only after considerable pressure, either from government or from minority organizations:

> Only three or four years ago, the climate in white-collar employment changed to some degree, but not because of any new-found social consciousness or social conscience toward Negroes. Rather, two factors prevailed: one, the threat of boycott of products by Negroes; and two, the directive of the Federal Government requiring that there be no discrimination in businesses where government contracts exceed $50,000. I am saying, therefore, that the impetus towards placing Negroes on the payroll in white-collar positions came from outside forces and pressures, and not from within the hearts of employers.[17]

The first pressure consists of the consumer economic power exerted by a minority group; the second pressure remains only a threat, at this writing. No company has actually been faced with cancellation of its federal contracts, despite strong evidence that compliance is less than satisfactory. Although both federal and state civil rights agencies have found violations of federal antidiscrimination laws, the Executive Order of 1961 that called for their enforcement by threatening the cancellation of contracts, and the later requirements of Title VII of the Civil Rights Act of 1964 have never been put into effect. Despite the existence of laws, therefore, the actual changes in hiring and employment practices which effectively reduce discrimination or widen opportunity occur more readily when *economic* pressures exist. By the same token, the economic power of large firms or unions has important meaning for effective changes in employment.

The construction industry illustrates both the impact of aggregate economic policy and specific economic pressure on employment. Many ghetto problems stem from a lack of new building: there is overcrowded, substandard housing, rundown schools and poorly equipped hospitals, streets and parks and fences and lighting in need of maintenance or renovation. All these physical characteristics of urban slums, now denoting a ghetto area, could be removed with massive construction efforts. New building could also mean jobs, if stores, offices, warehouses, service operations, and factories were located within reach of the underemployed ghetto residents. The potential demand for such building in the city far exceeds the ability of the construction industry to produce. Other demands also exist: the Housing Act of 1968 called for 26 million new housing units by 1978; at this writing there is no prospect that this goal can even remotely be approached. On the other hand, these demands remain largely potential.

In the fall of 1968, a tight monetary policy was adopted to reduce aggregate demand and thereby relieve inflationary pressure. Rising interest rates and a shortage of loanable funds made borrowing more expensive and difficult; investment spending was expected to fall. At the same time a surtax on the personal income tax would, it was hoped, make consumer spending fall. The consequent decrease in demand—or slowdown in the rate at which aggregate demand was increasing— would discourage firms from raising prices and workers from asking higher wages.

What happened during 1969 was that the surtax had very little effect. Retail sales stayed high and prices rose more rapidly than at any time since the late 1940's. But the impact of monetary policy was severe. Generally supposed (like fiscal policy) to be neutral in its effect on different sectors in the economy, tight money turns out to be highly selective. Small firms (but not the giant corporations) find their banks unwilling to make larger loans and their suppliers pressing for earlier payment; local communities and state agencies (but not the federal government) find it impossible to obtain funds at the legal interest rates specified for their borrowings; college students discover that loans and scholarships this year are half the amount they were last year (but money is available to others who can pay higher rates).

Most hard hit—in 1966 and recently—has been the construction industry, partly because of the multiple impact of tight money. To the extent that builders consist of small, independent firms, they suffer the disadvantage of size: the billion-dollar corporation may find the effective short-term interest rate is 10 per cent but it can still obtain money. To the extent that consumers have cut down on their saving in order to maintain consumption expenditures, fewer funds are available to invest in housing. To the extent that rising construction costs are beyond the builder's control (the price of both labor and materials being settled in markets in which the individual firm has little or no influence), profits may be squeezed or demand choked off.

Over this same period the building trades have shown wage increases among the highest in the country. Recent examples include the Buffalo contract for the Laborers' International Union which increased total compensation to $8.58 an hour, or by 64 per cent in 1971; an agreement in Kansas City increased pay and benefit for painters by 67 per cent to approximately $8.00 an hour by 1971. Average weekly earnings for workers on construction contracts rose, during three years from 1966 to 1969, by 25 per cent. Quite clearly a yearly rise of 10 per cent, 15 per cent, or higher does not reflect productivity gains of any such amount; these translate, therefore, almost entirely into cost increases and subsequent price increases, and add to the pressure on financing. Although the administration in 1969 shied from any hint of wage-price controls in favor of the classic indirect controls of fiscal and monetary policy, both labor and management in the construction industry opted for the direct approach.[18] Notwithstanding, the federal government moved to reduce construction spending by cancelling some $2 billion of bridges, highways, government offices, and housing, while maintaining projects with "social priority" like the Model Cities program or low-income housing. The anti-inflationary policy continued to rely on efforts to cut back demand.

This chapter, of course, has dealt with supply—increasing the number of workers and the productivity of workers by changing employment and training practices. It is reasonable to inquire, therefore, about the effects on inflation of expanding the supply of workers, rather than of cutting demand. Between 1967 and 1975, it is estimated, the construction industry should hire at least 100,000 skilled workers merely to maintain normal growth; if more became available, the pressure of wage rises on costs, prices, and financing would slacken, while the process of renewing cities and homes might accelerate. Clearly, the employment opportunities for a larger number of workers will not diminish in the foreseeable future. But if a larger number of workers is to appear, the apprenticeship programs must be expanded, and the employment of qualified craftsmen on massive construction projects stepped up: both require changes in the existing practices of construction unions and firms.

The building trades have a record of discriminating against nonwhites and minorities almost as outstanding as their record of wage increases; nor has this record been stained by government criticism. For example, between 1957 and 1968 the Department of Labor sponsored a program to assist and expand nonwhite recruitment into the unions' apprenticeship courses, and as a result, 1,750 young men were trained. Over ten years' time one might expect an industry that employs almost three million workers to find and train more than 175 black apprentices a year. But, of course, by reducing the barriers to entry and expanding the supply of workers, a potential source of gain to the existing labor force has been lost. Whenever the supply can be kept small, the suppliers can reap a high price: the building trades have so far possessed the market power to act in this way.

Although the market power possessed by unions can be offset by the market power of large firms, too often the interest of both coincides. The efforts of "Roger's Round Table," a group of executives from large firms organized by Roger Blough to influence the construction industry, is a case in point. The plans of the group called for resisting the use of overtime or premium payments in order to speed up building programs; as prospective buyers the firms would stand to gain, immediately, if the costs of new plant construction could be lowered (or kept from rising) by such means. They would, of course, have little impact on the structure of wages and prices within the industry. Such an agreement that wields the market power of large firms might be subject to accusations of antitrust conspiracy. But if these same firms agreed to insist on minority group workers being employed at construction projects for their companies, they would be exercising market power which could not be suspect, since it would be an agreement to enforce federal laws against discrimination. The immediate result of such an agreement, however, would not be to reduce costs paid by the companies, although it would help increase the supply of construction workers and reduce the pressure on prices and wages. Very few firms have chosen to use their influence in such a fashion; one exception is the letter from Stanley Marcus of January, 1968, offering to use Neiman Marcus' buying power to support firms which work positively and actively against discrimination.[19]

The most effective form of economic pressure that has so far been brought to bear on the construction industry is the picket lines and barricades to prevent further work on half-completed structures, until minority group workers have been employed. Such tactics threaten workers as well as management, and unions as well as business firms, with immediate and continuing economic losses from construction delays. The threat of contract cancellation, written into federal law, implies the same kind of economic loss, but the marches and demonstrations on construction sites in Chicago, Pittsburgh, and other cities have had more positive effect. And one new program—the so-called Pittsburgh plan which calculates specific numbers of minority group workers to be hired—has come into being.

CONCLUSIONS

Policies to remedy the unemployment and underemployment endemic in the ghetto consist largely of removing market imperfections between potential jobs and the people who are potential workers. New techniques in hiring and training can, by increasing productivity, benefit both worker and employer aside from the social gain of rescuing an "unemployable" from his dependent status. Reducing the barriers to entry in a labor market may also mean expanded supply with less upward pressure on prices. But potential gains do not always clearly exceed expected costs, and many programs come into existence only in response to economic pressure.

CHAPTER NINE

EDUCATION
AND HOUSING

Two AREAS of public policy, education and housing, encompass as much controversy as almost any other domestic concern. Nor do these two represent primarily ghetto problems: government has influenced the amount and kind of private housing through well-established tax and financial provisions,* while public housing has been visible for many years. The "housing needs" of the country have been counted and announced at intervals since the turn of the century, and if government authorities and private experts are getting more skillful at making reliable estimates of these needs, they do not seem any more able to attain their policy goals. In education, on the other hand, the problem is that of defining appropriate policy goals. Whether society should provide "free" education for all through college, preschool kindergarten or infant training, sex education or driver training—these and other questions about the purpose of education require choice-decisions by individuals and their governments at local, state, and national levels. Education and housing involve all of us, not merely the inhabitants of the ghetto, yet the existing conditions of housing and education interact with maximum impact on ghetto life.

*Cf. discussion in Chapter Three, p. 56.

For example, take the training programs discussed in the previous chapter. That such programs exist means that schools have failed, and have failed spectacularly. For a college graduate to study computer programming or shorthand does not reveal major defects in his college education, but for a youngster with ten years of school to have to learn how to read an instruction tag or figure a percentage tax suggests that his school acted only as his custodian for ten years. Where people live governs where their children go to school, and few people choose to live where schools do not provide education. The availability of housing, therefore, limits the availability of education. Housing can also limit the usefulness of the subsequent training programs that attempt to remedy educational deficiencies. People expect to find jobs when they complete their courses, and if employment opportunities continue to decrease in the urban core while expanding in outlying districts, the ghetto resident may not be able to find housing where the jobs are.

These two problems for the ghetto dweller arise, of course, from conditions of segregation, the discrimination in both housing and schools which has produced the racial ghettos and inferior education that characterize so many American cities. After the factual evidence on housing and education in previous chapters, it does not seem necessary in the year 1970 to argue that segregation lowers the quality of life. Following the theme of this part of the book, therefore, we shall look at some policies designed to change these conditions: first at the economics of public schools and then at housing programs.

EDUCATION AND SCHOOLS

Who goes to school and how it is defined are matters of state legislation: in most states children are required to attend school from age seven to age sixteen. "Public schools" supported by federal, state, or local governments exist for every age level from kindergarten through university graduate school, yet nonpublic schools educate over eight million young people, over half of them in the elementary grades. (The highest *percentage* of nonpublic enrollment, of course, occurs at the college level where only two-thirds of the students, over four million, attend government-supported schools.) Providing children with "free" schools during the years of compulsory attendance means that education is the most important government-owned and operated industry in the country: the government unit responsible is the local town, municipality, or school district.

Figures for school enrollment summarize some dramatic shifts in population and economic development since 1960. In the past decade the number of white children in school (between five and seventeen years old) increased by 15 per cent; the number of nonwhite children by much more—25 per cent. This reflects the higher birth rate among Negroes and other nonwhites compared to whites. But the seven million additional pupils represented by the total increase were distributed quite differently among urban and suburban schools, which has little to do with the birth rate. Between 1960 and 1967, central city schools suffered an absolute decline in white student attendance and a 35 per cent increase in nonwhite attendance, so that at the later date the school population in these areas consisted of nine and one-half million white children, and three and one-half million nonwhites. Outside the central city, despite a substantial rise in the number of nonwhites, the school population has a ratio of sixteen white children to one nonwhite child.

The economic burden of "free" public schooling falls largely on states and localities; as of 1967, federal aid to education provided only 7.9 per cent of the total funds, while states contributed 39 per cent and local governments the remainder. And despite the obvious economic fact that the source of *all* government revenue is the income earned by its citizens, localities finance their public schools by relying on the property tax or some kind of school tax unrelated to income. Such a tax base typically produces wide variation in the resources available within a narrowly circumscribed region: the 124 elementary school districts of Cook County, Illinois, range in assessed valuation from $8,200 per pupil to $243,000 per pupil. The figures represent, obviously, the uneven distribution of both wealth and population. Expenditures on public schools also differ dramatically, sometimes within an area small enough to be thought of as a single metropolitan unit. In Brookline, a

Boston suburb, expenditures of $990 per pupil contrast sharply with the $390 per pupil allotted in Millville, less than forty miles away.

While most consumers and taxpayers decide how much to spend and save in terms of income and the command over economic resources it provides, the reliance of most local governments on the property tax means that spending on schools is not so determined. Comparing education expenditures to income gives some strange results: Connecticut has the highest per capita income of any state, but ranks seventh in per pupil expenditure, devoting some 19 per cent of its income to education. In New York, school expenditures are the highest in the country and take 18 per cent of personal income. On the other hand, spending per pupil is exactly the same in Colorado and Illinois, yet because these two states have quite different income levels, the first devotes 21 per cent of its per capita personal income to education and the second only 18 per cent. In Louisiana and North Carolina, where income figures are the same, school expenditures differ widely, amounting to 27 per cent of income for the first state and only 20 per cent in the second. Spending on schools, like other forms of consumption, reflects not only income but also people's choices or preferences.

A particularly unfortunate effect of depending on a tax on property to support schools occurs in economically depressed areas, where education suffers. Not all inadequate public school systems exist in black urban ghettos as the following quotation suggests[1]:

> The average age for public schools is 63.7 years. Twenty were built before 1900; three are more than a century old. Almost two-thirds were constructed prior to the existence of a state fire code for schools. Twenty-three buildings are hazardous for children because of combustible interiors and exterior construction, inadequate heating and ventilation, and unsound and unsafe roofing materials. Tests show that although the children score at or above national norms at the third-grade level, their average score at higher grade levels falls below. Reading scores, considered alone, reflect the same pattern. These tests indicate

the severity of the need for enrichment and a dramatically
different program.

The words refer to Lowell, Massachusetts, a largely white,
small city in an old manufacturing district whose schools were
evaluated by the Harvard Center for Field Studies. Noting that
the local tax base had not expanded in recent years, the report
criticized the local school system for failing to seek federal and
state aid.

In the affluent suburbs, on the other hand, the property tax
base may not correspond either to available income or to the
demand for education. The inadequacies in suburban schools
frequently consist of overcrowding or double sessions, inex-
perienced personnel, a high rate of staff turnover and curricu-
lum change—all symptoms of rapid growth. As some communities have found to their cost, a growing population does not
necessarily mean that tax revenues will grow as much as the
increase in local services required. And it takes more time to
expand the supply of education—building and staffing schools—
than it does to expand the demand. With the supply of schools
fixed over the short run, an increase in the demand for education may very well mean a deterioration in quality.

So far in American history, such economic choice questions
have been answered by voters in separate localities. With federal and state aid to education increasing, the questions of
how much for schools and *who benefits* from schools must be
resolved over a wider area. How to define this "wider area"
poses a fundamental problem. One way of analyzing it relies
on the political scientist's knowledge of intergovernmental
relations, power groups, and organizational structures.* Another
way calls on sociologists and psychologists to explain community relations and social groups. The economist suggests, however, that input-output analysis can clarify much of the problem, and that we look at education as a process of production.

---

*Or relies on the existing political structure where state governments supervise
localities. If the Michigan legislature approves, voters of that state will decide
in November of 1970 whether or not to adopt a state property tax whose pro-
ceeds would finance public education and reduce the quality differential between suburban schools and those in rural and inner city areas.

EDUCATION AND INPUT-OUTPUT ANALYSIS

For education, as for any other type of human endeavor, the simple economic question is how to make the best use of the scarce resources available. If education is the output, teachers and buildings represent labor and capital inputs. They work with other types of labor and capital like the administrative staff, laboratory equipment, buses, and playgrounds. The amount of teaching labor depends on the number of teachers (student-faculty ratio), their quality (bachelors' or masters' degrees), and their duties (collecting lunch money or correcting papers). Most criticisms of existing schools and suggestions for their improvement would benefit from being stated in terms of inputs and outputs, because most school procedures lack an agreed-upon, universal rule. To say that teaching is only one input which can be combined with capital and other inputs to produce various levels of output may sound awkward. But it describes well-known situations: a large lecture course takes less labor but more capital per student, while acquiring the ability to speak a foreign language fluently takes resources different from merely learning to read a foreign language.

Unfortunately, as a moment's reflection will show, education in the United States has always been defined in terms of inputs. State laws do not call for compulsory education; they require children to go to schools. And what are schools?

> The Office of Education defines a "school" as "A division of the school system consisting of a group of pupils composed of one or more grade groups, organized as one unit with one or more teachers to give instruction of a defined type, and housed in a school plant of one or more buildings."[2]

The school plant, "one or more buildings," is fixed capital—an input factor. The teachers (one or more) represent labor—an input factor. The children themselves can be regarded either as inputs who work with the labor and capital available to them in the schools, or they can be viewed as inert raw material to be worked over by the schools. Their "education" is defined in terms of time—the required number of school days in a year, the years spent in obeying the state law—a kind of sentence passed on all children between the ages of six or seven and fifteen or sixteen. That it has always been so seems evident; most explanations of the American system resemble this one[3]:

> Education for their children has always occupied a special place in the hearts of Americans. Probably in no other country has so much been done to assure education for so many children. However, the policy . . . developed over time, first slowly and then in this country precipitately and massively. Minimal goals were continually escalated, from grammar or elementary school education a century ago to a high school education as the desired objective in the first part of this century. And in our own time we have seen this objective expanded to a widespread desire for some education at the college level.

Like the Office of Education definition quoted earlier, this discussion relies on grades and years and schools to define American education—and these are all input factors. Nowhere is there a simple description of the *output* of the productive process known as education, or a specification of the final product of the public schools. Nowhere do we learn about the educated child turned out by the grammar or elementary school of a century ago, or by the high school today. Even the "minimal goals" mentioned discuss input factors: "some education at the college level" specifies only where one goes, not what one learns. But the usual statement of goals refers only to inputs, as in this recent declaration about the future of Catholic schools[4]:

> We are not getting out of the "education business"; we belong there and we will stay there. Our aim will be to strengthen our educational resources wherever this is possible and to continue the pursuit of excellence in all our institutions.

In the few cases where American education is discussed as a productive process, its end result or purpose is nearly always defined in abstractions which can be interpreted in many ways. For example, the Kerner Commission found that "education in our democratic society must equip the children of the nation to develop their potential and to participate fully in American life. . . . For the children of the racial ghetto, the schools have failed."[5] But an answer to this high-sounding statement claims, "I think there are some fallacious assumptions there. One is that the concept of democratic society applies to black people, and secondly, that the system has failed to educate black people. I think first of all, that the society does not apply to black people. . . . If you really look at the attitudes of the people who are in control of the system you find out that, in a way, they haven't failed. In a way they succeeded because they don't want to make black people first-class citizens."[6]

Most attempts to define more specific goals merely list more specific types of education.[7] "Reading, writing, calculation, and analysis of information are becoming basic requirements for independence, productive work, political participation, and wise consumption." This emphasis on the economic rewards of education is echoed by some[8]: "The local education system [has] the goal of preparing youth for a productive and prosperous role," and questioned by others: "Education is the principal route to a high status occupation, but it is not obvious whether, on balance, it promotes social mobility."[9]

Linking education to specific goals in this fashion poses a knotty problem in policy. We define "educated people" by the inputs of our system—the most frequently used measure of educational attainment, by the way, is the median school year completed. When high school or college graduates obviously lack "productive work" or "political participation" (to say nothing of "high status occupation"), does the fault lie with the education process or with the organization of work, the political process, or social status?

If, instead of describing education in terms of years and teachers, grades and school buildings, we regard it as a productive process, we should be able to list specifications for the output of this process. We could describe an "educated child" in terms of skills and attributes and formulate policy more efficiently as a result.

For example, suppose that we established the ability to type fifty words a minute as a minimum educational requirement for all children to attain by the age of fourteen. The specification of output then leads to a fairly clear-cut problem in analysis: how best to achieve this minimum requirement. Various types of production functions can be assessed; that is, schools could try small classes and large classes, programmed instruction and personal supervision, letting children type from age five up or instituting a crash course at age thirteen, and so on. Once the relation between inputs (the machines, space, and human beings involved) and the level of output (the ability to type 50 words a minute) has been established, it then becomes a matter of choosing that method which minimizes costs, of relying more on people and less on machines if the latter are relatively more expensive. School systems will differ in the efficiency (cost) with which they attain the minimum level of output, and some systems will provide much more than this level. Parents and children will criticize whatever method is chosen, and there may be some controversy about whether 50 words or 60 words a minute should be required. These problems are familiar, and they would continue to be so, but setting standards in terms of output rather than input would at least disentangle them from others which exist today.

In particular, two disputed areas are susceptible to this type of resolution. One is the demand by teachers to assume greater responsibility for what is taught, on the grounds that their professional competence in the field of education entitles them to authority. Opposing such a claim makes a parent or school committee member uneasy (although it does not deter students from demanding the right to determine their own education). But the uneasiness stems largely from the confusion between inputs and outputs. Teachers may indeed know more about educational production functions: the relation between inputs and outputs, or how to get a child to master the twelve times table or irregular French verbs. Many parents or school committees rightly regard this knowledge as an art or even a mystery. But this does not mean that teachers know best about whether children *should* learn to multiply twelve times sixteen, or whether they should be able to follow a French film without the aid of subtitles. Presumably the purchasers of education, the parents or citizens or taxpayers or voters, should determine what it is they wish produced. They can best do so by defining schools in terms of output rather than the inputs involved. (Students will continue to demand control over both output and input, that is, to determine both what they learn and how they learn it. But this is perfectly logical, since students have the dual role of being producers and consumers: they help educate themselves and they benefit from their education.)

The second problem is that of government aid to education and the appropriate locus of control. The recent demand for community control of schools causes many citizens to be uneasy. For the residents of ghetto neighborhoods to demand a greater voice in the schools their children attend can scarcely be opposed without hypocrisy by suburbanites, whose local school districts or even municipal school boards do not approach the enormous size of big city school bureaucracies. And at least part of the opposition to suggestions for metropolitan school systems stems from the fear that a small-scale and familiar school setup will be replaced by intransigent rules and unresponsive administrators. Yet with the steady increase in federal aid to education and a growing awareness of the disparity in educational opportunities within the same state, pressures for imposing controls beyond the local level will increase. Again, distinguishing between inputs and outputs would help.

The justification for federal or state aid to education can only be that local resources are insufficient to provide acceptable education and must be supplemented by income transferred from other areas. Aid to education therefore resembles welfare programs in the implicit assumption that some minimum level of education exists, below which the American public will not permit its children to be. The trouble is that this minimum level has never been defined in terms of *output*. The only standard that now exists consists solely of an input requirement: that every child between the ages of (roughly) seven and fifteen "go to school." There is no legal requirement that every child demonstrate his competence to read, write, speak a foreign language, explain the United States Constitution, fill out a federal personal income tax form, or perform any other feat as a result of "going to school." But to provide transfer payments so as to improve a school system requires an improved definition of minimum standards. Rethinking education in terms of its output is the first step.

First, it would give some criterion for determining the amount of aid and the amount of "community" control. If American public school education were defined in terms of output, society could demand some minimum standard as the price of assistance to localities that lack resources by insisting that a given level of competence or accomplishment in certain fields be produced by the schools receiving government aid. But the local community would then be free to provide other types of education, whether ballet dancing or Black history. The locality could also determine how to educate: whether to require children to attend school in one building or to use neighborhood resources for learning, whether to organize instruction for toddlers or adults, whether to open schools at night or on a year-round basis. Finally, the community could determine whether, and how, it would raise the education provided above the minimum standards. By defining the required output of schools, the amount of aid required could be calculated with a minimum of outside control.

The difference between standards for inputs and standards for output is not trivial; judicial decisions about segregation have shifted from one to the other with significant results. The former standard for education in the South referred to "separate but equal" *facilities*—a standard for inputs. In its 1954 decision, Brown v. Board of Education, the Supreme Court abandoned this standard and demanded that education strive for equal outputs. Pointing out the impact of segregation itself, the Court found that "separate educational facilities are inherently unequal" because the child who emerged from a segregated school (its output) was not the equivalent of one turned out by an integrated system.* The Court's original finding gains support from empirical data in the Coleman report which found that the input factors, the teachers and facilities, of segregated schools could not produce a finished article (an "educated" child) equal in quality to that of the nonsegregated schools.

*I am indebted to my former student, Susan Nelson, Wellesley College 1970, for this example.

The danger in *not* shifting from input to output definitions is very real. As the analysis of welfare payments made clear, there is a limit to the amount of resources that can be transferred from one group in the economy to another. If programs for assistance to schools are constructed solely in terms of inputs, that limit may be reached without solving any of the problems of uneducated teen-agers. Merely adding inputs cannot, of course, guarantee any improvement whatever in output: the fact is that very little is known about the production function implicit in any educational process. (The argument about large lectures versus small classes, for example, has been raging for generations and is no nearer solution.) That pioneer effort to appraise American society, the 1969 document *Toward a Social Report,* emphasizes our ignorance:

> It is generally assumed that . . . increases in the length of schooling and expenditures on education have brought about an increase in the amount children have learned. There is, however, almost no direct evidence on this point. . . . The *Digest of Educational Statistics,* for example, contains over a hundred pages of educational statistics in each annual issue, yet has virtually no information on how much children have learned.[10]

Clearly, therefore, there is no way to evaluate the relative merits of competing programs, to decide that resources should be shifted from a "remedial" project to one of "enrichment," simply in terms of input factors. Their relative merits cannot be weighed without reference to the educational output: which will produce more education in a given school, books or blackboards? It is equally impossible to set minimum standards in terms of inputs: should every school system have a library? every school building a library of 5,000 books? every school staff a full-time librarian? Such questions can only be answered by knowing the impact of these input factors on output. Finally, there is no way to justify shifting resources from one type of school to another, or from one segment of the population to another, as long as education is defined solely in terms of inputs.

A definition in terms of output, and minimum standards in such terms, would also go far to solve the problem of management—who should run the schools. (Merely reiterating the long-standing rule that public schools are a matter for "local control" does not answer the question, for then comes the need to define "local.") Phrases like "decentralization," "community control," "Black power," or "the neighborhood school" reflect the political and ideological facets of this problem: the economist may phrase it, instead, in terms of efficiency and the economies of scale. What kinds of schools teaching what kinds of students can achieve minimum standards of competence with least cost?

Given the existing proliferation of governmental units, some considerable economies of scale undoubtedly exist. The 228 Standard Metropolitan Statistical Areas designated by the Bureau of the Census correspond to no governmental entity. But they contain over twenty thousand local governments. The largest number surrounds Chicago: that SMSA contains 1,113 authorities, including counties, municipalities, school districts, and special districts. Other fragmented SMSA's include Philadelphia, with 871 local governments, and New York with 551. One-quarter of the local units in all SMSA's consist of school districts, of which one-third manage one school, and one-fourth contain fewer than 300 pupils. Merely recognizing that continuous production exists over the ten-year span the child is required to attend school suggests that the total system, rather than the single building, is the more efficient unit of management.

The second and more profound potential of scale economies has to do with achieving racially integrated schools. Given that segregation, de jure or de facto, is no longer an admissible social goal in this country, the question of how to desegregate the schools, how to change the existing patterns, has usually been posed in political and ideological terms: it can also be thought of in terms of efficiency. The question then becomes, "What is the minimum size of a school system to manage an integrated educational process?" Its answer would take the racial mixture desired (whether it was eight to two, seven to three, six to four, or fifty-fifty) as a kind of fixed factor, and design a school system accordingly. Most studies of racially integrated education have focused on particular schools or existing communities, and it is becoming apparent that these units are frequently too small to accomplish integration efficiently. The many different types of school arrangements (educational parks, pairing of grades, magnet schools, and the like) depend on the size of the area they are to serve. Rather than limit the means by which schools can be integrated to those methods which fit the existing array of school districts, why not define the school district so as to allow efficient integration? In both cases, to increase efficiency means lowering costs or releasing scarce resources for other uses. A recent observer of school desegregation in the North comments,[11]

> If complete integration is to take place in the schools of northern cities, the needed number of white children must come from the suburbs . . . requiring control of the schools on a metropolitan basis. A county-wide system would not be large enough. For example, no fewer than nine counties border on the twin bays of San Francisco and San Pablo, yet there is almost no break in the housing. Still it is very difficult, because of the long-established American practice of local control of schools, to think about schools except in local terms.

If tradition and inertia make it "very difficult" to think about schools in other than local terms, the simplest economic understanding of costs and benefits makes it very easy to do so. The past few years have seen a beginning and expansion of remedial programs, carried on by business, the federal government, and local agencies, for the failure of the schools. Such programs obviously cost more than setting the educational process within the schools to rights. No one doubts that these remedies, and their costs in manpower, equipment, and materials, must continue, along with an expansion of support programs for those unequipped by their schooling to support themselves. To these costs must be added the loss of production by the young people whose potential for thinking and working and accomplishing has never been tapped. The benefits from public schools used to be explained by referring to the gains for the local community in reducing crime and delinquency and increasing human productivity. If the incidence of dropouts and functional illiterates makes us begin to doubt whether such benefits any longer exist, it does not relieve us from bearing the costs of public schools. The crassest kind of economic calculation, with no moral or ethical judgment whatever, forces the conclusion that the country as a whole is now concerned with the input-output process of the local public school.

HOUSING

Some Americans have worked to abolish slum housing since the turn of the century: whether their goal has ever been wholeheartedly adopted as a national policy, despite the slews of legislation, seems less certain. Housing programs cover a broad range[12]: there are proposals to create entirely new cities,[13] to develop the urbanized area by merging some of the SMSA's along carefully planned lines,[14] to scatter the existing population of the inner city among outlying districts and suburbs,[15] to rebuild urban centers so as to attract business and residential occupants, to find space within the city for housing projects, and to rehabilitate the existing slum areas.[16]

Any or all of these programs would rely on massive public funds, but we lack sufficiently precise data to determine the least-cost approach that would maximize the use of these funds.[17] (Economic analysis does, however, allow some pertinent observations: the first of which may merely be the reminder that housing and schools are, at least under existing practice, inexorably tied together. Any scheme for housing, therefore, should include a specific statement of its educational provision: where the children in the proposed housing will go to school and what will happen to the schools formerly supported in the areas which these children left.) Also worth examining, however, is the economic foundation for such reliance on public funding. We have been told for years that private enterprise cannot do the housing job, that providing decent housing for low-income families (or even for moderate-income families in many areas) must be the responsibility of the federal government, and through constant repetition of the statement most people have come to accept it. One of the most authoritative versions of this statement occurs in the final report of the President's Commission on Urban Problems[18]:

To expect the free market to supply housing for all Americans without subsidy requires a flight from reality. We have to turn to government at every level to help finance an adequate supply of minimum standard housing, especially in the inner cities.

But this statement, and its incorporation into social policy and government programs, surely contains a severe criticism of the entire economic system of the United States. If private enterprise and the American version of capitalism cannot produce and sell housing for American citizens, what will be the next failure of the system? How should we prepare for the ultimate collapse of capitalism, what should we plan to replace private enterprise? These questions quite reasonably follow from the unquestioning acceptance of the need for federal assistance to build adequate housing.

THE HOUSING SHORTAGE

Some simple arithmetic, based on rule-of-thumb calculation rather than sophisticated analysis, may be helpful. The advice (or rule) for buying or renting links housing expenditure to income: thus, one should not spend more than two-and-a-half times one's income in buying a house, and the rental payments should not exceed twenty per cent of income. Using these guide lines, a poverty level income of $3,000 per family allows rent payments of $50 monthly and a purchase price of $7,500. In 1968 (when about 10 per cent of all families, or 5.2 million, received *less* than $3,000 income), the average cost of construction for single-family houses was over $18,000, and for units in multi-family structures about $10,000. As for rental housing, of the vacant units available fewer than one-third rented for $50 monthly or less, and two-thirds of these, containing only one or two rooms, did not constitute "family" housing. Recent low-cost, limited-profit housing built in New York State shows a median rent of $33 *per room*, again clearly exceeding the "rule-of-thumb" for family expenditures.

The chief cost components for housing include land, construction costs, and financial charges or interest on investment, and prices for all these have increased over the past decade at a much more rapid pace than has family or personal income, as can be seen from a few indicators.

Table IX-1
Housing Costs

Item	Percentage increase 1957–59 to mid-1968
Median family income	21
Building cost indexes:	
American appraisal	40
Associated General Contractors	36
Wholesale prices, lumber	25.3
Construction materials	10.2
Construction workers, earnings per week	57
Land	60

Source: Income figures from Bureau of the Census, *Current Population Reports, Series P. 60.* Other figures from Elsie Eaves, *How the Many Costs of Housing Fit Together,* Research Report No. 16 (Washington, D.C.: National Commission on Urban Problems, 1969).

It seems fairly clear, therefore, that poor families, and even those with incomes below the median, cannot pay for housing. But how much "free market" or "private enterprise" do all these figures represent? Upon examination, few of the cost increases appear to have resulted from anything like the market operations of supply and demand: instead, they reflect years of conscious and unconscious government policy and intervention.

First, the cost of investment in housing. The list above omits figures on financial costs and their increase, because when money gets scarce it not only carries a higher price tag (interest rate) but tends to disappear altogether from the housing and construction industry. An index of price rises cannot show the impact of absolute shortages. But money, or more precisely the supply of loanable funds to prospective investors in housing, is a matter of federal government action in this country, not of private enterprise; monetary policy is the responsibility of the Federal Reserve Board, the Treasury, and Congress.

The costs of a restrictive monetary stance fall on consumers who are actual or potential home buyers or renters: those families who move (or decide not to move although they'd like to); who set up their own home (or continue sharing a house with relatives); those couples who marry and form new families or those individuals who grow up and form new consumer units. In the ghetto such costs weigh on families and individuals displaced by highways, high-priced office or business structures, or by the expansion of government and nonprofit institutions, as well as those with better jobs and higher incomes who seek to escape the restricted supply of housing in the inner city. Studies of this phenomenon—the impact of tight money on housing—abound; what is less clear is how far these costs have been consciously weighed against the benefits to be gained from tight money. (We may think of the Phillips Curve, which also shows how overall economic policy can affect one sector.) But under no circumstance can we characterize the financial circumstances of the housing situation as a failure of American capitalism or private enterprise.

Next, rising land prices also reflect government's intervention; federal, state, and municipal programs have had their impact. These programs are of two kinds: the land-use regulations (zoning, restrictions, planning, and so on) enacted at the local and state level, and the public buildings erected by all three types of government. (Other types of public development, like transportation or sanitation or parks or pollution control, also affect land prices.) Any one of these changes the demand for land for housing, or the supply of land for housing, or both: consequently the price rise (or fall) that results cannot be attributed to "private enterprise" or to "market capitalism." For example, a zoning law allowing for cluster zoning or an extension of the commercial area in a locality may cause land prices in the newly zoned section to rise, while those immediately adjoining fall. When the city extends its sewer system to an outlying district, it extends windfall gains (or losses) to land owners in the area; the proposed route for an expressway or bus line can mean unexpected (and unearned) wealth (or financial reverses) to those in its way, who may or may not be innocent bystanders.

As seems true of schools, it is probable that the sheer number of governmental units that influence land prices is inefficiently large. Since land abuts land except for natural divisions like rivers and chasms (which can always be bridged), the ownership and use of any parcel inevitably involves costs and benefits to those in neighboring areas. These two observations lead the economist to search for scale economies in planning and executing land development and to conclude that the historical accidents which we call cities or towns may be totally inappropriate as areas for rational development. Again, it is impossible to characterize either the present structure of land and property values, or the price rises which have occurred over the past decade, as the result of private enterprise and a capitalistic, free market system.

But what about the third segment of housing costs, summarized on the previous page in two building indexes and price indicators for materials and labor? Granted that the United States is a "mixed economy," rather than one of pure capitalism as it is so often considered, do not business and labor, privately owned and operated, produce and distribute most of the goods and services in the country, and do not the price rises in building materials and labor therefore reflect the harsh facts of supply and demand? Here, also, the impact of government regulation and market intervention must be reckoned with. The demand for materials and labor obviously depends almost entirely on the demand for construction as a whole, and government-built schools, hospitals, jails, courthouses, expressways, warehouses, and the complex installations for defense and space activities make up a major part of total demand. The government also influences the supply of materials and labor, not least by perpetuating market imperfections like those discussed in the last chapter. A housing shortage is evidently the permanent condition of the country, but it must be attributed directly to the failure of government, not to defects in the free market system.

Government housing policy, therefore, consists largely of programs that attempt to increase the supply of housing. (In scattered communities, government policy also includes various forms of price control to hold rents down from the heights they would attain under conditions of increased demand and too little supply.) Federal and state housing legislation embodies a variety of measures to subsidize either housing construction, home buyers, or tenants. Only a few isolated attempts at other solutions to the housing shortage have appeared, yet there is room for considerable innovation.

HOUSING POLICY

One area of experimentation includes the wholesale encouragement of technological change in the nature of housing.

Operation Breakthrough, a major effort by the Department of Housing and Urban Affairs in 1969, attracted over 500 companies who submitted plans for low-cost housing, presumably involving the development of mass production techniques. Development contracts announced in the winter of 1969–70 will lead only to prototypes and "demonstration" projects, and most experts agree that the program will not turn up any revolutionary building methods hitherto unknown in the field.

More immediate is the impact of mobile homes, which represent technological change just as much as any example of prefabrication, modular units, or factory-built components. Shipments of the industry have risen steadily from 96,000 units in 1960–61 to an estimated 400,000 units or more in 1969.[19] Many units priced below $10,000 offer a solution to the impossible arithmetic of low-income housing cited above, and have the further advantage of being familiar if not totally accepted on the American scene. (One of the obstacles to developing unconventional low-cost housing is that people may very well refuse to buy or live in houses which do not seem, to them, like a home.) Expanding the supply of mobile homes will require government action on the local level, where many zoning restrictions prohibit such units, and on the federal level, where mortgage money has not yet been made available.

In Chicago and in Greenburgh, New York, families dislocated by urban renewal have been housed in mobile homes parked within the neighborhood; similar use of the units for temporary housing has been urged in other cities as well. To the residents, it means being able to stay in familiar surroundings without the costs and tensions of moving away. To the housing program, it means providing continuous shelter to families with a minimum of effort in relocating or moving tenants. To the community, it means an opportunity to find out about such housing: in some areas a local ban against mobile homes has been lifted to allow for temporary arrangements like these. Once people see what modern mobile homes look like, what they consist of, and how they can be located on planned sites, some of the opposition embodied in zoning restrictions disappears. In areas where such bans do not exist, the development of mobile home sites is already underway.

Financing for mobile homes has until recently been excluded from the money market for housing. (One reason for the recent rapid growth of such units has been the shortage of mortgage money which has shifted prospective home buyers into the mobile home market.) In the summer and fall of 1969 regulations and legislation were modified to allow savings and loan associations to finance mobile homes, and to provide FHA guarantee of mortgages. Such moves recognize the units as a new type of permanent housing; and it may very well be the technological breakthrough that reduces much of the housing shortage.

Aside from technology, some of the institutional surroundings of housing have also been subject to change. Allowing welfare families to purchase multi-family homes frequently solves the housing problem for large families, and sometimes at lower costs to society. Building housing on scattered land parcels owned by the city can increase supply without the delays and dislocations of large-scale housing projects. Changing housing patterns, so that middle or upper-income areas will include low-income families, has been proposed in a variety of ways.

At present, public housing can be rented only by families at certain income levels: if their income rises, the family may no longer be eligible to stay in the housing provided. In several areas this policy is beginning to arouse protest, prompting the alternative suggestion that, if family income rises beyond the limits of eligibility, the tenant be allowed to remain and contribute either the full cost of the rent or some fraction, perhaps 25 per cent, of family income in payment for housing. Tenants argue that they don't wish to leave friends and neighbors, that a mixture of occupational and social characteristics of families benefits everyone, and that housing maintenance and upkeep can be improved if some residents earn more than minimum income. In short, there may be gains from diversity.

Diversity may also be the aim of legislation that nullifies local zoning restrictions, in carefully defined situations, that have prevented public housing or low-income housing developments in suburban areas. The President's Committee on Urban Housing recommends that the federal government should have the power to "preempt local zoning ordinances which exclude the development of subsidized housing." In 1969, state legislation to this effect (called antisnob zoning) was passed in Massachusetts, but at this writing no action had been taken. If such housing is not to create pocket ghettos in suburban areas, both local authorities and developers will need to plan very carefully. Putting low-income families in high-income areas may succeed in giving people shelter; but unless there are transportation, shops, schools, and employment available, these families may not be any more able to escape their low-income class.

The weakness of these programs—for new technology, for new institutions, for new legislation—in dealing with ghetto housing is that they are all merely permissive. They allow change to be made, but change is not inevitable or immediate. Like the laws forbidding discrimination in housing (or segregation in schools), these programs merely set the stage for action. In themselves, they have not moved many ghetto dwellers out of their substandard housing.

POSITIVE ACTION

The difference between permissive and positive action should be clear. During the 1930's, the local city government set the stage for action on housing when the Metropolitan Life Insurance Company built Stuyvesant Town in New York City. The government condemned land, turned over public streets, and provided tax exemptions for a period of years, which encouraged the company to add to the housing supply. The city also permitted the company full discretion in the selection of tenants. The company took the positive action, building and leasing housing units of the project, providing no schools or playgrounds, and restricting the tenants to white families. (In 1943, the Chairman of the Board, Frederick Ecker, was quoted as saying "Negroes and whites don't mix. A hundred years from now they might.") Stuyvesant Town combined a public subsidy to housing with private enterprise in housing.

Twenty-five years later, the government has reset the stage for action. Antidiscrimination legislation, city planning, and government appropriations mean that a similar action would not occur today. But what does occur still depends, like the

Stuyvesant Town of the 1930's, on positive action and, to a considerable extent, private enterprise with the emphasis on enterprise. To quote one authority, "stable racially inclusive housing patterns do not occur through law or by chance. They result from motivation, imaginative planning, and painstaking management."[20]

Various types of innovators along these lines have recently appeared. One is the private foundation, established in a few white suburban communities, which not only helps nonwhites find housing but which also buys and builds housing for sale or rent to families looking for a way out of the ghetto. The second is the college or university that develops low-cost housing on its own land or in its neighborhood, which frequently consists of a slum or racial ghetto. The third is the real estate investment trust, which buys and operates rental property on a profit-making business, but which introduces integrated housing into a previously all-white area. These are all forms of private enterprise which widen the market for housing and offer more economic choice to the ghetto resident. A strong argument exists for encouraging such private enterprise among black people themselves, as voiced, for example, by the president of the National Business League[21]:

> At this crucial point in history, you must not build a system to subsidize General Motors to come into low-income housing business and ignore the alternative we present to you of stimulating minority-owned business. . . . We have the architects, the engineers, the planners, the builders, and the labor force to do the job that has to be done. These men and women have the same or superior formal education backgrounds as have their white contemporaries. They don't have any money. . . . If the government of the United States is going to guarantee the security of the white builders' projects, guarantee him a profit on his effort, pay him to train the local population to work for him and guarantee him a market, then for the sake of peace, Let Us Do It Ourselves!

CONCLUSIONS

In both housing and education, the existing methods of

production have proved exceedingly costly: we have a housing shortage and substantial numbers of uneducated people. Nonetheless, public policy for housing consists largely of giving subsidies to the existing housing industry, although innovations in both technology and marketing may be needed to solve the housing shortage for ghetto residents. The programs for public education lack a definition of output, while allowing the proliferation of management. But in both cases, public policy also requires removing the barriers of segregation and discrimination. These, in themselves, have costs which must finally be recognized.

CHAPTER TEN

THE GHETTO ECONOMY

LOOKING AT the economics *of* the ghetto leads finally to the question, "*Is* the ghetto an economy?" Should programs to remedy conditions in the ghetto be designed in terms of a separate entity, an area ripe for economic development? What does "an economy" consist of?

While in some contexts it may be helpful to speak of "the computer economy," "the twentieth-century economy," or "the market economy," in most cases we use the term for an identifiable area, defined geographically and in some sense politically, like "the New England economy" or the "eighteenth-century French economy." This usage also hints that "an economy" is viable: we don't refer to the "suburban economy" or "the high school economy," because these are so clearly only parts of a larger framework. In what sense, therefore, can we speak of "the ghetto economy?"

PROTECTION AND FREE TRADE

Although any area contains economic resources that consist of the people who live there (actually their abilities and productive potential) plus whatever capital assets (including land) they own, not every area, and particularly not a ghetto area, can be self-sufficient. The income earned by people depends on how their resources are used, and ghetto residents have been limited in opportunities to use their abilities or their enterprise. But simple application of economic analysis—in this case, of a theory developed to explain international trade—shows that the road to increased productivity and income within the ghetto does not lie in developing separate ghetto economies. Rather, it means breaking down the barriers between the ghetto and the larger economic framework within which it operates. People on both sides of the invisible ghetto wall must opt for free trade rather than protection.

This conclusion needs spelling out, because it is so frequently misunderstood. Take, for example, this quotation from Malcolm X:

> Our economic philosophy of Black Nationalism means that instead of our spending the rest of our lives begging the white man for a job, our people should be reeducated to the science of economics and the part that it plays in our community. We should be taught just the basic fundamentals: that whenever you take money out of the neighborhood and spend it in another neighborhood, the neighborhood in which you spend it gets richer and richer, and the neighborhood from which you take it gets poorer and poorer. This creates a ghetto, as now exists in every so-called Negro community in this country. If the Negro isn't spending his money downtown with what we call "the man," "the man" is himself right in the Negro community. All the stores are run by the white man, who takes the money out of the community as soon as the sun sets. We have to teach our people the importance of where to spend their dollars and the importance of establishing and owning businesses. Thereby we can create employment for ourselves, instead of having to wait to boycott your stores and businesses to demand that you give us a job. Whenever the majority of our people begin to think along such lines, you'll find that we ourselves can best solve our problems. Instead of having to wait for someone to come out of your neighborhood into our neighborhood to tackle these problems for us, we ourselves may solve them.[1]

These words echo those of thirty years earlier, recorded by Drake and Cayton in their classic study of Chicago[2]:

> "No community can hope to thrive," insists one newspaper editor, "where people come from other communities and operate businesses in this community, and at the close of the day you see the money taken out of the neighborhood never to return, except in the form of some more second- or third-grade goods to take the rest of the Negro's money." The Baptist minister . . . commented bitterly: "The Negro in Chicago spends billions on merchandise. All of that money goes into the white man's pocket and then out of our neighborhoods. It is used to buy white men cars and homes, and their wives mink coats and servants. Our money is being used by the white man to pay us for being his cook, his valet, and his washwoman."

In its most extreme form, the dream of controlling the Negro market visualizes a complete separate Negro economy: "The idea is to be able to support ourselves instead of being wholly dependent on the white race."

Aside from the very powerful impact of these words, what is the economic validity of this reasoning? To what extent should black people (or anyone else) be taught that "whenever you take money out of the neighborhood and spend it in another neighborhood, the neighborhood in which you spend it gets richer and richer, and the neighborhood from which you take it gets poorer and poorer?"

These ideas trace back not merely thirty years but more than three hundred, to the sixteenth- and seventeenth-century mercantilists who were arguing for self-sufficient nations instead of neighborhoods, but who used much the same words about getting richer and poorer. Englishmen argued that spending money on French textiles made the French richer and the English poorer; Frenchmen argued that spending money on Spanish lace made the Spanish rich and the French poorer; so the English should try to build up a textile industry at home and the French a domestic lace industry to keep the money from going out of their countries. Another goal of the mercantilists, a favorable balance of trade or an excess of exports over imports, could be stated in the same terms: if the English sent more wool to France, then they could buy French textiles, but the balance must be in England's "favor" so as not to send money to France. (The French, of course, would argue exactly along the same lines.)

But the idea that there is something favorable about such a "favorable" balance of trade—an excess of exports over imports, or a situation where money is not being taken out of the country—can be easily disposed of by anyone with an elementary knowledge of economics sufficient to distinguish money from economic resources. Since nobody can eat money, or wear it, or live in it, economic policies that bring *money* into the country bring no real advantage, in terms of either productive resources or desirable goods and helpful services. Since both businessmen and consumers gain from an increase in the *supply of goods and services,* then an excess of exports over imports means that the country is poorer, not richer, for it is sending abroad some of the abundance of its production without an equal return of tangible goods or useful services. Consequently, the notion that "money leaving the country" leads to economic impoverishment proves to be quite fallacious.

Does this conclusion hold for other economic areas? If it is true that a nation loses more *real* income from an unfavorable balance of trade than a favorable one, is it equally true for Bedford-Stuyvesant? or Watts? or any ghetto area? The argument that you should spend money "at home" to prevent your neighborhood from getting poorer and poorer occurs over a wide spectrum of political and social attitudes. Malcolm X's interpretation resembles another statement from quite a different source. Advertisements in many local newspapers, paid for by local business (usually retailers and service firms or the chamber of commerce), use the same arguments.

One example (a full-page spread) reads:

> Practically everything we buy in our home community stores is a Bargain. It's a Natural Law of Economics . . . that the costs of community building and operating must be included in the prices we pay. And if that part of our money goes to build and operate somebody else's community instead of ours, it's no Bargain. . . . It pays to buy where you live. . . . Trade at Home where your money benefits you.[3]

This statement refers to the "natural Law of Economics" (note the capital letters) and Malcolm X referred to the "basic fundamentals," but clearly they agree on the importance of keeping money in the neighborhood.

But the mercantilist argument applied to communities is, if anything, more fallacious than when it purports to explain international economics. If people in a suburb support their local stores—if they trade at home as this advertisement urges —in what sense do they benefit? If they can obtain goods or services at lower prices elsewhere than *in* the community, then their real income is *reduced* by trading at home. If residents in one suburb can choose from a wider variety or receive more skilled services from outlets in neighboring suburbs, or in the central city, or in a far-distant metropolis, then buying in the "home community" is no bargain.

The answer to Malcolm X's proposal—"We have to teach our people the importance of where to spend their dollars"—was voiced decades ago, by black people themselves in response to attempts to build up black businesses. Drake and Cayton explain the failure of this movement in Chicago and emphasize that what people buy, for a given price, includes quality and service:

> Over and over, Negroes in Bronzeville reveal a conflict between the economic imperative of "making ends meet" and the social demands of "race pride." They insist that Negro merchants cannot give equivalent goods and services for the same price:

> "I'd like to do all my shopping—what little I do—with colored, but I can get things cheaper at the chain stores. I buy there for that reason. . . ."

> "My real friend is a dollar. I try to patronize my people, but when it comes to saving a penny, especially at this time, I do so, even if I have to buy from whites. . . ."

> "I try to spend as much as I can with Negro stores, but most of them don't have what you want, or they are too high. . . ."

"The Negro must learn to be independent and have the same type of goods the white man has for the same price. The Negro should not be expected to trade with another Negro because he is a black man. People of any race should have some respect for their people, but any people naturally want to get things where they can get the best bargains."[4]

And indeed, most *consumers* understand the *disadvantages* of a so-called "favorable" balance of trade and tend to ignore the special pleading of local businessmen.

Free trade increases rather than decreases the welfare of people, and this is true within a country as much as between nations. Indeed, the generally high levels of production and income attained by the United States reflect, at least partly, the enormous market within which free trade exists. The European Common Market and other regional economic associations attempt to secure such benefits of free trade for inhabitants who do not wish to keep their money at home—either in the locality or in the country of their residence. Only if the local tradesman is more efficient, and efficient in the real sense of providing the same goods or services at *lower* prices or providing *more* goods and services at the same prices, will local support or local buying be justified to the consumer.

Business exists, however, not only for its customers but for its employees, and the drive to support local business, or to build up ghetto firms, also aims to provide employment. Malcolm X and the speakers living in Black Metropolis refer specifically to employment as a part of community development, and this meaning is implicit in the advertisement quoted, as it was also a goal of mercantilist economics. Creating a favorable balance of trade (an excess of exports over imports) might impoverish consumers within a country by denying them access to cheaper imports, but in another way it might enrich them by ensuring employment in the expanding export industries. (Just as military spending provides jobs and incomes to workers but not products or services for consumers to buy, so export industries can offer jobs and income, but not products or services for domestic consumers to buy.) If this led to higher incomes from more work, the net effect might indeed be "favorable."

In a brilliant appendix to his *General Theory,* John Maynard Keynes restated mercantilism from this point of view, to show that self-sufficiency policies might be developed not to prevent "money leaving the country" but to provide jobs. Another example, it can be argued, was the United States' postwar policy of supplying massive amounts of foreign aid to finance a "favorable" balance of trade which helped maintain income and employment at home while shipping goods abroad.

This method of expanding income and production (creating a favorable balance of trade) is, however, available only to nations, not to communities within a nation, precisely because it requires control over the system of money and banking that finances transactions. This proviso is important because the notion of the ghetto as an economic entity appears frequently, not only as a figure of speech but in programs for community development that refer to "exports from ghetto industries," or to "the multiplier effect" from expanded employment. Such phrases originate in economic analysis but omit any reference to the financial transactions required.

It is possible, of course, to draw up balance of payments statements for regions *within* countries, and to show that what one area produces, another consumes. Thus, the Pacific Coast "exports" aircraft to buyers in the rest of the country, while obtaining textiles (for its garment industries) from the South, education and research (for its technical industries) from the Northeast, beef and pork from the interior, and so on. Of course, what actually happens is that the firms and consumers of the Pacific Coast transact such business, and their payments to other parties in the country can be calculated along with the payments *from* other firms and consumers for aircraft, sports clothing, films, and the other goods and services produced in Pacific Coast industries. If these payments do not precisely balance, business and consumers must have some means of settling the difference: perhaps by using past savings, perhaps by borrowing on a short-term or long-term basis, perhaps by sending or receiving gifts and donations. Drawing up such a balance of payments statement for ghetto areas vis à vis the rest of the economy might reveal an unfavorable balance of trade for the ghetto: that is, people there may consume more than their current earnings.

Certainly one large item on the statement would be transfers, income paid to welfare recipients in the ghetto but earned by taxpayers there and elsewhere. Indeed the goal of community development, of making the ghetto self-sufficient, is to replace such welfare "handouts" and the meagre consumption levels they allow with earned income (wages and salaries) from productive jobs. But merely "trading at home" will not build a community, nor will spending dollars in the neighborhood establish business or expand employment in the neighborhood.

First, the market in ghetto areas is limited to begin with: poor people live there, and a business that gets all that poor people have to spend may have lower sales than one getting only a part of what richer people spend. Second, unless the firm is efficient it cannot capture all of the spending in its limited market, for consumers will be well aware of competitive offerings elsewhere. Finally, even if the total spending of ghetto inhabitants were concentrated on ghetto business, such firms could not grow and provide more employment than the minimum required for a limited market, unless they were both efficient and profitable. Business profits can be a source of capital, and for a business to expand requires both capital and manpower. The firm whose sales double so that it needs additional employees also needs additional inventory and more equipment to handle it. To open up new jobs requires investing new capital, for the American economy typically uses men with machines, manpower with capital.

Those who expect ghetto-owned businesses to create ghetto employment assume that such business will be profitable, and that they will thereby accumulate the capital to invest in expanded production or new jobs. What both Malcolm X and other proponents of black-owned and operated business leave unexpressed is this notion of business profits as a source of capital. When they refer to the white man "taking the money out of the community," they use "money" to mean "profits." When they speak of "all of that money going into the white man's pocket," they object to the white man's earning *profits* in the black community and disposing of these profits by investing in the white community. For they see clearly that it takes investment to create jobs and employment, and they also realize that business profits can add to the funds for investment.

But it is not true that all business is profitable, nor that all business profits are available for investment. Nor is it true that all ghetto business is profitable, nor that if ghetto businesses were owned by ghetto residents, that, in and of itself, would make the business profitable. To expect profits generated by ghetto business to yield significant amounts of investment capital is to ignore all the economic facts of ghetto life—primarily, the facts of poverty and of a limited market.

Empirical data support this analytical conclusion. A study of Puerto Rico during the 1950's revealed not only poverty but a proliferation of retail and service establishments that provided employment but little or no income to the workers. This form of disguised unemployment, or underemployment, also appears in other sectors like agriculture, and in other underdeveloped countries; it is evident that employment and entrepreneurship does not necessarily mean an end to poverty.[5] Quite parallel to these findings, a recent analysis estimated unemployment rates among residents of inner city ghetto areas at about twice the urban average, but *underemployment* rates from eight to ten times as high.[6] Not all of this represents the part-time or sporadic work discussed earlier,* for it also includes employment in marginal business, where sales are low and costs are high, which leaves little income for either the owner or his employees. Investigations of ghetto retailing reveal the prevalence of small, inefficient stores whose high prices do not yield high profits**; at least one market research analysis suggests that the number of ghetto establishments should be thinned out rather than increased.[7] Finally, almost three-quarters of the businesses presently owned by black people "operate within the strict confinement of their own community,"[8] and have been unable to add substantially to a self-contained economic development.

*Cf. Chapter Five, p. 108.
**Cf. Chapter Six, pp. 139, 143.

This last statistic, however, prefaces the valid complaint about ghetto business: if 73 per cent of black business operates within the black community, 80 per cent of the business volume in the black community is controlled by whites. And although these estimates also mean that one-quarter of black business operates within *white* markets, the overall volume makes up a very small amount—less than three per cent of all American industry, and less than one per cent of the manufacturing sector where most of the jobs (and most of the productive, high-income jobs) are found. The drive to establish business as a source of employment opportunities, therefore, makes economic sense to minority groups who want more control over the jobs available to them. It also means a demand for specific jobs—the managerial and executive positions that go along with owning and operating business, and that to date seem almost totally closed to blacks or other minorities. From this point of view, the notion of a ghetto economy as a self-contained unit must be reexamined.

Part of the drive toward community development or Black Nationalism stems from the realization that a ghetto is, to some extent, a self-contained economy, whether this makes economic sense or not. Barriers to trade exist: if ghetto consumers can import goods produced elsewhere, ghetto businessmen cannot readily import capital, and ghetto workers find that their exports of labor are restricted. Such barriers make production less efficient and everyone on *both* sides of the ghetto walls worse off, but they cannot be removed by those who live in the ghetto. If the theory of international trade casts considerable doubt on the maxim that spending one's money at home is a good idea, it also suggests that working or investing at home are not useful procedures either. If ghetto consumers recognize that they can sometimes get more for their money by trading outside the area, nonghetto employers and investors should recognize that trade is a two-way street and that ghetto consumers would have even more to spend if they had higher incomes that include dividends or profits from business enterprise. Programs to increase the number of minority-owned business enterprises are, in effect, efforts to promote the flow of capital in new directions, just as efforts to expand and upgrade employment among minority groups consist of programs that widen the market for labor.*

TRADE BARRIERS TO MANAGEMENT

If opening new employment opportunities takes capital because capital and manpower work together in American industry, opening new businesses takes not only capital but management—specifically, managerial skills. To establish a business requires two sorts of know-how. The first consists of competence in the particular field, whether it is servicing appliances, running a restaurant, making children's toys for gift shops, or filling special orders for laboratory equipment. Either the employer or his workers must be familiar with production techniques and with the means of marketing the final product. An incompetent repairman, a lackadaisical counterman, or a careless shop worker will waste materials, alienate customers, and will cost more than he brings the firm in sales. But a trained serviceman who gets no calls, a lunchroom invisible to the passerby, manufactured products priced too high to sell or too low to cover costs will bankrupt the business just as surely, so the second type of competence, which is more obviously located in the manager's office, has to do with knowing how to run a business. Part of the barrier between the would-be minority entrepreneur and the sources of capital lies in his inexperience with business management. (In this he is not alone: the failure rate of new business enterprises is extremely high because more people than have the requisite combination of skills want to go into business for themselves.)

But barriers also exist for the minority businessman who wants to obtain these skills. Many new businesses result from established firms. Sometimes a product line or market area or other project expands out of proportion to the rest of the business and becomes a separate entity, organized with a good deal of autonomy within a corporate structure or set up as a subsidiary with even more independence. More frequently a dissatisfied employee strikes out on his own, with or without other members from the "founding" firm. (Possibly the dissatisfaction consists merely of not owning the business.) In

*Cf. Chapter Eight, pp. 175–81.

either case, the new entrepreneurs possess business experience which they gained as employees of established firms. Their knowledge of management (which may be insufficient but consists of more than casual acquaintance) stems from their having occupied executive positions, or from having carried some share of authority and responsibility. And these are precisely the sorts of jobs which are not open to all comers: minority group members rarely if ever hold such management positions. So the would-be ghetto entrepreneur may lack access to capital because he has been denied access to the employment that would give him the skills to manage capital.

Two kinds of programs exist to remedy this lack. One encourages able young people to enter graduate schools of business management, and the other encourages ambitious businessmen, who want to expand their existing firms or start their own, to seek advice from consulting centers. The first can take effect only over the long run and will also require sustained effort, on the part of existing business, to hire and promote these newly trained executives. The second includes agencies set up by local and federal governments, community and business organizations, academic institutions, and other ad hoc efforts. They supply an essential economic resource—knowledge and know-how—but there are barriers to its free movement into the ghetto.

To minority groups, owning a business means more than merely occupying a managerial or executive position: the symbolic value of entrepreneurship, representing independence, is very high. To accept counseling about how to manage one's own business can easily appear to limit this independence, and specific advice to slow down or cut back on a business venture can readily be interpreted as denying independence. The needed technical knowledge can be lost in a cloud of suspicion on one side or condescension on the other. The disgruntled black businessman can be quoted: "No matter how far a black person goes, no matter how good we are, there's a limit you (whites) put on us,"[9] while the frustrated consultant maintains, "Their initial picture of the company was rather grandiose."[10] And probably both might find the following an understatement: Tony Pickman, a white suburbanite who runs a 100-volunteer "skills pool" for the aid of Roxbury businessmen has observed, "There's a problem of confidence. . . . Our biggest difficulty is that the black man doesn't necessarily want to do what the white man tells him." [11] Transactions can rarely be completed where confidence, on either side, is lacking; if information and technical assistance does not, in fact, flow to minority businessmen, the origins of the barriers should concern us less than the means to remove them.

Some observers point out that franchising allows such a flow of technical assistance; for example, Federal Trade Commissioner Mary Gardiner Jones states:

> The biggest disadvantage of being small is the inability to absorb error or to ride out even relatively short periods of adversity. The franchise relationship, offering as it can and usually does the continuing guidance, counselling, and expertise of the larger more experienced franchisor, constitutes at least a partial answer to this fact of life for the developing small entrepreneur.
>
> Thus franchising can be used as a means for existing national businesses to expand into ghetto areas, or as a means of developing new minority businesses in ghetto areas. It can also be looked at as a potentially effective means for ghetto residents to gain practical business and entrepreneurial experience either inside or outside ghetto areas. Finally, it can be a tool to enable small minority entrepreneurships starting perhaps from an inner city base to expand their own operations through a franchise operation of their own.[12]

A business representative, Al Lapin, Jr., says:

> Franchising provides the most rapid, viable, and proven means of creating successful small business opportunities. The potential to dramatically increase the number of minority business owners is great. . . .
>
> Franchising also serves as a vehicle for creating new jobs at the franchise level. In the restaurants, we train and employ cooks. In the automobile repair shops, we train and employ mechanics. In the apparel stores, we train and hire salespeople. . . . As these employees develop their skills to an efficient and productive level and recognize

the benefits of the franchise system, they can and do become outstanding prospects for ownership of their *own* franchise operations. . . . As franchisors we can generate a vast array of new small business ownership opportunities. Our new minority franchises, in turn, can offer countless opportunities for positions of skill and responsibility for minority employees through the training apparatus of the franchise system. . . .[13]

TRADE BARRIERS TO CAPITAL

Any business venture also requires a capital investment, and programs for stepping up the flow of capital to would-be ghetto entrepreneurs include efforts by the Small Business Administration, by various pools of investment funds controlled by banks and financial intermediaries (insurance companies, pension plans, and other institutions which funnel people's savings to the business users of capital), by established business enterprise, and by new forms of enterprise that include banks or development corporations owned and managed by minority groups or local communities. There seems to be general agreement that existing arrangements for collecting and channeling investment funds will not succeed as purveyors of capital to the ghetto without fundamental changes.

Despite a variety of political promises for new efforts, the federal government acts chiefly through the Small Business Administration, which can make loans or guarantee loans for commercial banks to make. Until a very few years ago the SBA record for helping minority entrepreneurs was abysmal: with a change in procedures and staff, it is now criticized for delay and penny-pinching. In an economy where rising prices and monetary stringency make investment delays more costly each day, these are both harsh strictures.

The primary source of capital or investable funds, however, is not the government but the private financial structure, and it has been criticized even more severely. Conventional standards for assessing risks shut out many, for the financial community has long since abandoned J. P. Morgan's principle of relying on a man's character rather than his references. Instead:

We make black men loans when they make sense—when

there is a reasonable assurance that the money will be paid
back. In making our decisions, we use a business' past
performance, or in the case of a new company, our pro-
jection of its cash flow.[14]

In some cases, the conventional standards exclude entire areas:

He turned to commercial banks for a loan, Mr. Bailey
recalled, but was repeatedly rejected without an explanation, "usually after I told them the place was in Bedford-
Stuyvesant." This is the slum-ridden section of Brooklyn
regularly shunned by businessmen as a place to invest.

"It's the system, that's all," Mr. Bailey said recently of
his rebuffs without a trace of bitterness.[15]

Some signs exist that "the system" is changing, and that
bankers can no longer use customary standards in evaluating
requests for funds. "Perhaps in years past it was permissible or
acceptable under the 'prudence' theory to turn the corporate
back on the requirements of urban society, but such is not the
case today."[16] Ironically, the change may mean reverting to
J. P. Morgan's criterion, as one bank official explained, "It's
usually more important to get to know the man rather than
investigate his background."[17] But in the case of ghetto businessmen, "knowing the man" may require technical assistance
from ghetto residents. "Some banks are inviting minority group
members to join their boards of directors or to sit on advisory
boards for branches located in areas populated primarily by
minority groups. . . . Such representation may be a promising
vehicle to enable the banks to reach out to minority groups in
the urban ghettos."[18]

In other cases, changing the system means establishing new
channels for capital flow. The suggestion of Federal Reserve
Board Governor Brimmer that commercial banks be authorized
"to meet a larger share of the equity capital needs in urban
areas . . . via means similar to those which they can now use
abroad"[19] has not yet been turned into legislation, but other
innovations already exist. In some localities, bankers have
worked out various cooperative arrangements to provide
mortgage financing or venture capital on unconventional
terms.[20] In others, newly formed corporations mingle funds
obtained from government grants, private contributions, and

financial investors to shift capital from the largely white business community to the largely black ghetto community.[21] For some of these, equity has been reserved to local supporters of a new ghetto business by selling stock priced within the reach of small savers. Thus, in St. Louis, Central City Foods, Inc. raised equity capital for a supermarket by selling 20,000 shares at $10 apiece to people in the ghetto area who would be customers, while mortgage and working capital funds came from two banks and an insurance company. In Venice, California, a conglomerate obtained capital for expansion by placing preferred stock with corporate, institutional, and private investors and by offering common stock at $2.00 a share. In Roxbury, Massachusetts, one firm planned to sell voting stock only in the ghetto community, while another obtained permission to sell shares on the installment plan to put ownership within reach of low-income families.

Some banks have been set up in this way, and the number of black-owned banks grew rapidly during the late 1960's. Of twenty such banks in existence in 1967, half were less than five years old (and the other half were over twenty years old). Ten banks planned to open in 1968–69. The record of these banks, however, shows high operating costs and losses on loans, suggesting again that the notion of a self-contained ghetto has grave weaknesses:

> Obviously, the difficulties do not spring from the fact that the banks are owned and operated by Negroes. Rather, the problems seem to arise partly from the fact that the market for their services is circumscribed by the general conditions in the ghetto—high unemployment, low incomes, a low rate of savings, and the marginal character of local business. But these obstacles are reinforced by the severe shortage of trained management personnel.[22]

Nor does black ownership necessarily equip a bank with large amounts of loanable funds. More effective are corporate efforts to maintain sizeable deposits in black-owned banks; for example, the Chrysler Corporation offered to set aside $100,000 monthly in each of three Negro banks, and Olin Mathieson formed a plan to deposit $600,000 of its payroll tax deductions at six banks and $400,000 of its working capital at six others.

These sums will have a significant impact, for the average deposits of Negro-owned banks totalled only $8.6 million (1967).

It is worth stressing the scope for innovation here; some of these new arrangements must seem as strange to established business as federally insured mortgages must have appeared, during the 1930's, or Euro-dollars in the 1950's. Yet even though technical innovations can link ghetto resources with the rest of the economy, they will not be implemented without some motivation. What incentives exist to break down the existing barriers to allow the links to be established?

THE ECONOMICS OF DISCRIMINATION

Most of the barriers which maintain the ghetto in economic isolation are due to racial and ethnic discrimination. Most people associate the term "discrimination" with prejudice and both with ethical or emotional judgments. But discrimination can also be a topic for economic analysis, highly dependent on the work of Gary Becker.[23]

We recall that people play economic roles in two markets and that their personal choices depend on income, tastes and preferences, and market prices. We offer labor in the market for productive services,* depending on our liking for leisure instead of work, or for real income over leisure; and we choose goods and services in the final market, depending on our preferences or tastes or likes and dislikes of the things for sale. The *origins* of tastes and preferences may be safely left to psychologists or sociologists, but if their *result* is economic or social discrimination, then it concerns all of us. How do we distinguish harmful discrimination and its economic effects from the consumer's freedom to choose what he likes and doesn't like? What is the economic process of discrimination?

Any consumer may have a strong *preference* for ripe olives over green olives, and when he is shown two bottles of olives, one ripe and one green, the consumer may also exhibit *prejudice,* a predetermined bias in favor of ripe olives, if he refuses even to taste the green. The impact of such likes and dislikes on total market demand depends on the number of such consumers and their market power: those who dislike green olives

*Cf. pp. 82, 103, 175.

may be matched by consumers who dislike ripe olives. Furthermore, since processors can make either green or ripe olives, society will deem it unnecessary to protect either industry or consumers from the effects of preference or prejudice.

There can be, however, a taste for discrimination itself with serious economic effects. Gary Becker reminds us that the antithesis of discrimination is nepotism, and if today's social concern is with discrimination *against* an individual or group, tomorrow's may be with discrimination *for*. The usual charge of nepotism refers to individuals—the boss appointing his son to a vice-presidency or the governor appointing his brother to a state commission—but nepotism, or reverse discrimination, can also apply to groups of people, like the veteran's preference in some civil service systems. Illustrating the symmetrical relation between nepotism and discrimination, the quota system, used for years to keep people out, is now being advocated as an effective method of getting people in.

Any economic impact of discrimination requires the individual or economic unit involved to act *as if* he were willing to pay for fulfilling his taste for discrimination. For example, the consumer who effectively discriminates in favor of ripe olives must be willing to pay a premium over the money costs of producing the olives. (The extra sum does not reward any productive factor used in making and selling the olives.) The worker who effectively discriminates against black people must be willing to accept a lower wage than would otherwise be offered to elicit his labor. The employer who discriminates against women must be willing to pay a higher wage to men than would otherwise prevail.

This analysis specifies that the discriminating person must behave *as if* he were willing to pay for satisfying his taste in discrimination; whether or not he actually does so is a separate matter. (The reader may *be willing* to pay $5.00 per pound for fresh lobster, but the market price, which may not be $5.00, determines what he *must* pay for fresh lobster.) Discrimination may stem either from an acquired taste or from ignorance. For example, the white worker, informed that management has plans for hiring blacks, may believe that he will suffer an economic loss because black workers, being less productive, will only slow down the assembly line and reduce his chances of a bonus. If this belief proves false, and black workers demonstrate equal productivity, the white employee may or may not continue to discriminate, that is, be willing to forfeit some wages rather than accept the presence of blacks. If removing ignorance does not dispel discrimination, then it represents a fundamental taste or preference.

The distinction between ignorance and taste bears on the argument that education can get rid of discrimination by wiping out racial prejudice, which so frequently meets the rebuttal that "you can't legislate human nature." Information which may do away with ignorance cannot be provided without *cost;* that is, it entails using economic resources of materials and manpower either in basic education or in publicizing specific facts about a specific situation.

On the other hand, there is nothing inherently inadmissible in the taste for discrimination. There is no economic reason why people should not satisfy their tastes, as long as they are willing to pay for the costs involved. This analysis applies to private clubs with segregated facilities whether their exclusiveness represents WASP clubs or all-black Afro-American societies. Any of these can be a means of satisfying personal tastes for associating with a particular group, and as long as the costs of satisfying such tastes are borne by the members of the group and not shifted in any way to nonmembers, there is no economic question of equity. It should be possible for any private organization to restrict its membership to white people, or black people, or cross-eyed people. In recent years, various public persons have resigned in protest from private organizations that discriminate against black people, but this probably reflects the fact that having a taste for discrimination, these days, may involve other costs such as social disapproval if the taste becomes widely known. It is like the practice of homosexuality between two consenting adults, which is not a matter of *public* morality nor social legislation. The costs of publicly announcing such a practice, however, are at the moment considerable.

Our *social* concern with discrimination arises because the costs of discriminating have not been paid at the source, but have in fact been shifted to those who are discriminated against. Inequity arises when people who may be *willing* to take lower wages rather than work among black colleagues do not have to, because they have shifted the cost to others, particularly to black workers. Inequity exists if whites who would in fact pay higher prices to live in a segregated community need *not* pay a premium for satisfying this taste, because nonmarket methods of harassment or persecution keep the neighborhood white, and the costs fall on families living in the segregated ghettos. If each person paid the full economic cost of satisfying his own personal tastes, most of the evils we associate with "discrimination *against*" would disappear, or be reduced to the same scale of evil we apply to lesser social prejudices like those against pantsuits or plastic flowers. It is because costs are shifted that inequity occurs; and it is up to the economist to delineate the nature of such costs, if he cannot precisely estimate their magnitude.

Most civil rights legislation has its economic rationale in this phenomenon of shifting costs: the 1954 Supreme Court decision on segregated schools is a case in point. That decision said, in effect, that black children were paying the costs of satisfying the white taste for discrimination. The 1966 Survey of Equality in Educational Opportunity and later studies confirmed this interpretation with data on the inadequate school facilities available to Negroes, and on better achievement on reading and mathematical tests by Negro children who had moved to integrated schools. The survey also concluded that "improving the school of a minority pupil will increase his achievement more than will improving the school of a white child increase his."[24] But it should be recognized that not *all* the costs of segregation have been met in this way, by lowering the quality of education available to black children, for the quality of education available to white children has also been lowered by the extra costs of discrimination.

As in education, so in other areas the costs of satisfying a taste for discrimination have not, in fact, been successfully shifted. Those who discriminate, as well as those who are discriminated against, lose economic welfare as a result, and the economist's response to all suggestions for segregation, from "separate but equal" to "Black power" or a "gilded ghetto" must finally be "Do you know what it will cost?"

Let us summarize these costs, which have been dealt with throughout this book. First, the direct costs: a loss of production which exceeds that during the Great Depression and both World Wars, and a loss which continues each day.

1. Estimates of the output to be gained from using idle resources must be crude, but they may not be dismissed. If unemployment among blacks were reduced to the rate prevailing among whites in 1969, some $5 billion annually would have been added to output. Between 1968 and 1969, the number of black unemployed workers *increased* by almost 100,000: this meant an absolute loss of output during the year which exceeded by almost $1 billion that wasted during the year previous.

2. Because additional output from hitherto idle resources has a multiplier effect on the total economy, this calculation, based on average productivity and employment figures, underestimates the potential gains. Another crude estimate, based on eliminating the difference of median *income,* suggests that some $16.5 billion would be added to total income within the country, were the Negro population equally as well off as the whites. For consumer goods industries—for firms that make clothing, food, furniture, appliances—it would be the equivalent of adding several small states, or one the size of Florida or Massachusetts, to their markets. It may be argued that deliberate discrimination is not responsible for *all* the income differences, that low incomes are not entirely a matter of prejudice, but some significant part of the cost of discrimination takes this form.

3. The loss from *under*employment rather than *un*employment must be added to the shortfall of production and income estimated above. Any attempt to quantify this loss, based on present data, would give only a tenuous figure, but the facts of involuntary short-time, sporadic employment, part-time work, and employment in jobs which do not utilize available skills suggest that it is sizeable.

4. Another source of potential output exists, besides the underemployed people, in those who are undereducated owing to discrimination. The mechanic who would be a supervisor if he

had been taught more mathematics, the sweeper who could be a clerk if he knew how to read, the gas station attendant who could be a manager if he had some business training—these are examples where potential production cannot be captured by removing discrimination in employment. Nor is there any way at all to estimate the potential productivity in jobs that now exist, or in jobs that may exist, which has been lost in this way. Some of the impact of discrimination has been on physical and mental health, and this also means a loss of potential output.

5. One awesome characteristic is shared by all these types of economic loss: they are irreparable. Like the production which did not take place during the 1930's when millions of men were idle, the loss of output from discrimination in 1968, 1969, 1970 or at this very moment can never be made up. The time has passed for that production to be forthcoming. What loss do we expect for the future?

Most of society has been able to avoid many of these direct costs by allowing the persistence of poverty, among *both* blacks and whites. To some unknown extent, the burden of discrimination, insofar as it has meant fewer goods and services available, has fallen on all poor people: the elderly, those with large families, the women without husbands who support their children. But poverty has begun to submit its own bill of costs; and these, plus other indirect charges, must be added to the direct costs noted above.

1. Both present and planned systems of welfare to relieve poverty add billions of dollars to governmental budgets. The vast majority of welfare recipients cannot be self-supporting through productive employment, and for many of them this is true because of discrimination that has left them, or the heads of their families, poorly educated, disabled, or saddled with family responsibilities.

2. The present costs of medical care, which will grow as Medicaid expands, could be sharply reduced with the simple preventive medicine of providing healthy surroundings, nourishing food, and personal or household care. Again, some part of this reflects poverty in general, yet the incidence of infant mortality and disease is lower for poor white families than for

poor black families. The starkest form of discrimination appears in life expectancy: the white baby born today can expect to outlive the nonwhite by seven years.

3. So far, the costs of discrimination have been figured in terms of people, and the production or income or well-being they lose. Yet recently we have come to reckon the loss of natural resources in pollution of air and water, in the destruction of wilderness or countryside, in the erosion of coastline, and the scars of strip mining. Some of this, like yesterday's production, can never be restored; some of it can be won back. It is appropriate to couple the exploitation of our land with the exploitation of people, for both represent a type of social cost frequently shifted by those who incur the cost to others, or to the public at large. Many of these costs stem from urban crowding and the rapid development of land outside the central cities. Both these phenomena have their roots in discrimination: the definition of the ghetto with which we began speaks of people in the city, who live under conditions of involuntary segregation. Because they are confined to the city, the problems of urban congestion multiply; because the exodus of others has been so precipitate, the problems of land use proliferate. We are only beginning to recognize that such social costs exist, so the time for quantifying is still in the distance.

If no hard estimates can be cited for the total costs of discrimination, the economic burden of these costs is no less real. And if the economist dwells on production, income, the loss of output, the costs of pollution, he does so to reiterate the economic facts of life: that resources are scarce, that there are not enough men or materials in the world to make everyone comfortably well off. Not until we use what we have efficiently, by putting men and materials in the places where they can be most productive, can we devote our *entire* attention to questions of ethics, of justice, of morals. But it should not escape notice that the ethical man who refuses to discriminate because he respects the integrity of an individual person comes to the same decision as the economist.

NOTES

NOTES TO CHAPTER ONE

1. Eugene Foley, *The Achieving Ghetto* (Washington, D.C.: The National Press, 1968), p. 8.

2. Stokely Carmichael and Charles Hamilton, *Black Power* (New York: Random House, Inc., 1967), pp. 19–20.

3. J. P. Davis, ed., *op. cit.* (Englewood Cliffs, N.J.: Prentice-Hall, Inc., 1966).

4. Hearings before the Committee on Labor and Public Welfare Relating to Equal Employment Opportunities (U.S. Senate, 68th Congress, 1st Session, Washington, D.C., July and August, 1963).

5. U.S. Department of Commerce, Bureau of the Census, "Trends in Income Distribution in the United States," Technical Paper No. 8 (Washington, D.C., 1963).

6. *Rich Man Poor Man* (New York: Thomas Crowell, 1964).

7. U.S. Bureau of the Census, "Income Distribution in the United States" (Washington, D.C.: U.S. Government Printing Office, 1966).

8. Bureau of the Census, "Censuses of Population and Housing (1960)," Introduction, p. 3.

9. Kenneth E. Boulding, "Economics as a Moral Science," *American Economic Review,* LIX: 1 (March, 1967), p. 7.

10. *Ibid.,* p. 8.

11. *Report of the National Advisory Commission on Civil Disorders* (Washington, D.C.: U.S. Government Printing Office, 1968), p. 6.

12. Jacob S. Siegel, "Completeness of Coverage of the Nonwhite Population in the 1960 Census and Current Estimates, and Some Implications," in David M. Heer, ed., *Social Statistics and the City* (Cam-

bridge, Mass.: Joint Center of Urban Studies of the Massachusetts Institute of Technology and Harvard University, 1968); and also Dennis F. Johnston and James R. Wetzel, "Effect of the Census Undercount on Labor Force Estimates," *Monthly Labor Review* (March, 1969).

NOTES TO CHAPTER TWO

1. Simon Kuznets, "Economic Growth and Income Inequality," *American Economic Review,* LXV:1 (March, 1955) 1–28.
2. *Ibid.,* p. 23.
3. Robert Bremner, *From the Depths* (New York: New York University Press, 1956).
4. U.S. Department of Agriculture, Agricultural Research Service, *Household Food Consumption Survey 1965–66,* Report No. 1 (Washington, D.C.: U.S. Government Printing Office, 1968), pp. 34, 41, 44, 49.
5. Faith Clark, "Food Costs of Families," address before the American Association for the Advancement of Science, (Boston, Dec. 28, 1969), pp. 7–8.
6. Mollie Orshansky, "Counting the Poor: Another Look at the Poverty Profile," *Social Security Bulletin* (January, 1965).
7. *Idem.,* "How Poverty Is Measured," *Monthly Labor Review* (February, 1969), p. 37.

NOTES TO CHAPTER THREE

1. Charles Booth, *Life and Labour in London, 1889–1902;* B. Seebohm Rowntree and May Kendall, *How the Labourer Lives* (London: Thomas Nelson and Sons, 1913); Charles B. Spahr, *America's Working People* (New York: Longmans, Green & Co. Ltd., 1900); Robert Coit Chapin, *The Standard of Living Among Workingmen's Families in New York City* (New York: Charities Publication Committee, 1909).
2. Bureau of the Census, *Census of Population and Housing, 1960.*
3. National Conference of Charities and Correction, Cleveland, 1912, quoted in Edith Elmer Wood, *Recent Trends in American Housing* (New York: The Macmillan Company, 1931).
4. American Public Health Association Committee on the Hygiene of Housing, *Construction and Equipment of the Home* (Chicago: Public Administration Service, 1961).
5. *Report* of the National Commission on Urban Problems, (Washington, D.C., 1969), p. 9.
6. Patricia Leavey Hodge and Philip M. Hauser, *The Federal Income Tax in Relation to Housing,* Research Report No. 5, The National Commission on Urban Problems (Washington, D.C.: U.S. Government Printing Office, 1968), pp. 158–59.
7. As well as *Building the American City,* the report of the National Commission, three research reports to the commission deal with this

subject: The American Society of Planning Officials, *Problems of Zoning and Land-Use Regulation* (Washington, D.C.: Communication Service Corporation, 1968); Allen D. Manvel, *Local Land and Building Regulation* (Washington, D.C.: U.S. Government Printing Office, 1968); Raymond and May Associates, *Zoning Controversies in the Suburbs: Three Case Studies* (Washington, D.C.: U.S. Government Printing Office, 1968).

8. *Urban and Rural America: Policies for Future Growth* (Washington, D.C.: U.S. Government Printing Office, 1968).

9. For a review of research findings on the impact of housing, particularly substandard housing, on health, behavior, family, and social relationships and attitudes, see Alvin Schorr, *Slums and Social Insecurity,* Research Report No. 1, U.S. Department of Health, Education, and Welfare, Social Security Administration Division of Research and Statistics (Washington, D.C.: U.S. Government Printing Office, 1966).

10. Jane Jacobs, *The Death and Life of Great American Cities* (New York: Random House, Inc., 1961).

NOTES TO CHAPTER FOUR

1. National Commission on Urban Problems, *Building the American City* (Washington, D.C.: U.S. Government Printing Office, 1969), p. 3.

2. National Citizen's Committee for Community Relations, *Putting the Hard-Core Unemployed Into Jobs* (Washington, D.C.: U.S. Government Printing Office, 1969), p. 86.

3. Muriel Cohen, "Mattapan Faces Up to a Crisis," *Sunday Herald Traveler* (January 5, 1969).

4. Bureau of the Census, *Census of Population and Housing: 1960,* Final Report, Introduction, p. 3.

5. Cf. Monroe W. Karmin, "Polish Hill: The White Ethnic's Complaint," *The Washington Monthly* I:7 (August, 1969), 35–39.

6. Gary Becker, *Human Capital* (Princeton: Princeton University Press, 1964).

7. Alfred Marshall, *Principles of Economics,* 8th ed. (New York: The Macmillan Company, 1950), p. 564.

8. Becker, *op. cit.,* p. 101.

9. Marshall, *op. cit.,* pp. 561–2.

10. *Op. cit.,* (New York: McGraw-Hill Book Company, 1962), p. 373.

11. U.S. Department of Health, Education, and Welfare, *Toward A Social Report* (Washington, D.C.: U.S. Government Printing Office, 1969).

12. Cf. Thomas I. Ribich, *Education and Poverty* (Washington, D.C.: The Brookings Institution, 1969), p. 7. "The poor may have biases against the classroom that lead them to systematically underrate the power of education, thus implying that society should counter this

'irrationality' by greatly increasing its efforts on the education front. But it may be that the poor will not respond effectively to education unless poverty itself is ameliorated."

13. See for example, *Equality of Educational Opportunity—Summary Report* (Washington, D.C.: U.S. Department of Health, Education, and Welfare, 1966), and James G. Conant, *Slums and Suburbs* (New York: McGraw Hill, 1961).

14. William C. Knaraceous, John S. Gibson, and Thomas J. Curtin, eds., *Poverty, Education and Race Relations,* (Boston: Allyn & Bacon, Inc., 1967), p. 16.

15. Daniel Seligman, "What They Believe: A *Fortune* Survey," *Fortune* (January, 1969), p. 70.

NOTES TO CHAPTER FIVE

1. James Morgan et al., *1967 Survey of Consumer Finances* (Ann Arbor: Institute for Social Research, 1968) pp. 13–14.

2. Dorothy S. Projector and Gertrude S. Weiss, *Financial Characteristics of Consumers* (Washington, D.C.: Board of Governors of Federal Reserve System, 1966), pp. 14, 151.

3. *Ibid.,* p. 41.

4. A. W. Phillips, "The Relation Between Unemployment and the Rate of Change in Money Wage Rates in the United Kingdom, 1862–1957," *Economica* (November, 1958), 283–99.

5. Dorothy K. Newman, "The Decentralization of Jobs," *Monthly Labor Review* (May, 1967).

6. National Committee Against Discrimination in Housing, *The Impact of Housing Patterns on Job Opportunities* (New York: NCADH, 1968), p. 5.

7. Richard W. Epps, "Suburban Jobs and Black Workers," *Business Review* (Philadelphia Federal Reserve Bank, October, 1969) pp. 3–5.

8. National Committee Against Discrimination in Housing, *op. cit.,* pp. 26–7.

9. Cf. Joseph D. Mooney, "Urban Poverty and Labor Force Participation," *American Economic Review,* LVII: 1 (March, 1967), 104–119.

10. Paul O. Flaim, "Persons Not in the Labor Force," *Monthly Labor Review,* 92:7 (July, 1969) p. 11.

11. These and other data can be found in the Department of Labor publication, *Negro Women . . . in the Population and in the Labor Force* (Washington, D.C.: U.S. Government Printing Office, 1968).

12. Seth Low and Pearl G. Spindler, *Child Care Arrangements of Working Mothers in the United States,* U.S. HEW and USDL, Children's Bureau Publication Number 461–1968 (Washington, D.C.: U.S. Government Printing Office, 1968).

13. *Ibid.,* p. 9.

14. Hearings before the Subcommittee on Fiscal Policy of the Joint Economic Committee, *Income and Maintenance Programs,* Congress

of the United States, 90th Congress, 2nd Session (June 11 to 27, 1968), Vol. I: *Proceedings*, p. 77.

15. Herbert Hill, "The Racial Practices of Organized Labor," in Arthur Ross, ed., *Employment, Race, and Poverty* (New York: Harcourt, Brace & Company, 1967); and Ray Marshall, *The Negro Worker* (New York: Random House, Inc., 1967).

NOTES TO CHAPTER SIX

1. Parke D. Gibson, *The $30 Billion Negro* (Toronto: The Macmillan Company, 1969), p. 80. The book contains some provocative examples of reliable research findings.

2. Bronson E. Sawyer, "An Examination of Race as a Factor in Negro-white Consumption Patterns," *Review of Economic Statistics,* 44:217, 220 (August, 1962).

3. James Duesenberry, *Income, Saving, and the Theory of Consumer Behavior* (Cambridge: Harvard University Press, 1949).

4. *New York Times* (October 23, 1966), quoting Dr. Parke Gibson and Hilton J. Hill.

5. Cf. "Whites have more places to put their discretionary income while Negroes, even in the same income level as whites, use their dollars differently because of their narrower selectivity." "Is There Really a Negro Market?," *Marketing Insights* (January 29, 1968), p. 14; and also "Most Negro families have little opportunity to base their self-respect on occupational, educational, or other accomplishments. This poverty of opportunity tends to reinforce for those families the significance of consumption." James E. Stafford, Keith Cox, and James Higgenbotham, "Some Consumption Pattern Differences Between Urban Whites and Negroes," *Social Science Quarterly* (December, 1968), p. 621.

6. Bureau of Labor Statistics, Bulletin 1517, *The Consumer Price Index* (Washington, D.C., 1966), pp. 66–68.

7. U.S. Department of Labor, Bureau of Labor Statistics, "A Study of Prices Charged in Food Stores Located in Low and Higher Income Areas of Six Large Cities, February, 1966," (Washington, D.C.: U.S. Government Printing Office, June 12, 1966), p. 1.

8. *Ibid.,* p. 15.

9. *Ibid.,* pp. 10–11.

10. *Ibid.,* p. 11.

11. Margaret Morris, "Grocery Shopping in Washington, D.C.," *United Planning Organization* (Washington, D.C., 1966), pp. 1–2.

12. Baltimore Community Relations Commission, "Findings of the Supermarket Pricing Survey" (May, 1968), p. 4.

13. Charles S. Goodman, "Do the Poor Pay More?," (Philadelphia: University of Pennsylvania, 1967); Cf. *idem,* "Do the Poor Pay More?," *Journal of Marketing,* 32:1 (January, 1968).

14. *Economic Report on Food Chain Selling Practices in the District*

of Columbia and San Francisco, a staff report to the Federal Trade Commission (Washington, D.C.: U.S. Government Printing Office, July, 1969), p. 3.

15. George Katona, William Dunkelberg, Jay Schmiedeskamp, and Frank Stafford, *1968 Survey of Consumer Finances* (Ann Arbor: University of Michigan Institute for Social Research, 1969), p. 87.

16. Federal Trade Commission, *Economic Report of Installment Credit and Retail Sales Practices of District of Columbia Retailers* (March, 1968), pp. 48–49.

17. Sar Levitan, *The Great Society's Poor Law* (Baltimore, Maryland: Johns Hopkins Press, 1969), p. 187.

18. *Door-to-Door Sales Regulation,* Hearings before the Consumer Subcommittee of the Committee on Commerce, United States Senate, 1968, pp. 28–31, quoting William M. O'Brien, Department of Health, Education, and Welfare.

NOTES TO INTRODUCTION TO PART TWO

1. Cf. Harry Johnson, "The Economic Approach to Social Questions," *Economica,* New Series, February, 1968, XXXV:137:1–21.

2. Report to the Congress, Review of Economic Opportunity Programs, Comptroller General of the United States, March 18, 1969, p. 1.

3. Sar A. Levitan, *The Great Society's Poor Law,* (Baltimore: Johns Hopkins Press, 1969), p. xii.

4. David Wallace and Jesse Smith, "The Study: Methodology and Findings," in *The Multi-Problem Dilemma,* edited by G. E. Brown, (Metuchen, N.J.: The Scarecrow Press, 1967), p. 126.

5. These people are likely to be in two different population groups; as Lester C. Thurow points out, the distribution of income is intimately involved. Cf. his *Poverty and Discrimination* (Washington, D.C.: The Brookings Institution, 1969), pp. 182–187.

NOTES TO CHAPTER SEVEN

1. Jay L. Roney, "Twenty Years of Public Assistance," *Social Security Bulletin* (August, 1955), p. 18.

2. Wilbur J. Cohen, "Social Security Objectives and Achievements," *Social Security Bulletin,* (August, 1955), p. 2.

3. Hearings before the Subcommittee on Fiscal Policy of the Joint Economic Committee (June, 1968, I:70), quoting Mrs. Beulah Sanders, Chairman, New York Citywide Coordinating Committee of Welfare Groups.

4. Gordon E. Brown, *The Multi-Problem Dilemma* (Metuchen, New Jersey: The Scarecrow Press, 1968), pp. 20–22, p. 30.

5. Cohen, *op. cit.,* p. 2.

6. Robert Lampman, "Approaches to the Reduction of Poverty," *American Economic Review, Papers and Proceedings* LV: 2: 524 (May,

1965). Cf. Alvin Schorr, *Poor Kids* (New York: Basic Books, 1966), and *Explorations in Social Policy* (New York: Basic Books, 1968), and the data in Chapter Four, p. 120.

7. *Boston Globe* (June 18, 1968), p. 21.

8. Robert J. Lampman, "Approaches to the Reduction of Poverty," *American Economic Review, Papers and Proceedings,* LV: 2 (May, 1965), 524.

9. Edward C. Banfield, "Welfare Reform," *Wall Street Journal* (August 14, 1969).

10. The first report, on methodology, is by the Director of the Institute, Harold R. Watts, "Graduated Work Incentives: An Experiment in Negative Taxation," *American Economic Review, Papers and Proceedings,* LIX:2 (May, 1969), 463–72.

11. Hearings before the Subcommitte on Fiscal Policy of the Joint Economic Committee of Congress, *Income Maintenance Programs,* I:210 (June, 1968), quoting Professor Albert Rees of Princeton University.

12. *Wall Street Journal,* Aug. 21, 1969, p. 1.

13. *Income Maintenance Programs,* I:1–2.

14. Lampman, *op. cit.,* p. 528.

NOTES TO CHAPTER EIGHT

1. John B. Lansing and Eva Mueller, *The Geographic Mobility of Labor,* (Ann Arbor, Michigan: Institute for Social Research, 1967), pp. 341–342.

2. National Citizens' Committee for Community Relations, *Putting the Hard-Core Unemployed Into Jobs* (Washington, D.C.: U.S. Government Printing Office, 1968), p. 11, quoting Edward N. Hodges, III, General Employment Supervisor of Michigan Bell Telephone Company.

3. U.S. Equal Employment Opportunities Commission, *Hearings in New York City, January 15–18, 1968* (Washington, D.C.: U.S. Government Printing Office), p. 44, quoting Robert W. Feagles, Senior Vice President, First National City Bank, N.Y.

4. Chamber of Commerce of the United States, *Proceedings of the National Workshop on The Urban Poor,* March 26, 1968, quoting Dave Hicks, ex-Harlem Globetrotter and now a neighborhood worker in New Haven, Connecticut.

5. Harvard Business School Special Report to Management, *Management of Racial Integration in Business* (New York: McGraw-Hill Book Company, 1964); and Jack Gourlay, *The Negro Salaried Worker,* (New York: The American Management Association, 1965).

6. *Hearings Before the U.S. Equal Employment Opportunities Commission, Held in New York City, January, 1968,* (Washington, D.C.: U.S. Government Printing Office, 1969), p. 123, quoting Stanley Rasch, Vice President of Personnel, Bache and Company.

7. William E. Burrows, "A T & T," *The Wall Street Journal* (Monday, June 2, 1969), p. 1.

8. *Hearings Before the U.S. Equal Employment Opportunities Commission, Held in New York City, January 15-18, 1968* (Washington, D.C.: U.S. Government Printing Office, 1969), p. 377, quoting Marie McWilliams, Director of Personnel, American Broadcasting Company.

9. National Citizens' Committee for Community Relations, *op. cit.,* p. 47, quoting Dr. Carl B. Kludt, Director, Community Affairs Program, Los Angeles.

10. *Hearings Before the U.S. Equal Employment Opportunities Commission Held in New York City, January 1968* (Washington, D.C.: U.S. Government Printing Office), pp. 47-48, quoting Robert W. Feagles.

11. National Citizens' Committee, *op. cit.,* p. 35, quoting Monrose Sullivan, Coordinator, Tri-Faith Employment Project, Chicago, Illinois.

12. V. E. Boyd, President, Chrysler Corporation, Speech delivered at the 46th Annual Conference of the Association of Industrial Advertisers, June 24, 1968.

13. George A. Higley, Director, Training Center, Raytheon Company, *Boston Sunday Herald Traveler* (March 9, 1969), Section Five, p. 5.

14. David Rogers, *110 Livingston Street* (New York: Random House, Inc., 1968), p. 516, quoting "New York City Businessmen."

15. The quotation and some of the analysis come from a study prepared by my former student, Karen Williamson, Wellesley College, B.A., 1969.

16. Marion K. Sanders, "James Haughton Wants 500,000 More Jobs," New York *Times* Magazine, Sept. 14, 1969, p. 133, quoting Mr. Haughton.

17. Hearings, *op. cit.,* p. 387, quoting Mr. Emanuel Robinson.

18. In an interview in September, 1969, Mr. George Meany stated that federal wage-price controls were the only way to end inflation, and a week later this was echoed by the president of a building trade association: "If there are going to be massive cutbacks in construction, as far as this industry is concerned, I think wage-price controls would be preferable," Carl M. Halvorseon, President of the 9000-company Associated General Contractors of America, quoted by Associated Press, September 4.

19. See Appendix 1.

NOTES TO CHAPTER NINE

1. Harvard University Center for Field Studies, quoted in the *Boston Herald Traveler* (January 26, 1969), p. 39.

2. *Statistical Abstract of the United States, 1968* (Washington, D.C.: U.S. Government Printing Office, 1968), p. 104.

3. Frederick M. Wirt, "Policy Outcomes of Desegregation Cases," in *School Desegregation in the North,* ed. T. Bentley Edwards and Frederick M. Wirt (San Francisco: Chandler Publishing Company, 1967), p. 4.

4. Cardinal Cushing, quoted in *The Boston Globe* (September 12, 1969).

5. National Advisory Commission on Civil Disorders, *Report* (Washington, D.C.: U.S. Government Printing Office, 1968), p. 236.

6. Dexter D. Eure, "Tell it like it is," *The Boston Globe* (July 16, 1968), p. 15, quoting Mrs. Toye Lewis, Education Director of the New Urban League of Greater Boston.

7. James S. Coleman, et al., *Equality of Educational Opportunity* (Washington, D.C.: U.S. Government Printing Office, 1966), p. 218.

8. Arnold Schuchter, *White Power/Black Freedom* (Boston: Beacon Press, 1968), p. 259.

9. U.S. Department of Health, Education, and Welfare, *Toward A Social Report* (Washington, D.C.: U.S. Government Printing Office, 1969), p. 19.

10. *Ibid.,* p. 66.

11. Bentley T. Edwards and Frederick M. Wirt, *School Desegregation in the North* (San Francisco: Chandler Publishing Company, 1967), p. 130.

12. Cf. John B. Willmann, *The Department of Housing and Urban Development* (New York: Frederick A. Praeger, Inc., 1967), and the various reports of the National Commission on Urban Problems for an overview.

13. Cf. Frederic J. Osborn and Arnold Whittick, *The New Towns* (London: Leonard Hill, 1963); Derek Senior, ed., *The Regional City* (New York: Landon Longmans, Green and Co., Ltd., 1966); Edward P. Eichler and Marshall Kaplan, *The Community Builders,* and especially Donald Canty, ed., *The New City* (New York; Frederick A. Praeger, Inc., 1969).

14. Cf. Advisory Commission on Intergovernmental Relations, *Urban and Rural America* (Washington, D.C.: April, 1968); J. Gottmann, *Megalopolis—The Urbanized Northern Seaboard of the United States* (New York: Twentieth Century Fund, 1961); and *idem.,* R. A. Harper, *Metropolis on the Move: Geographers Look at Urban Sprawl* (New York: John Wiley & Sons, Inc., 1967).

15. Cf. Martin Anderson, *The Federal Bulldozer* (Cambridge: The M.I.T. Press, 1964); Jerome Rothenberg, *Economic Evaluation of Urban Renewal* (Washington, D.C.: The Brookings Institution, 1967).

16. Jane Jacobs, *The Death and Life of Great American Cities* (New York: Random House, Inc., 1961).

17. Cf. U.S. Department of Housing and Urban Development, *Benefit-Cost Applications in Urban Renewal* (Washington, D.C.: U.S. Government Printing Office, 1969).

18. *Op. cit.,* p. 10.

19. The figures come from the Department of Commerce *Construction Review,* which distinguishes mobile homes from travel trailers. The former is defined as a "vehicular portable structure built on a chassis and designed to be used without a permanent foundation as a year-round dwelling when connected to utilities. Mobile homes are

defined as units 29 feet or longer and weighing over 4,500 pounds; travel trailers, as units less than 29 feet long, regardless of weight, and weighing less than 4,500 pounds, regardless of length. Excludes units designed for commercial uses, pickup cabs, folding campers, and amphibious units."

20. George Schermer, *Housing Guide to Equal Opportunity*, quoted in letter to author.

21. Burell G. Berkeley, President, National Business League, quoted in *Housing and Urban Development Legislation of 1968*, Hearings before the Subcommittee on Housing and Urban Affairs of the Committee on Banking and Currency, United States Senate, 90th Congress, Second Session, Part 2, p. 869.

NOTES TO CHAPTER TEN

1. *The Speeches of Malcolm X at Harvard*, ed. Archie Epps (New York: William Morrow & Co., Inc., 1968), pp. 141–142.

2. Clair St. Drake and Horace R. Cayton, *Black Metropolis* (New York: Harper and Row, Publishers, 1962), p. 439.

3. D. E. Scott, *Trade at Home* (Wellington, Texas: D. E. Scott Newspaper Service), 1969.

4. Drake and Cayton, *op. cit.,* pp. 443–45.

5. Richard H. Holton, "Marketing Structure and Economic Development," *Quarterly Journal of Economics,* LXVII:3 (August, 1953), 344–61.

6. *Manpower Report of the President, 1969* (Washington, D.C.: U.S. Government Printing Office, 1969), p. 410.

7. William E. Cox, Jr., "A Commercial Structure Model for Depressed Neighborhoods," *Journal of Marketing,* XXXIII:3 (July, 1969), 1–9.

8. "Black Economic Development," Report of the 35th American Assembly (New York: Arden House, 1969), citing Small Business Administration estimates, 1968.

9. Burt Schore, "Ailing Entrepreneurs," *Wall Street Journal* (September 23, 1969), p. 30.

10. Everett Groseclose, "A Black Businessman Finds It's Hard to Get New Firm Off Ground," *Wall Street Journal* (September 17, 1969), p. 29.

11. Schore, *loc. cit.*

12. Mary Gardiner Jones, "A Federal Trade Commissioner Looks at Franchising," Address in Ann Arbor, Michigan, September 7, 1968, pp. 19–21.

13. Al Lapin, Jr., "Franchising: Power for Economic Equality," Address at Boston College, April 12, 1969.

14. Thomas Oliphant, "Blacks Get Together with Boston Banks," *Boston Globe* (December 9, 1968), p. 44, quoting Walter F. Taube, Vice President, State Street Bank and Trust Company.

15. Francis X. Clines, "Some Businesses in Slum Assisted," *New York Times* (January 12, 1969), p. 56.

16. Hearings before the Senate Subcommittee on Financial Institutions, January 12, 1970, quoting George W. Miller, President, Bank of the Commonwealth.

17. Oliphant, *loc. cit.,* quoting Paul P. McLaughlin, National Shawmut Bank.

18. Andrew F. Brimmer, "The Banking System and Urban Economic Development," Address before the American Finance Association, Chicago, Illinois, December 28, 1968, p. 7.

19. Brimmer, *op. cit.,* p. 35.

20. Opportunity Through Ownership, San Francisco; Georgia Plan, Savannah; and B-Burg, Boston, to name a few.

21. Capital Formation, N.Y.; Economic Development Corporation, Detroit; Harlem Commonwealth Council; United Inner-City Development Foundation, Seattle; Cleveland Now; Economic Resources Corp., Los Angeles; FARMICCO, Washington, D.C.; and the five-city Negro Industrial and Economic Union, for example.

22. Brimmer, *op. cit.,* p. 22.

23. Gary Becker, *The Economics of Discrimination* (Chicago: University of Chicago Press, 1957).

24. U.S. Department of Health, Education, and Welfare, Office of Education, *Equality of Education* (Washington, D.C.: U.S. Government Printing Office, 1966), p. 21.

Neiman-Marcus
Dallas, Texas   75201
January 5, 1968

HAPPY NEW YEAR:

As we start a New Year, I should like to express my appreciation to you for having served us so well during the past year. As one of America's fine specialty stores we are dependent on manufacturers and suppliers who can *understand* and *appreciate* the principles of *quality* for which we stand.

1967 will have been a good year for most retailers and manufacturers, but it was a bad year for our country. We witnessed riots and civil disturbances in many of our major cities which threatened to disrupt the nation. *None* of us can feel secure in our businesses, however prosperous or well managed they may be, if we have disorder and destruction in the land. A large part of the problems facing our cities is caused by poverty and discrimination which lead to frustration then to violence. Steps must be taken beyond those contemplated in current programs, and in our opinion the *business community* must assume a *greater* degree of *responsibility* than it has heretofore.

Specifically we feel that despite obvious difficulties, a greater effort must be made to create job opportunities for members of minority groups. I am sure that you have given thought to positive ways in which businessmen can work to help *correct* the situation.

The Federal Government, as you know, requires that every one of its suppliers of goods and services certifies that it is an equal opportunity employer. We believe a *private company* should do *no* less, and we maintain an equal opportunity policy in our employment program.

It is our intention to include notice on each of our purchase orders that we expect our suppliers to follow fair employment practices as a condition of the order. We shall, in our purchasing activities, look with *favor* upon those companies which are taking *positive* steps toward employing and training people of minority groups.

In implementing this policy, we will continue to buy primarily based on quality, service, and price, but this *additional* factor of an affirmative equal opportunity employment policy will also be considered by all of our buyers. In the future we would rather do business with a company which is actively and sincerely pursuing a policy of equal opportunity, than to continue to do business with one which is not.

In our belief that the private sector should take the *lead* in this country, we recommend our policy to you and *hope* that you will implement it with your own suppliers.

Again may I thank you for what you've done for this past year. With the opening of our great new store in Houston in the fall of 1968, we look forward to achieving new sales records, to which I hope your company will be an active participant.

Sincerely,

Stanley Marcus

BIBLIOGRAPHY

THIS LISTING reflects the fact that the footnotes, each with complete bibliographic references, themselves provide an extensive list of sources. Here follows a short list of works, each a major contribution to basic knowledge, and a longer list of books and articles containing original research or analysis, most of which are not well known.

ESSENTIALS

Advisory Commission on Intergovernmental Relations. *Urban and Rural America: Policies for Future Growth.* Washington, D.C.: U.S. Government Printing Office, 1968.

Canty, David., ed. *The New City.* Frederick A. Praeger, Inc., 1969.

National Advisory Commission on Rural Poverty. *Rural Poverty in the United States.* Washington, D.C.: U.S. Government Printing Office, 1968.

National Commission on Urban Problems. *Building the American City.* Washington, D.C.: U.S. Government Printing Office, 1969.

_____. *Hearings Before the National Commission on Urban Problems.* 5 vols. Washington, D.C.: U.S. Government Printing Office, 1969.

_____. "Research Reports Submitted to the National Commission." Nos. 1–18 to date. Washington, D.C.: U.S. Government Printing Office, 1969. (These publications have been called the blueprints for future America; see Fischer, John, "The Easy Chair." *Harper's* (November, 1969).

Myrdal, Gunnar. *An American Dilemma*. New York: Harper and Row, Publishers, 1944.

Urban America, Inc. and the Urban Coalition. *One Year Later*. Frederick A. Praeger, Inc., 1969. (Follow-up to the Kerner report.)

United States Commission on Civil Rights. *Racial Isolation in the Public Schools*. Washington, D.C.: U.S. Government Printing Office, 1967.

United States Equal Employment Opportunity Commission. *Hearings, 1968*. Washington, D.C.: U.S. Government Printing Office, 1969.

United States Department of Health, Education, and Welfare. *Toward A Social Report*. Washington, D.C.: U.S. Government Printing Office, 1969.

United States Congress: The following hearings, before various congressional committees, are merely a sampling of the invaluable data gathered.

Financial Institutions and the Urban Crisis. Hearings before the subcommittee on financial institutions, Committee on Banking and Currency, U.S. Senate, 1968.

Door to Door Sales Regulation. Hearings before the consumer subcommittee of the Committee on Commerce, U.S. Senate, 1968.

Income Maintenance Programs. Hearings before the subcommittee on fiscal policy of the Joint Economic Committee of Congress, 1968.

Report of the Joint Economic Committee of Congress. "Employment and Manpower Problems in the Cities: September 16, 1968."

Report to the Joint Economic Committee. "Guaranteed Minimum Income Programs Used by Governments of Selected Countries." 1968.

Hearings before the Senate Committee on Labor and Public Welfare Relating to Equal Employment Opportunities, 1963.

Washington Inner City Poverty Survey. Report to the subcommittee on employment, manpower, and poverty of the Committee on Labor and Public Welfare, U.S. Senate, 1968.

Economic Development Opportunity. Hearings before the Select Committee on Small Business, U.S. Senate, 1968.

United States Department of Labor, Bureau of Labor Statistics. *Survey of Consumer Expenditures, 1960–61*. BLS Report 237–93, Supplement 2, Part A to BLS Report 237–38. See other reports for particular localities. Washington, D.C.: U.S. Government Printing Office.

United States Department of Commerce, Bureau of the Census. *Current Population Reports: Series P-20, Population Characteristics; Series P-23, Special Reports; Series P-25, Employment Characteristics; Series P-27, Education Characteristics;* and *Series P-60, Consumer Income* are issued irregularly.

United States Department of Commerce, Bureau of the Census. *Maps of Major Concentration of Poverty in Standard Metropolitan Statistical Areas of 250,000 or More Population, 1966*. Washington, D.C., U.S. Government Printing Office, 1968.

ORIGINS AND CHARACTERISTICS

Anderson, W. Locke. "Trickling Down: The Relationship Between Economic Growth and the Extent of Poverty." *Quarterly Journal of Economics,* 78:511–24.

Cooper, William H. "Economics and Non-Economics of Poverty." *American Economic Review, Papers and Proceedings,* 58:2; 521–46.

Day, Richard H. "The Economics of Technological Change and the Demise of the Sharecropper." *American Economic Review,* 57:427–49.

Detroit Urban League. *A Profile of the Detroit Negro.* Detroit: 1959, 1967.

Heer, David, ed. *Social Statistics and the City.* Cambridge: Joint Center for Urban Studies, 1968.

Lampman, Robert J. "Population Change and Poverty Reduction, 1947–1975." In *Poverty Amidst Affluence,* ed. Leo Fishman. New Haven: Yale University Press, 1966.

Maitland, Sheridan T. and Stanley M. Knebel. "Rural to Urban Transition." *Monthly Labor Review,* 91:6–12.

Miller, Andre L. "Economic Growth and Minorities." *American Journal of Economics and Sociology* (July, 1967).

Mueller, Eva. "Negro-White Differences in Geographic Mobility." In *Geographic Mobility of Labor,* ed. Lansing and Mueller. Ann Arbor, Michigan: Institute of Social Research, University of Michigan, 1967.

Schorr, Alvin L. "The Family Cycle and Income Development." *Social Security Bulletin* (February, 1966).

Staples, Robert E. "The Lower Income Negro Family in St. Paul." St. Paul, Minnesota: Urban League, 1967.

United States Department of Labor, Bureau of Labor Statistics. *The Negro in the West.* San Francisco Bureau of Labor Statistics, n.d.

Wall Street Journal. "Kelley Street Blues." (January 6, 10, 16, 20, 1969).

POVERTY, INCOME, AND EMPLOYMENT

AFL–CIO Department of Research. "The Low-Paid Worker." *American Federationist* (August, 1964).

Aigner, D. J. and A. J. Heins. "On the Determinants of Income Equality." *American Economic Review,* 57:175–84.

Batchelder, Alan B. "Decline in the Relative Income of Negro Men." *Quarterly Journal of Economics,* 78:525–48.

Bluestone, Barry. "The Poor Who *Have* Jobs." *Dissent* (September–October, 1968).

Delhanty, George E. and Robert Evans, Jr. "Low-Wage Employment: An Inventory and An Assessment." Unpublished manuscript, March 1969.

Ferman, Louis A., *The Negro and Equal Employment Opportunities.* New York: Frederick A. Praeger, 1968.

Gordon, David M. "Income and Welfare in New York City." *The Public Interest,* Number 16, 1969.

Miller, Herman. "Present Value of Estimated Lifetime Earnings." Technical Paper 16, U.S. Bureau of the Census, 1967.

Monthly Labor Review, current articles. Typical of the excellent analysis to be found are:

    Perrella, Vera C. "Low Earners and Their Incomes." (May, 1967).

    ———— and Edward J. O'Boyle. "Work Plans of Men Not in the Labor Force." (August and September, 1968).

    Russell, Joe L. "Changing Patterns in Employment of Non-white Workers." (May, 1966).

    Ryscavage, Paul M. and Hazel M. Willacy. "Employment of the Nation's Urban Poor." (August, 1968).

Mooney, J. D. "Urban Poverty and Labor Force Participation." *American Economic Review,* 54:104–117.

Survey of Current Business. "Personal Income, Standard Metropolitan Statistical Areas, 1929–66." (August, 1968).

CONSUMPTION AND MARKETING

Alexis, Marcus. "Some Negro-White Differences in Consumption." *American Journal of Economics and Sociology* (January, 1962).

Bullock, Henry. "Consumer Motivations in Black and White." *Harvard Business Review* (May–June, July–August, 1961).

Community Council of Greater New York. *A Family Budget Standard.* New York: Community Council, 1963. Rev. ed., 1969.

Consumer Problems of the Poor. Hearings before and report by the Committee on Government Operations, House of Representatives. Washington, D.C.: U.S. Government Printing Office, 1967, 1968.

Cox, William E. "A Commercial Structure Model for Depressed Neighborhoods." *Journal of Marketing* (July, 1969).

Dixon, Donald F. and Daniel J. McLaughlin, Jr. "Do the Inner City Poor Pay More for Food?" *Economic and Business Bulletin of Temple University* (Spring, 1968).

Klein, L. R. and H. W. Mooney. "Negro-White Savings Differentials and the Consumption Function Problem." *Econometrica,* 21: 425–56.

Lamale, Helen H. "Changes in Concepts of Income Adequacy in the Last Century." *American Economic Review, Papers and Proceedings,* 48: 291–99.

———— and Thomas J. Lanahan, Jr. "Income and Levels of Living," *Monthly Labor Review* (March, 1968).

National Commission on Food Marketing. "Retail Food Prices in Low and Higher Income Areas." Special Studies on Food Marketing, Technical Study No. 10. Washington, D.C.: U.S. Government Printing Office, June, 1966.

Petrof, John V. "Customer Strategy for Negro Retailers." *Journal of Retailing* (Fall, 1967).

Progressive Grocer. *Consumer Dynamics in the Supermarket.* New York: Progressive Grocer, 1965.

Sommer, M. and G. D. Bruce. "Blacks, Whites, and Products." *Social Science Quarterly,* 49:631–42.

Stafford, James, Keith Cox, and James Higginbotham. "Consumption Pattern Differences Between Urban Whites and Negroes." *Social Science Quarterly,* 49:619–30.

Sturdivant, F. D. and W. T. Wilhelm. "Poverty, Minorities, and Consumer Exploitation." *Social Science Quarterly,* 49: 643–50.

U.S. Department of Agriculture, Consumer and Marketing Service. *Comparison of Prices Paid for Selected Foods in Chain-stores in High and Low Income Areas of Six Cities.* Washington, D.C.: June, 1968.

U.S. Department of Commerce, Bureau of Defense Services Administration. *Bibliography on Marketing to Low-Income Consumers.* Washington, D.C.: 1969.

U.S. Department of Health, Education, and Welfare. *Low Income Life Styles.* Washington, D.C.: U.S. Government Printing Office, 1966.

U.S. Department of Labor, Bureau of Labor Statistics. *Consumer Expenditures and Income, with Emphasis on Low-Income Families.* BLS Report No. 238-6. Washington, D.C.: U.S. Government Printing Office, 1964.

_____. *Levels of Living Among the Poor.* BLS Report No. 238-12. Washington, D.C.: U.S. Government Printing Office, 1965.

Wright, John S. and Carl M. Larson, *A Survey of Brand Preferences among Chicago Negro Families.* Chicago: Stipes Publishing Company, 1968.

DISCRIMINATION AND EMPLOYMENT

Gilman, Harry J. "Economic Discrimination and Unemployment." *American Economic Review,* 55: 1077–196.

Hiestand, Dale L. *Economic Growth and Employment Opportunities for Minorities.* New York: Columbia University Press, 1964.

Hill, Herbert. "Racial Inequality in Employment: The Patterns of Discrimination," *Annals of the American Academy of Political and Social Science* (February, 1965).

"Industrial Conflict and Race Conflict." Proceedings of the 1967 annual spring meeting, Institute for Industrial Relations, Madison, Wisconsin: 1967.

International Labor Office. *Fighting Discrimination in Employment and Occupation: A Workers' Education Manual.* Geneva: International Labor Office, 1968.

_____. *Discrimination in Employment and Occupation: Standards and Policy Statements.* Geneva: International Labor Office, 1967.

NAACP. *Labor Manual,* 1968 ed. New York: NAACP, 1969.

Northrup, Herbert R. *The Negro in the Automobile Industry.* Philadelphia: University of Pennsylvania Press, 1968.

Rowan, Richard. "Discrimination and Apprentice Regulation in the
Building Trades." *Journal of Business,* 40:435–43.

Sovern, Michael I. *Legal Restraints on Racial Discrimination in Employment.* New York: Twentieth Century Fund, 1966.

Thurow, Lester C. *Poverty and Discrimination.* Washington, D.C.: The
Brookings Institution, 1969.

"White and Negro Attitudes Towards Race Related Issues and Activities." CBS New Public Opinion Survey. Princeton, N.J.: Opinion
Research Company, 1968.

U.S. Department of Labor, Wage and Labor Standards Administration. *Negro Women in the Population and in the Labor Force.* Washington, D.C.: U.S. Government Printing Office, 1967.

Via, Emory F. "Discrimination, Integration, and Job Equality."
Monthly Labor Review (March, 1968).

EDUCATION AND TRAINING

Dentler, Robert A., Bernard Macklet, and Mary Ellen Warshauer, eds.
The Urban R's. New York: Frederick A. Praeger, Inc., 1967.

Fogel, Walter. "The Effect of Low Educational Attainment on Incomes: A Comparative Study of Selected Ethnic Groups." *Journal of
Human Resources* (Fall, 1966).

Main, E. D. "A Nationwide Evaluation of MDTA Institutional Job
Training." *Journal of Human Resources* (Spring, 1968).

*Manpower Research and Training. A Report by the Secretary of Labor,
March, 1965.* Washington, D.C.: U.S. Government Printing Office,
1965.

Masters, S. H. "The Effect of Family Income on Children's Education." *Journal of Human Resources* (Spring, 1969).

Mincer, Jacob. "Investment in Human Capital and Personal Income
Distribution." *Journal of Political Economy,* 66:281–302.

Patten, Thomas H. and Gerald E. Clark. "Literacy Training and Job
Placement of Hard-Core Unemployed Negroes in Detroit." *Journal
of Human Resources* (Winter, 1968).

President's Task Force on Manpower Conservation. *One-Third of a
Nation: A Report on Young Men Found Unqualified for Military
Service.* Washington, D.C.: U.S. Government Printing Office, 1964.

Schultz, T. W. "Investment in Human Capital." *American Economic
Review,* 51: 1–17.

———. "Rise in the Capital Stock Represented by Education in the
United States, 1900–1957." In *Economics of Higher Education,* ed.
Selma Mishkin. U.S. Department of Health, Education, and Wel-
fare. Washington, D.C.: U.S. Government Printing Office, 1962.

Smolensky, Eugene. "Investment in Education of the Poor." *American
Economic Review,* 66:2: 370–78.

U.S. Senate Committee on Labor and Public Welfare, Subcommittee on Employment. *Manpower and Poverty, Hearings.* Washington, D.C.: U.S. Government Printing Office, 1967.

HOUSING AND RESIDENCE

Abrams, Charles. *Forbidden Neighbors.* New York: 1955.

Epps, Richard W. "Suburban Jobs and Black Workers." *Business Review,* Federal Reserve Bank of Philadelphia (October, 1969).

Kain, John F. "Housing Segregation, Negro Employment, and Metropolitan Decentralization." *Quarterly Journal of Economics* (May, 1968).

Laurenti, Luigi. *Property Values and Race.* Berkeley, California: University of California Press, 1960.

Lowenstein, Louis K. *The Location of Residences and Work Places in Urban Areas.* Metuchen, N.J.: The Scarecrow Press, 1965.

National Committee Against Discrimination in Housing, New York. "The Impact of Housing Patterns on Job Opportunities." New York: National Committee, 1968.

Neutze, Graeme M. *The Suburban Apartment Boom.* Baltimore: John Hopkins Press, 1968.

Schneider, Lewis M. "The Fallacy of Free Transportation." *Harvard Business Review* (January–February, 1969).

Watts, Lewis G., Howard Freeman, Helen Hughes, Robert Morris, and Thomas Pettigrew. *The Middle-Income Negro Family Faces Urban Renewal.* (Waltham, Mass.: Brandeis University, 1964).

Wolf, Eleanor P. and Charles N. Lebeaux. "Class and Race in the Changing City." In *Social Science in the City,* ed. Leo Schnore. New York: Frederick A. Praeger, Inc., 1968.

Wunderlich, Gene. "Costs of Communicating by Transportation." *Journal of Economic Issues* (September, 1967).

PROGRAMS AND POLICIES

American Assembly, Arden House. *Black Economic Development.* New York: Arden House, 1969.

American Business Press, Inc. *Solving the Crisis in Our Cities.* New York: American Business Press, Inc., March, 1969.

Business and Society. New York. (This is a newsletter reporting the activities of business firms in the area of urban crisis.)

Brimmer, Andrew F. "Black Capitalism." *American Economic Review* (May, 1970).

Contact. New York, Richard Clarke Associated. (This is a monthly employment information publication from equal opportunity employers.)

Collins, Lora S. "Public Assistance Expenditures in the United States." In *Studies in the Economics of Income Maintenance,* ed. Otto Eckstein. Washington, D.C.: The Brookings Institution, 1967.

Etzkowitz, Henry and Gerald M. Schaffner. *Ghetto Crisis.* Boston: Little, Brown, and Company, 1969.

Feldman, Paul. "The Pathos of 'Black Power.'" *Dissent* (January–February, 1967).

Hamilton, David. "The Political Economy of Poverty." *Journal of Economic Issues* (December, 1967).

Kasper, Hirschel. "The War on Poverty." *Quarterly Review of Economics and Business* (Autumn, 1968).

Kalish, James A. "The Urban Problems Industry." *The Washington Monthly* (November, 1969).

Marcus, Stanley. "Who Is Responsible?" *Business Horizons* (June, 1968).

McKersie, Robert B. "Vitalize Black Enterprise." *Harvard Business Review* (September–October, 1968).

Robinson, Susan. "Moving Money Into Ghetto Business." *Business Review,* Federal Reserve Bank of Philadelphia (October, 1968).

Sturdivant, Frederick D. "The Limits of Black Capitalism." *Harvard Business Review* (January–February, 1968).

INDEX

INDEX OF NAMES